KING CHŎNGJO, AN ENLIGHTENED DESPOT IN EARLY MODERN KOREA

KING CHŎNGJO

AN ENLIGHTENED DESPOT IN

EARLY MODERN KOREA

CHRISTOPHER LOVINS

Cover art: King Chŏngjo, Chosŏn, painting of a chrysanthemum, 1777–1800, Korea. Dongguk University Museum, Seoul, Republic of Korea.

Published by State University of New York Press, Albany

For information, contact State University of New York Press, Albany, NY
www.sunypress.edu

Library of Congress Cataloging-in-Publication Data

Names: Lovins, Christopher, 1980- author.
Title: King Chŏngjo, an enlightened despot in early modern Korea / Christopher Lovins.
Description: Albany, NY : State University of New York, [2019] | Includes bibliographical
    references and index.
Identifiers: LCCN 2018021867 | ISBN 9781438473635 (hardcover : alk. paper) | ISBN
    9781438473659 (e-book)
Subjects: LCSH: Chŏngjo, King of Korea, 1752-1800. | Korea—Kings and rulers—
    Biography. | Chŏngjo, King of Korea, 1752-1800—Correspondence. | Despotism—
    Korea—History. | Korea—Politics and government—1392-1910.
Classification: LCC DS913.392.C53 L68 2019 | DDC 951.9/02092 [B] —dc23 LC record
    available at https://lccn.loc.gov/2018021867

10   9   8   7   6   5   4   3   2   1

FOR MY FATHER.

The sleeper has awakened.

CONTENTS

ACKNOWLEDGMENTS

THIS BOOK BEGAN WHEN BONNIE CHENG, PROFESSOR OF ART HISTORY AND East Asian studies at Oberlin College, asked me during an interview for a visiting professor position there, "What do you mean by *absolutism*?" I filibustered some kind of nonanswer to this question, which fortunately Bonnie did not press me on, since doing so would have quickly revealed that I, having never bothered to ask the question myself, *had* no answer. In my dissertation I concluded that King Chŏngjo was not an absolute ruler because I really had no idea what an absolute ruler was. What did I mean by *absolutism*? Well, what everybody means, right? Tyranny and oppression and let them eat cake and all that. None of this described Chŏngjo. Ergo, he was not an absolute ruler.

Once I set out to determine what exactly *absolutism* meant, I was confronted by a forest of confusion. I have done my best here to wend my way through it and make some kind of use of the concept. I am under no illusion that my effort will end that confusion. But I do hope that offering the perspective of a Korean monarch on the concept will clarify at least some aspects, even if it proves to obscure others in the process.

This book could not have been completed without the generous support of the faculty and staff of the Department of East Asian Studies at Oberlin College, the Department of Asian Studies at the University of British Columbia, and the Division of General Studies at the Ulsan National Institute of Science and Technology. Special thanks must go to Ross King, head of Asian Studies at UBC, and the Academy of Korean Studies. My postdoctoral year, supported by an Academy of Korean Studies grant funded by the Korean government (MEST) (AKS-2011-AAA-2103), was vital to the completion of this manuscript. A substantially different version of a portion of chapter 7 was published in volume 52 of the *Journal of Asian History*. Finally, I must thank my editor at State University New York Press, Christopher Ahn, and two anonymous reviewers, whose constructive criticism made possible the transformation of a jumbled manuscript into an actual, readable book. Any remaining omissions and errors are mine alone.

INTRODUCTION

Alas! I am the son of Crown Prince Sado.
—King Chǒngjo to his officials, November 20, 1776[1]

ON JULY 4, 1762, THE KING OF KOREA ORDERED THE EXECUTION OF THE heir to the throne, his son. In the four hundred years the Yi family—or Chosǒn, as it was called then—had ruled Korea, brothers had slain brothers and uncles had murdered nephews in the struggle for the crown, but thus far no king had killed his own son. The situation was a strange one, the execution itself stranger still. The crown prince had been suffering from madness for six years, attempting to kill himself in 1756, and committing his first murder the following year. Sneaking out of the palace at night, carousing with ruffians and prostitutes, beating servants to death in fits of rage—there seemed no end to the crown prince's bizarre behavior. The court lived in fear in the months leading up to the execution, paralyzed by the dread of being on the receiving end of his bouts of insanity. But what could be done? Crown Prince Sado was the only legitimate son of the king. There was no precedent in Korean law for disinheriting him in favor of another candidate. And what of Sado's son, the future heir, who under Chosǒn law would be punished along with his father should any action be taken?

It was not until the summer of 1762 that Sado finally made the mistake that would seal his fate. He committed the unforgiveable crime of threatening the survival of the dynasty, and therefore, the state itself. In a fit of madness, he threatened regicide, to take his father's life. The king vacillated for three weeks while the prince awaited punishment, but in the end even Sado's mother urged the king to act: Sado had to die. In order to protect the line of succession, the crown prince could not be executed as a common criminal. Some alternative had to be found, something that would result in Sado's death without the stigma of a legal judgment impugning his own son's legitimacy. Suicide would have served, but Sado's tutors prevented him from strangling himself, much to the king's ire, if Yi Kwanghyǒn's diary is to be believed.[2] As the king shouted in exasperation, "Why don't you just kill yourself?," Sado's son, a boy of ten, begged the king for his father's life until he was physically dragged out of the palace. Sado was ordered to enter an empty rice chest—a sturdy wooden box about four feet high and wide—which then was sealed. His wife and son were expelled from the palace, and eight days later, during a mighty thunderstorm, the crown prince died.

Fourteen years after the tragedy, that boy ascended the throne. Born Yi San in 1752, he is best known by the posthumous title Chŏngjo 正祖 ("Rectified Ancestor"). Now a man of twenty-five, Chŏngjo never forgot that he was his father's son, and his first statement to his officials upon his accession, quoted above, reflects this. A child at the time of Sado's death, Chŏngjo never understood his father's illness. He was convinced Sado had fallen victim to the endemic, deadly court factionalism that had held the Chosŏn government in its grip for two centuries. Chŏngjo's overriding goal was to free the throne from domination by any faction so that he and his descendents would never be manipulated into tragedy, as he believed his grandfather had been. This goal took time, intensive effort, and extraordinary talent to accomplish, as revealed by his inability to prevent his half-brother's execution on what were likely false charges of treason in his first year on the throne. In his relentless drive to make the king the ultimate arbiter in the land, the singular figure from which all power flowed, Chŏngjo—like Louis XIV and the Qianlong Emperor—acted as an absolute monarch in an early modern world.

For most of the twentieth century, the late Chosŏn period (roughly 1700–1910) was regarded as a long, slow decline into corruption and chaos, ending with the ignominy of Japanese colonialism. This is in large part due to the justifications put forward by Japanese scholars in the years leading up to the annexation of Korea and throughout the colonial period: that Chosŏn was backward and had failed to modernize on its own (as Japan had) and so needed Japanese colonial guidance. Korean scholars writing in the early decades of independent South Korea sought to recover their history, but they had been trained in modern historiography by scholars steeped in the colonial paradigm and so accepted many of its assumptions, even as they sought to refute or refine that paradigm. They adopted the Marxist perspective of their former occupiers and looked for evidence of Korean development out of the "feudal" stage of late Chosŏn, finding varying degrees of what they sought.[3] This is exemplified in the "sprouts of capitalism" argument, the claim that proto-capitalism had developed in Korea and that therefore the country's impending modernization had been derailed by the Japanese colonial project.

Thus, even through the 1980s, late Chosŏn Korea was viewed as a period of missed opportunity and failure. Locked into rigid Confucian ideology and riven by hereditary factions that argued over minutiae like proper mourning reforms and the failure to achieve them. This, he argues, mirrored the King's reform-mindedness and tragically short life. The 1980s view of Chŏngjo itself stands in contrast to the view of the King's near-contemporaries in the nineteenth century, who looked at his reign as a dynastic high point. His reign served as a model for reform in Kojong's time, even as a modernized Japan was knocking at Korea's door. Evaluations by postliberation scholars, having been trained under Japanese colonialism, judged it a failure—an example of the failings and backward "feudal" nature of the dynasty as a whole according to such influential historians as Ki-baik Lee and Han Woo-keun. It was not until the 1980s that the dynasty's achievements began to gain recognition (such as surviving for 300 years after the devastating Imjin War that would have toppled another government). However, even in the 1980s, with South Korea struggling under a dictatorship, Korean scholars were reluctant to praise strong kingship, leaving Chŏngjo to be seen as well-meaning and filial, tragic, but still inept, the puppet of Hong Kuk-yŏng, remembered primarily for dying young and leaving a legacy of in-law government. Passing unmentioned were many of the aspects of the Chŏngjo reign emphasized in the 1990s: the Royal Library, the Illustrious Fortress, the Robust and Brave Garrison. In connection with the '90s push to retrieve Korean books brought back to France during the 1866 French Incursion and the 1997 publication of Han Yŏng-u's *Finding Our History Again* (*Tasi ch'anŭn uri yŏksa*), Chŏngjo received a new evaluation, in tandem with the emerging movement to "rescue" Korean history from colonial historiography and its goateed mirror-universe counterpart, nationalist historiography. In Kim's view, the "syndrome" of Chŏngjo is the pinning of Korea's failure to resist Japanese colonialism on his early death, allowing Korea's fall to be treated as an inevitable tragedy that avoided the need to take a hard look at the actual failures. Kim points out that King Sŏngjong died at age thirty-seven, a full ten years younger than Chŏngjo, and having reigned less than half of the time Chŏngjo did. Yet Sŏngjong's death is not viewed as a tragedy, making the tragedy of Chŏngjo's death image rather than fact, or history that reflects the desires of people in the present.[12]

This "syndrome" survives into the twenty-first century, as exemplified by Song Ki-ch'ul's *T'onghap ŭi chŏngch'iga Yi San* (Chŏngjo, the Complete Politician), published in 2012. In this history of the reign, "Chŏngjo the Great" is the representative case of one who overcame all obstacles through the exercise of creative leadership, as the maverick King escapes from the constrictive Confucian framework to undertake modernizing reforms according to his "democratic consciousness"(!), which he apparently does by maximizing his own autocratic power to crush the resistance of the stodgy old aristocrats who disapprove of the King's efforts to empower the people of the nation.[13] In accounts like these, Chŏngjo is unmoored from history, affecting the future while seemingly unaffected by the past, since his Policy of Impartiality is explicitly described as not a continuation of Yŏngjo's but singularly his own creation. The old "sprouts of capitalism" argument is trotted out (though the term itself does not appear), along with the dubious claim that Chŏngjo shook off Sinocentrism as part of his nationalist consciousness. (Chŏngjo was very conscious, it seems.) Chŏngjo's processions are discussed under the section heading "The Realization of Direct Democracy [Chikchŏp minjujuŭi ŭi silhyŏn]"! Thus, the Chŏngjo period is seen as a turning point in both Korean nationalism and democratization, though Song is hardly alone in making such grandiose claims.[14] Yi Tae-Jin, to take another example, also attributes Korea's more rapid democratization than neighboring China and Japan to Yŏngjo's and Chŏngjo's focus on the common people.[15] How North Korea's continuing brutal totalitarianism fits into such a model is not addressed. Taking the diametrically opposed, if not altogether any more useful, view is Kim Ki-bong, for whom Chŏngjo was not an enlightened ruler but a reactionary who tried to block the dawn of the modern age in Korea, and his success in doing so at the expense of the modernizing "advanced intellectuals" (sin chisik'in) condemned the country to the fate of Japanese colonialism. Kim contrasts him with Louis XIV, whose legacy was the French Revolution and, in consequence, modernity in France.[16]

This account will endeavor to be a little more sober in dealing with Chŏngjo, examining how he expanded and modified while also being constrained by the policies inherited from his predecessors and the cultural and social conditions under which he operated. Chŏngjo's primary goal was not to empower the people or modernize the country, as these are two concepts were hardly known in eighteenth-century Korea, where the notion of allowing the masses to choose their leaders sounded like chaos.[17] Instead, he sought to expand his power to carry out his own will as ruler of the country. Convinced that his grandfather had been manipulated by others into executing his father, Chŏngjo's goal was to be the law unto himself, relying on his own judgment, manipulated and controlled by no one. Although as a good Confucian monarch he may have believed that his expanded power would be good for the state and the people, since only the king was able, through effective rule, to benefit the people's livelihood, this was not his main intention. He pursued policies that would put not only himself but his successors in the unassailable position of final decision-maker, which meant not only increasing his own power but setting up structures that would solidify the king's power for the reigns to follow his. But controlling the course of events after one's death is perhaps the most challenging thing for any ruler. Louis XIV had his will annulled and his envisioned joint-regency for his young son and heir was instead dominated by the Duke of Orleans. Qianlong's powerful and fabulously wealthy favorite, Heshen, was disgraced and executed almost immediately after his patron's death. And while Chŏngjo himself ruled as a true absolutist, his institutional reforms meant to ensure his enhanced power would be passed to his descendants were not so successful.

The 2000s have seen an explosion of Chŏngjo literature in Korea. From Yi Tae-Jin, who views Chŏngjo as having pretensions to absolute monarchy, to Park Hyunmo and Yu Pong-hak, who see him as a shrewd politician with no firm agenda responding to the vicissitudes of the times, to Yi Han-u, who argues he had a vision rather than a plan and learned the game of politics through his early mistakes, to Jung Jae-hoon, who put forward that he sought to roll back the clock to early Chosŏn—there are a number of ways Chŏngjo's reign can be interpreted.[18] The present work builds primarily on that of Yi Tae-Jin to argue for Chŏngjo's Chosŏn as an early modern absolute polity. I contend that he maximized his political and legal discretion within the constraints imposed by the Korean elite's shared understanding of acceptable use of power in accordance with the Confucian Way. His strategy for reform might best be summarized with William Beik's concept of "conservative innovation," that is, the appropriation and revitalization of traditional ruling techniques in new but recognizable ways in the service of goals that are fundamentally conservative—stability, maintenance of elite privilege, and security of the state and the dynasty. Chŏngjo was a masterful politician who fully understood the system in which he had to operate, what he could accomplish and what he could not, how to accomplish what he could, and importantly, how long such accomplishment would take, which he measured in years or even decades. Like Louis XIV, he "strove to fulfill and exercise the fullness of royal sovereignty as it was understood in the context of his time," and his "great achievement was to take up the existing potential of the royal state to exert its power in [Korean] society and push it to its limits."[19]

Chapter 1 explores Chosŏn as an early modern polity and interrogates the meaning of the term *absolutism*. Chapter 2 lays the groundwork of eighteenth-century Korea and for Chŏngjo's royal project as arising from the death of his father. It introduces the political world of the Eastern Kingdom, a careful balancing act between the throne and the aristocratic *yangban* ruling class. It also addresses both Chŏngjo's personal grief at his father's tragic end and his Machiavellian willingness to play on the sympathy generated by that tragedy in the service of his political ends. Convinced that nefarious ministers manipulated Yŏngjo into executing his son, Chŏngjo's overriding goal was royal autonomy so that he might never be subjected to such manipulation.

As the boundaries between politics and culture were not strongly policed in Chosŏn, any analysis of one cannot afford to ignore the other. Chapter 3 deals with political philosophy, as Chŏngjo struggled with the *yangban* over the proper interpretation of Confucian ideology. With his mastery of the Confucian canon—the fundamental basis for governing in Chosŏn—the King was in a position to engage in intellectual combat with the *yangban* over his role in government. He brought his formidable intellect to bear on reinterpreting the classical texts of Confucianism to permit a greater degree of royal latitude. Chŏngjo sought to position himself as a scholar-king who instructed his ministers from a superior position, and he drew on earlier commentaries on the classics that stressed loyalty to the ruler as the supreme Confucian virtue. Through expanding the scope of "discretion" 權 (*kwŏn*)—the ruler's power to depart from accepted practice as the need arose, what in Europe might be termed "royal prerogative"—Chŏngjo sought to build an ideological justification for a strengthened kingship. Just as absolutists in Europe thought the ruler should obey the law except in emergencies, when it is acceptable to violate it,[20] Confucian scholars accepted violations of law and ritual in times of crisis.

Chapter 4 addresses how Chŏngjo dealt with the various power groups at court. After looking at his early struggles with the betrayal of a trusted friend—a betrayal that could only have reinforced his commitment to royal autonomy—we examine the intrigues against several members of his family, revealing how the King sought to protect royal relatives in order to preserve the majesty of the royal clan and to make a clear statement that he would be dominated by no one. The chapter then turns to Chŏngjo's handling of the major political factions and his subtle refinement of his predecessor's factional policy. It takes advantage of the recent discovery of Chŏngjo's "secret" letters to a consistent and prominent opponent of his policies, using them to illustrate how the King navigated the labyrinthine webs of power in late Chosŏn. This chapter reveals that Chŏngjo was willing both to sacrifice his friends and to work with his enemies in pursuit of his goals.

Chapter 5 looks at Chŏngjo's efforts to institute a system that would perpetuate royal power. After briefly examining his struggles with the bureaucracy over a key government position, the chapter investigates his creation of two new administrative organs to centralize royal power: a system to train future administrators in his own particular throne-centered interpretation of Confucianism and a locus of power outside the traditional bureaucratic ladder, the Royal Library. The former involved relatively young officials being selected and trained under the king's direction, sometimes receiving lessons directly from the king himself. Men reeducated in this way were the pool of talent from which Chŏngjo drew his support; by the closing years of Chŏngjo's reign, half of all officials to serve in the government came through the system. It is telling that, as soon as Chŏngjo died, his opponents successfully managed to exclude these men from power.

The Royal Library, while on the surface simply a place to store texts deemed important by the king, was given extensive powers by Chŏngjo in exchange for supporting his reforms. Established the very day after he ascended the throne, the Royal Library once again served a dual purpose. It brought prestige to the monarchy and, more pertinently, to Chŏngjo himself, and it also quickly assumed an important role in the politics of his reign. Strikingly, the officials of the Royal Library had the power to impeach officials in the existing government organs but were not subject to impeachment in turn by those in the regular bureaucracy who should have had the power to do so. This vesting of importance in the Royal Library weakened the traditional aristocratic strongholds of power. It is little wonder that Yi T'aek-ching 李澤徵 wrote in a memorial to the King in 1782 lamenting that "[t]he Royal Library is Your Majesty's private institution, not a public institution, and its officials are your private officials with no connection to the court [是閣卽殿下之私閣。而非國中共公之閣也。 是臣卽殿下之私臣。而非朝廷隣哉之臣也]."[21]

The chapter then moves on to address Chŏngjo's efforts to expand the pool of men from which he could draw officials. Throughout his reign, he sought to select men as he saw fit, including those who had long been excluded from positions at court, allowing him to make use of talented men who had no independent power base in the bureaucracy. The rapid removal of these men from power after the King's death is testament to their dependence on him for their positions. The chapter concludes with an examination of the King's attempts to increase direct royal influence by expanding the use of commoner petitions to the throne and the elimination of slavery.

Chapter 6 addresses Chŏngjo's military reforms to increase direct royal power over the military. After gutting the established military organizations— a stronghold of aristocratic authority—the King set up a new army under command of his personally selected governor in the city of Suwŏn, perhaps with an eye toward retiring there in order to escape from aristocrat-infested Seoul, or even transferring the capital there; this force eventually became the central army unit. Central to his reform was the construction of the Illustrious Fortress to guard his father's grave. While it is certainly true that Chŏngjo was intensely concerned with his father's memory, Sado's tomb also provided a convenient excuse for building a fortress to "protect" it, an excuse that would prove difficult for opponents to challenge on ideological grounds. Thus, the Illustrious Fortress is an excellent illustration of Chŏngjo's understanding of kingship: Everything is political and can be used for political ends. To this end, Chŏngjo stationed royal guards at the fortress and designated it as an administrative center. These guards, known as the Robust and Brave Regiment, began as a token tomb guard that the King slowly and patiently built up into a formidable force outside the regular bureaucratic structure of the military.

Chapter 7 evaluates the King as an absolute ruler as compared to his rough contemporaries: the Qianlong Emperor in China and Louis the XIV in France. Because social and political conditions in eighteenth-century Korea—namely the persistence of a landed aristocracy—more closely resembled those of early modern France, Chŏngjo's effectiveness as a ruler was more similar to Louis than to Qianlong, despite Korea's close cultural and diplomatic ties to China. Politically, Korea and France were more typical early modern states, while China emerges as the conspicuous exception due to its enormous size and population and its place as the central power dominating its region to a degree not possible for any state in early modern Europe. The chapter concludes that, according to the definition of "absolute ruler" discussed in chapter 1, Chŏngjo was as much an absolute ruler as these contemporaries, whose rule was made possible by the long-term trends of early modern societies—the further penetration of the state into local affairs and increased interaction between the center and the local, the spread of a shared culture and identity, and bureaucratized administration centered on the king.[22] This strengthens the case for an early modern world in the seventeenth and eighteenth centuries.

The eighth and final chapter concludes with an assessment of Chŏngjo's reforms. A testament to the power Chŏngjo centered in himself is that, after his death, his chosen ministers were quickly ousted from their posts and his reforms were rolled back or co-opted by those who had opposed them. Chŏngjo's son Sunjo 純祖 was only ten years old when his father died, and control of the country passed into the hands of Chŏngjo's opponents. Chŏngjo's plan to end hereditary slavery in Chosŏn was reduced to the mere emancipation of the by-then economically unnecessary palace slaves. Since this supposedly represented a loss of central government revenue, the "shortfall" was made up by the disbanding of Chŏngjo's Robust and Brave Guards. The King's major reforms—such as the abolition of hereditary slavery and the removal of discrimination against the sons of concubines—were only partially carried out by the succeeding regime, or perhaps we should say they were partially blocked. To Chŏngjo belongs whatever credit may be given for these limited reforms. The

1

EARLY MODERNITY AND ABSOLUTISM

ABSOLUTISM DOES NOT ARISE UNTIL THE EARLY MODERN PERIOD, BROADLY defined by Victor Lieberman as that period in world history roughly between 1400 and 1800. It is only in early modern states that the government is centralized enough and its bureaucracy strong enough,[1] with a shared political culture extensive enough, that the ruler can be recognized as the sole legitimate power, subject to no other earthly authority. Lieberman lists the criteria for an early modern state as follows:

> territorial consolidation; firearms-aided intensification of warfare; more expansive, routinized administrative systems; growing commercialization, which (especially from the eighteenth century) contributed to greater social mobility; wider popular literacy, along with a novel proliferation of vernacular texts; more vigorous dissemination of standard dialects and cultural symbols, and an unprecedented intersection between specifically local culture and state power.[2]

Chosŏn Korea fits all of these criteria,[3] which fostered Korean-style absolutism. By the eighteenth century, the Korean king appointed all government officials, including the head of each and every one of the country's three hundred counties and the mayor of every town. Supported by state printing of both official documents and private writings the state deemed worthy of dissemination throughout the country, the Korean elite became more involved than ever in a national culture.[4] With the fall of China to the barbarian Manchus in the seventeenth century, Korea's elite regarded themselves as the last bastion of true Confucian culture, stimulating a flurry of interest in the Korean heritage: local landscape painting, novels with Korean settings and characters, and an emphasis on the "Koreanness" of the ancient kingdom of Koguryŏ 高句麗, which at its height in the sixth century controlled not only the northern half of the Korean peninsula but most of modern-day Manchuria as well.[5]

Paradoxically, the eighteenth century also saw an increased openness to intellectual currents in the Qing Empire, especially among a group of intellectuals known as the "Northern School" 北學 (*Pukhak*), and King Chŏngjo himself shared some of that openness. The continued centralization and routinization of administration, the expansion of the ranks of the *yangban* ruling class and erosion of its status, and the spread of a "Korean" culture and vernacular writing all made absolutism possible.[6] Like Joseph II of Austria, early modern Korean kings interacted directly with the common people through a petition system. The kings traveled away from the capital, meeting the people along the way and adjudicating cases to deal with their grievances, many of which were against the local village heads and administrators. So committed was Chŏngjo to direct royal rule that he revived oral petitions so that those illiterate even in the vernacular could reach him. The elite's cultural disdain of the Manchus, who ruled China as part of their empire in the eighteenth century, reinforced the Korean monarch's claim to be the highest judge and the final arbiter in the land. Regardless of its geographical and cultural distance from Europe, Chosŏn Korea exemplified many of the trends evident in Lieberman's conception of early modernity.

This is not to suggest that the European experience of modernity was either inevitable or universal. In fact, the Korean experience of early modernity illustrates the very opposite—namely, that similar long-term trends and a shared world of growing interconnectedness do not necessarily lead to a loss of cultural distinctiveness or homogenization of societies. Sanjay Subrahmanyam's call to abandon the developmental perspective of who succeeded and who failed to modernize along European lines is welcome.[7] While it may have been true that in the 1970s the "early modern field was formed by backfill from the debris of the collapsed breakthroughs to modernity that had not quite come about,"[8] this is no longer the case. Amy Stanley offers a fine example of how early modern comparison can reveal continuity and connection without subsuming all human experience under a European model. She approaches agency in context in order to illuminate that "certain grooves worn into the social or economic landscape made some avenues of resistance or rebellion not only more possible but more thinkable than others," making macrolevel comparison easier.[9] Stanley examines how "[a]cross the Eurasian continent, a rise in demand for female domestic labor drew women into expanding cities" through a cross-cultural analysis of maidservants.[10] She finds that the "[i]ntimate, local details [of microhistories] . . . can also provide an illusion of specificity, obscuring broader patterns that can be seen more easily by employing a wider geographical frame." Thus, "[s]een through the eyes of these women, the 'early modern' world looks more contiguous—and lingers longer—than we might previously have imagined."[11] She concludes that "[f]rom the maidservant's point of view, London in 1620, Paris in 1750, and Edo in 1840 were surprisingly alike ... a basic story of urban migration, service, and settlement [that] was shared."[12]

As we shall see, while Chŏngjo as an absolute monarch faced similar challenges, operated under similar constraints, and sought broadly similar solutions as did the rulers of early modern Europe, he did so in distinctive ways that reflect the cultural context by which he himself was shaped, even as he exerted his considerable intellectual and political skills to shape it in turn. In our own period of increasing globalization through advanced communication technology and neoliberal free flow of capital and investment, fears of a bland, homogenized, indistinct world of conformity to dominant cultures and the loss of cultural expression are very real in many areas of the world that have long histories of cultural and linguistic unity. Chŏngjo's kingship in the early modern world shows us that a shared world need not be an interchangeable world. While Randolph Starn was correct to point out that all periods "can be thought of as being pulled between old and new, tradition and innovation,"[13] as Mary Elizabeth Berry pointed out when discussing Japan, "[l]ike all labels, the term 'early modern' is a blunt tool for detecting shared properties without leveling its subjects into uniformity. But insofar as it draws into relief the differences as well as the similarities in those subjects, the term abets the goal of historical analysis: understanding the reasons for convergence and divergence by examining the particularities of local experience."[14]

One of the most crucial aspects of early modernity that concerns absolute monarchy was the relationship between the throne and the aristocracy. Rather than the breakdown of the nobility, the trend across Eurasia (with China the conspicuous exception) was for centralization to increase the power of the powerful at the expense of those weaker than them, including lesser nobles. Hillay Zmora reveals that early modernity did not mean the nobility was replaced by the bourgeoisie, but rather "Western European societies underwent a process of aristocratization" in which the center and periphery often both got stronger—the center got greater powers even as local institutions saw their traditional freedoms strengthened.[15] Noble identity in Western Europe was much more in flux in the Middle Ages with no neat definition or criteria, leading Western European nobles to clarify and tighten both of these in the early modern period, such that "the more exact criteria of nobility may have made movement into it more difficult."[16] As other social groups sought to imitate the upper-class lifestyle, the nobles responded by "defining their behavioral norms still further" to keep themselves separate. Thus, court norms "filtered down from the Court to change lesser social groups, gradually transforming the whole of society."[17] The same trend is evident in Chosŏn Korea, where increasing centralization meant that the top *yangban* clans became even more restrictive and exclusive in their specific criteria for membership. Secondary sons were explicitly banned in the early fifteenth century, and the class known as the *chung'in* (middle people) were established, as formerly acceptable occupations were no longer considered noble enough. That is, with the high aristocrats increasingly refusing to serve in these vital positions, a hereditary class emerged below the aristocracy but above the common people to fill the need.[18] Over the course of the Chosŏn period, the filtering down of upper-class Confucian norms brought about what Martina Deuchler famously termed "the Confucian transformation of Korea," as Koreans at all levels of society adopted the cultural symbols and norms of the thoroughly Confucianized *yangban*, forcing more stringent policing of the boundaries like occupation and high office-holding that the most powerful clans used to distinguish themselves.[19]

As the high nobles sought to strengthen their superiority over the lower orders, they were helped by early modern monarchs, who co-opted them into their centralizing state. As the state got larger and the crown's extraction of wealth became more efficient, the nobles were drawn to and assimilated to the state. They competed with each other over access to it, which enhanced the ruler's role as arbiter among competing nobles. Absolutism can only emerge when the elite have been co-opted, such that they have a stake in the state and they consider it more worthy of controlling than obstructing; too much noble control paralyzes the state, as in eighteenth-century Poland, while having little stake in it can lead to outright opposition to it, as in seventeenth-century-century England. As Zmora concludes, "for all the inherent conflicts, a strong monarchy and a strong nobility were not mutually exclusive."[20] Loss of noble autonomy of the state—as expressed in open defiance and rebellion—does not equate to a loss of power but to a conversion of power from one type to another, from violent resistance to exercising influence at court. "Thus, despite differently configured sets of determinants, the crises of the fourteenth century had one similar net result in England, France and Castile: the formation of an alliance between the crown and the lordly class—an alliance which strengthened both to the marked disadvantage of the lower orders."[21] We see the same trend in Chosŏn, where the *yangban* have more to gain by working with the king than against him. After King Kwanghae's overthrow by his officials in 1623, no Chosŏn king faced a serious aristocratic revolt. The most dangerous of all, the 1728 rebellion against Yŏngjo, failed in large part because most of the Disciples faction supported the king rather than joining their brothers in revolt.[22]

Twenty-five years ago Hamish Scott wrote that "[f]ew historical concepts have had their obituaries written more frequently than enlightened absolutism, yet so obstinately refuse to die."[23] While Nicholas Henshall famously disparaged the term as meaning whatever historians want it to mean, Daryl Dee countered in 2009 that "the term *absolutism* still retains considerable analytical value,"[24] and it has indeed refused to die. For Peter H. Wilson, there is no point in constructing a single model of absolutism, since "what we are really dealing with here is a range of comparatively diverse and even partially contradictory ideas."[25] Indeed, it may be that the theoretical clarity scholars strive to get from the term would not reflect the messy realities of the practice of absolute monarchy, even assuming scholars were ever to achieve such theoretical clarity. Still, even if *absolutism* describes a cluster of related phenomena rather than a single theoretical model, it is still useful for demarcating that cluster from other manifestations of political power. Political actors have debated and contested, if rarely explicitly, different aspects of this cluster for centuries. As Michael Rappaport points out, in the early modern period itself there was "no clear demarcation between what constituted a just, 'absolute' monarchy and what was to be considered 'despotic' or tyrannical,'" and so royal powers' legal limits were a negotiated frontier rather than a fixed legal boundary,[26] just as the early modern French state itself was "a system of everyday practices" rather than "a static set of institutions."[27] Cesare Cuttica and Glenn Burgess, in their introduction to *Monarchism and Absolutism in Early Modern Europe*, note that absolutism is a problematic concept that few scholars have taken the time and effort to clearly define and that involved "seemingly incompatible conceptions of kingship [that] coexisted, and could be used, sometimes by the same writer, in defense of a particular monarch of type of monarchy." Nevertheless, they regard absolutism as an attempt "to elevate the (personal) authority of a monarch over other institutions."[28] In his chapter of the same volume, Johann P. Sommerville notes that scholars currently working on absolutism regard the ideas of absolute theorists as unrealistic and unworkable in reality. Absolutism may itself be a myth, a facade put on by kings to disguise how weak they really were. Sommerville counters that both of these claims are false. Instead, "theorists adopted views which accord better with the modern model of absolutism as social collaboration than with the older idea that absolutists aimed at autocratic centralization and bureaucratization." In fact, not only did absolutist theorists not advocate state-building in theory, but the two were not necessarily connected in practice. He points to Britain as an example, which in the eighteenth century had much higher taxes and functioned as a more efficient tax collector than contemporary absolutist France.[29] Derek Beales, who prefers the term *despotism* to *absolutism*, defines *enlightened despotism* to mean when a "ruler possesses or assumes the right to enact legislation without consent, exercises the right extensively and, in doing so, is influenced by" the capital-*E* Enlightenment, not small-*e* enlightenment "in some more general sense."[30] What does Beales mean by the capital-*E* Enlightenment? "[C]ritical, rational reformist opinion in the eighteenth century."[31] By that definition, though, I contend that eighteenth-century Korea counts, despite not being a direct partic-ipant in the capital-*E* Enlightenment. It certainly meets all of those require-ments.[32] Contrast Joseph II, for instance, who considered his edicts to have force of law with no one's approval, with his brother and successor Leopold, who wrote that his orders were not valid until the Estates had assented to them.[33] Joseph sought absolutism, while Leopold did not.

Of course, absolutism is not about unlimited authority, or authority limited only by the ruler's imagination, but "all legitimate political power,"[34] since even "the theory of absolutism never called for totally unrestricted royal power."[35] As Louis XIV himself reportedly said to an English ambassador, "you [must] understand that there are certain things that I can never do."[36] Omer Talon, Louis's attorney when he was a child-king, echoed this sentiment: "[T]here is no state in Europe where the royal authority is as absolute as in France," wrote Talon, yet a government "that accepts no limits, is not tempered by any mild-ness, would be good among Barbarians" but *not* absolutist France.[37] Absolutism lies in the *source* of limits on authority rather than the presence or absence of limits entirely. It is "characterized by compromise, negotiation, and sharing of resources in a manner which maintained and supported hierarchical differ-ences."[38] Early modern people distinguished between independent and unre-stricted, and so while the absolute ruler was theoretically subject to no earthly authority,[39] in practice there were always other political, social, and economic forces to contend with: the labor power and wealth within the state's control and the state's mechanisms for exploiting that power and extracting that wealth, the force of precedent and the legacies of previous rulers, and the necessity of issuing orders to subordinates who inevitably exert influence on how those orders are carried out, to name a few. Even totalitarian leaders of the twentieth and twenty-first centuries, who obtained power that early modern rulers could not even dream of, face at least two of those same limits. An absolute ruler in theory owns all land and is the sole dispenser of justice, the sole source of law, the sole perpetrator of violence, and others may only undertake these activities as delegations of the king's authority. But this power is not unlimited. The realm was "a public trust which a ruler must pass safely on to his successor"; he was not free to dispense with it however he saw fit or to meddle in the succession, as medieval rulers were able to do.[40] The king may rule by the divine right or the Mandate of Heaven, but he must exercise that power justly. The power does not come without the duty to use it responsibly in the eyes of the ruling class who have a stake in its use and abuse. An absolute ruler, then, is one limited by no human institution but instead by convention and a shared understanding among the elite of what constitutes reasonable use and unreasonable abuse of power. In Europe, this understanding was known as divine, or natural, law. "Political power indeed derived from God, but was not given freely and had to be earned by adhering to the true Christian principles of rule."[41] In Korea, the king was limited by the Confucian Way.

The dominant ideology of Chosŏn Korea was Confucianism. This was the philosophico-religious tradition that, Koreans believed, originated with the ancient sage-kings of Chinese antiquity and was explicated and transmitted by Confucius and Mencius, reaching its clearest formulation under the twelfth-century philosopher Zhu Xi (1130–1200). He and others of his school tied the ethical teachings of Confucianism into the cosmos itself. There was only one Way in the universe, one path to follow that was proper. It was not simply how humans ought to behave but how reality itself ought to behave. The ruler must lead the people to follow this Way, the Confucian Way, or risk disturbing the natural order of the universe. Thus, the ruler must use his power wisely—that is, for the furtherance of Confucian values such as filial piety, frugality, benevolence, and justice—lest disaster, including natural disasters like flood and famine, result. Just as the European absolute ruler was king by divine right, anointed by God, the Confucian monarch in East Asia—or, more properly, his family—ruled by virtue of possessing the Mandate of Heaven, the blessing of the cosmos itself that could be withdrawn due to misrule. The ideal of the sage-king in East Asia was not altogether different from the European saintly king who ruled in conformity with Catholic teachings. There was a similar tension between rigid adherence to religious requirements that was "inimical to political and moral compromises." It was still possible, that "a strong allegiance to monarchy could thus be combined with a tendency to find an individual king wanting by comparison with the ideal of truly saintly kingship" in Catholic France[42] and Chosŏn Korea.[43] French bishops, whose prestige and influence stemmed from their being successors to the Apostles, could draw on this lineage to oppose royal influence in ecclesiastical matters in the same way Chosŏn *yangban* scholars could call on their illustrious family background to dispute the king's interpretation of Confucianism.[44]

In the first volume of his *Origins of Political Order*, Francis Fukuyama discusses two types of absolutism: weak and strong. France's was of the former type, meaning the state "faced no formal constitutional constraints on its power," but there were still "a host of powerful individuals against whom it had limited power to act."[45] Fukuyama contrasts this with strong absolutist Chinese emperors on the grounds that the latter could confiscate land and arbitrarily alter tax rates, while French weak absolute monarchs "had to proceed very gingerly when confronting powerful elites."[46] Thus, the French monarchy was never "able to fully dominate the powerful elites in its society, and a heavier burden of taxation was placed on those least able to resist it,"[47] echoing the increasing tax burden on the Korean peasant.[48] Indeed, the French state was "normatively bound to respect the interests of the same social classes it was trying to dominate, and had to respect the laws inherited from the past."[49] While Louis XIV did have some success in relieving tax inequality in many villages,[50] Ronald Asch argues that "[i]f one looks for the limits of monarchical government in the eighteenth century, they are most apparent in the area of fiscal policy and tax reform."[51] In fact, many so-called enlightened reforms actually originated as attempts to sustain the established order *against* social and economic change, but because leaders' policies often have unexpected—and unintended—consequences, these measures altered the social order in unpredictable ways.[52] As one example, Chŏngjo's openness to imports of Japanese metals may have limited growth in the cash supply when the Tokugawa experienced a copper shortage and restricted those exports, the opposite of what the King intended. (He ordered limitations of domestic mining that were supposed to be made up by imports, which his successor was pressured to lift due both to demand and to Tokugawa export restrictions.)[53]

Why should the nobles want an absolute monarch? With struggles over control of the state apparatus, a more lucrative option than local autonomy for an elite increasingly assimilated to the overarching culture of the court, the king went from a rival for power to a mediator between competing claims, a disinterested party who could establish and guarantee privileges. The nobles wanted a strong king, but not *too* strong—powerful enough that he could bring reluctant magnates to heel and secure and separate enough that he had minimal personal stake in aristocratic competition and so could mediate conflict impartially.[54] In early modern France it was believed by absolutists that "freedom is ensured only by the existence of a strong, centralized authority (embodied by the king himself) rather than the absence of such authority,"[55] while in Central Europe an absolute ruler was considered necessary because ministers were "unable to see beyond their narrow class or local interests" and so "the common good was best served by trusting in the authority of an impartial king, standing above the petty squabbles and self-interest of lesser mortals."[56] Supporters of absolute monarchy in France thought that the "antidote" to "a state of civil war and the potential enslavement of the weak to the strong" was none other "an absolute sovereign who can manage the relationship of each member of the body politic to the other."[57] Even the rebellion of the Fronde was in favor of "a return to a balanced monarchy . . . when, [the Frondeurs] claimed, the king listened respectfully to their freely expressed opinions," what in Korea would have been called the channel of speech 言論 (ŏllon).[58]

Absolutism, then, was "essentially a renewed accommodation between monarchy and nobility, not a radical restructuring of their relationship in favor of the former."[59] Absolute authority "depended on the cooperation of other 'power holders' in the localities,"[60] and "the court provided the forum for the social bargaining processes at the heart of absolutism" that served to "domesticate the nobility."[61] Thus, absolute monarchy functioned in practice as a collaboration between the king and the elite, if one fraught with contradiction and sometimes bitter negotiation. Rulers like Chŏngjo and Joseph II would work to co-opt and assimilate the high nobility even as in court cases they tended to side with lesser nobles against the greater, with merit over heredity, and even with commoners against the noble.[62] Studies of France "have shown a continuing interdependence between the sovereign and noble subjects well into the eighteenth century."[63] The king's primary role in the eyes of the nobility was as a balancer, an impartial distributer of favor and support. He was mediator between social groups: between noble and noble, between noble and merchant, between noble and peasant.[64] "The cardinal rule of court politics" in an early modern absolute monarchy was that "a balance had to be maintained in the distribution of patronage so that families and factions remained in a state of equilibrium with the crown as the ultimate arbiter."[65] So Louis XIV, and Chŏngjo, "balanced collaboration and coercion"[66] in which they "preserved and even enhanced [elite] privilege so long as these advantages did not interfere with royal power."[67] Darryl Dee thus offers the following qualification to the revisionist paradigm of absolutism as collaborationism:

> The most important element in Louis XIV's drive to assert his authority was a reshaping of the rules that governed the relationship between the monarchy and the French elites. Revisionist historians of absolutism have rightly stressed that the king's success in ruling France owed much to his willingness to collaborate and compromise with these elites. What they have tended to downplay or even ignore is that he also successfully

strove to make his most powerful subjects accept the elevation of his interests above theirs. He demanded that they give him obedience as the sole possessor of sovereignty, the arbiter of conflict, the guarantor of privileges, and the ultimate source of all patronage. Only after they had accepted these terms did he collaborate with them. Moreover, he acknowledged and protected their interests just so long as they did not interfere with his own. Absolutism depended on a crown-elite alliance, as William Beik, David Parker, and others argue, but this alliance rested on an authoritarian foundation.[68]

Louis's divide-and-conquer strategy, adopted later in his reign, expanding royal prerogative through co-optation but exercising authority where necessary, was more effective than the attempts of Cardinals Richelieu and Mazarin to browbeat the nobles into obedience.[69] Louis's "genius lay in an uncanny knack for molding and consolidating the social order in a manner that both increased his own authority and benefited the traditional elites."[70] Neither Louis nor Chŏngjo had a master plan but "followed a policy of pragmatic opportunism,"[71] expanding royal power where possible, but being careful not to force it.

If kings "could not ride roughshod over the vested interests of office-holders who maintained the state,"[72] it should not be surprising that absolute monarchs have rarely been at the vanguard of radical reform or revolutionary political change, having the most to lose and the least to gain from unleashing the forces of radicalism. Early modern rulers in Eurasia more typically portrayed themselves as upholders of the status quo, protectors of the elite from the inevitable chaos and anarchy of mob rule. In the early modern world, "[a] government that tried a thorough-going overhaul of the system was courting a revolution. . . . Most innovations were apt to infringe on the privilege of some person, group, or institution."[73] Instead, kings concerned themselves with the most important task they had to deal with if they wanted to keep their realms stable and themselves on the throne—*management of the elite*, to use Nicholas Henshall's term.[74] Indeed, Andrew Lossky characterizes Louis's view of reform as "doing away with the accretions and innovations[!] that in the course of time corrupt all human affairs and restoring institutions and customs to their pristine state," just as Chŏngjo sought to "return" Korean institutions to those of ancient China, and Louis believed the "chief purpose of society was the maintenance of privileges."[75] William Beik notes that while the French monarchy was powerful, Louis XIV himself "was a king with a traditional view of his power" and that the French state was "still dominated by the interests of prominent nobles."[76]

This does not mean, of course, that absolute monarchs could not initiate real reform; indeed, I will argue that very thing in this book. Even for absolute monarchs, their early efforts at reform are rarely successful, as their youth and inexperience hamper their ability to effectively actualize the powers at their disposal in ways that placate the aristocracy. Early modern kingship was characterized by reform in the guise of restoration, in defense of rather than active diminution of upper-class privilege, reform that was "undertaken with the utmost caution and carried out piecemeal so as not to arouse general apprehension and resistance," from one end of Eurasia to the other. The king upheld the position of the nobles, because their positions stemmed in part from their relationship to him through office-holding and titles, making them partly dependent on him.[77] In the case of France, "what counted most for the absolute monarchy of Louis XIV during its darkest years was not the new and innovative but the more effective use of the old and traditional."[78] Early failures frequently lay the groundwork for later success, either by themselves or others. Thus, for both Louis and Chŏngjo, their greatest reforms came mostly at the end of their respective reigns.[79] Further, whatever their intentions, the decisions of political actors have effects they cannot anticipate. An example of this can be found in the conclusion to the present work, where I discuss the possibility that Chŏngjo's reforms paved the way for the so-called in-law politics of the nineteenth century that ensured a weak monarchy, certainly not the outcome he intended. Like Louis, Chŏngjo saw (or perhaps merely portrayed?) himself as restoring the system of the past, using monarchical power as the sages had meant for it to be used, rather than aggregating to himself new powers and working to institutionalize them for his heirs. Qianlong, too, reached back to the remote Chinese past—as evidenced by, among other things, the publication of the *Complete Library of the Four Treasuries* 四庫全書 (*Siku quanshu*)—and he did not hesitate to call on the legacy of earlier Chinese emperors, even those of the Ming dynasty that his ancestors cast down. Qianlong lamented the Manchus' loss of martial spirit and proficiency in the Manchu language, both of which he tried and spectacularly failed to restore, at least to his own satisfaction.

In early modern Korea, Confucianism was nearly universally accepted as the governing religion, philosophy, and ideology of not only politics but everyday life. Chŏngjo sought to maximize the throne's power within the confines of Confucianism as it was understood in eighteenth-century Chosŏn.

The aristocrats he faced were dedicated to upholding a robust kingship, but precisely *how* robust was a point of contention and negotiation with the reigning monarch. Each group could call upon strands of Confucian thought that supported their respective positions. Chŏngjo emphasized the king's role as instructor and interpreter of Confucian doctrine and the royal prerogative—termed *discretion* in Chosŏn—to nudge officialdom toward an expansion of royal power. These efforts are the focus of the next chapter.

2

POLITICS IN EARLY MODERN KOREA

All under a single Heaven and all within a single state, do they not together
do homage to a single person and together as one serve a single ruler?

[況一天之下。一國之內。共尊一人。同事一君者乎。]

—King Chŏngjo to his officials, November 2, 1776[1]

IN 1392, MILITARY GENERAL YI SŎNG-GYE OVERTHREW THE 450-YEAR-OLD
Koryŏ 高麗 state and founded Chosŏn. Though a few "new men" were added
to the powerful ruling clans at the time of the dynastic transition, this did
not continue over the rest of Chosŏn.[2] Once the makeup of the ruling *yangban* aristocracy that put Yi Sŏng-gye on the throne was set, there was little
change among the top clans. The term *yangban* existed in Koryŏ, but it was
under the new dynasty that the *yangban* succeeded in cementing its position
as the ruling class. Though the word itself means "the two branches"—that is,
the civil and military branches of the government bureaucracy—the civilian
branch had always been dominant, and this only became truer over the five
hundred years of Chosŏn. The *yangban* class has been aptly characterized
as an aristocratic-bureaucratic hybrid class.[3] The primary route to government office-holding was the civil service examination system, the *kwagŏ*
科擧, originally borrowed from China during the Koryŏ period (935–1392).
The examinations tested candidates' knowledge of the Confucian classics in
a three-tiered system of testing culminating in the *munkwa* 文科 ("literary
test"), the most coveted degree in the realm because it was required to serve
in any meaningful office in the capital. This, coupled with the king's power
to appoint and dismiss officials at will, was the bureaucratic side. Upon being
appointed to office, officials were given the appropriate "rank" for their new
positions. They maintained this rank after they left the office, even if they later
accepted an office with a lower rank. Consequently, many officials served in

offices below their rank. The official rank system was divided into eighteen divisions from one to nine, with a "senior" and "junior" within each division. Most officials only served in the bottom six ranks, junior ninth (9b) to senior seventh (7a). Reaching the middle ranks (6b to 4a) was a significant achievement, and the highest ranks (3b to 1a) were a distant dream for most, no matter how illustrious their ancestors were.

But the system was not entirely meritocratic. Despite lack of explicit laws against it, commoners were essentially unable to take the examinations due to the enormous time and expense required to prepare for it.[4] Sons of *yangban* fathers by their concubines were legally prohibited from taking the examinations. Even in the few periods in which they were eligible, they were still barred unless they could clearly establish their mothers' commoner status for at least two generations, and the mothers' "very identification as commoner precluded an advancement to the upper ranks of the bureaucracy."[5] Officials often held large private estates and commanded large numbers of private slaves wholly apart from their offices, meaning they, like French officials, did not depend on their government salary for their livelihood.[6] And while they did derive enormous prestige from success in the examinations and government service, they also drew on their ancestors' illustrious deeds and could gain moral credibility by refusing to serve in government on account of a noble desire to avoid the fame and power associated with office-holding.

In the eighteenth century, social mobility was on the rise in Korea. The technical specialists who existed uneasily between the *yangban* and the common people—appropriately enough known as *chung'in* 中人 or "middle people," though the name stems from their originating from the central districts of the capital rather than their place in society—were more and more attaining the trappings of the powerful, and slavery was entering a relatively steep and rapid decline after being a major social institution in Korea for at least a millennium.[7] Wealthy commoners were purchasing degrees and offices and, by extension, *yangban* status. Others were gaining that status through success on the military examinations, which had been the province of *yangban* but were increasingly seen as beneath the dignity of true *yangban*.[8] Still, the ranks of the powerful did not change substantially. The only true *yangban* were capital-based civilian families who were prominent at the time Chosŏn was founded. Reflecting early modern trends also seen in France, the families at the top were gradually squeezing out the lesser *yangban* and pretenders by tightening and clarifying the criteria for elite membership. James Collins notes that the high officials in France "formed a progressively more closed caste" and that "the main offices of the royal household passed permanently into the hands of small groups of families by the 1680s."[9] In both countries, the expansion of the ranks of the noble—reflected in the much bandied-about figure of 20 percent of Chosŏn families were *yangban* in the mid-nineteenth century—came even as much of the mobility consisted of certain groups' being pushed out of positions of real influence in the centralizing state. The upper class in early modern France and Korea consisted of "an aristocracy, a more sizeable middling nobility, and a large—sometimes very large—lesser nobility. At the apex were a group of families of real power and immense wealth."[10] This trend in France was reflected throughout sixteenth-century Europe, where "a relatively small group of well-placed families monopolized Crown favor, acquiring wealth, status, and titles to match."[11] Military families, those who bought *yangban* status, sons of *yangban* by concubines, upwardly mobile *chung'in*—all of these lived better than mere commoners, to be sure, but they held little influence in the central state, where power was increasingly located, and had no opportunity to serve in high office. That right exclusively remained with the twenty or so extremely wealthy and powerful civilian *yangban* clans who dominated the government at the dynasty's founding. It is these *yangban* that concern us here.

ARISTOCRATIC-BUREAUCRATIC BALANCE[12]

Politics in Chosŏn Korea could be described as, if not a tug-of-war between the king and his ministers, a tug-of-war between the throne and the aristocratic-bureaucratic hybrid that constituted the elite *yangban* class. The throne and the *yangban* needed each other, even as they struggled against one another with no clear "winner" over the course of five hundred years. The structure of Korean society set the parameters under which the new Chosŏn state could operate. Chosŏn was at its founding in 1392 a monarchical, centralizing, bureaucratic government on top of an aristocratic, hierarchical social system. The central government was in competition with the *yangban* aristocrats over access to land, slaves, and labor. Power, wealth, and prestige were not the province of the throne alone. Inherited status based on lineage put the *yangban* on equal footing with the early Chosŏn kings. Private land ownership was consistently condemned for being in conflict with the theoretical notion, inherited from sacred texts of Chinese antiquity, that all land in the state belonged to the king. Yet those same texts extolled the virtues of filial piety, part of which was understood as passing on enough property to provide an acceptable livelihood for one's children. Thus, effective private ownership and inheritance of land was never seriously threatened throughout the whole of the dynasty.

Further, Korea had a long tradition of local independence from excessive central authority. As in France, understaffed, overworked central government administrators operating in localities were dependent on local elite families for support in governing their areas, and the bureaucratic system discouraged vigorous leadership; most provincial governors wanted nothing more than to leave office without a scandal.[13] Provincial governors were also rotated frequently and were not permitted to serve in their home areas, creating space between them and the local *yangban* on whom they depended for assistance in administering their districts. The government clerks 鄉吏 (*hyangni*) who were supposed to support the governor, having lost their official salaries and their aristocratic status in the transition from Koryŏ to Chosŏn, also turned to corruption. Korea also had a long tradition of consensus-based decision-making. Rarely would a king in Koryŏ make a major decision that was opposed by a sufficient number of important officials, and even powerful early Chosŏn kings generally followed their model. Most major issues were decided by the *tangsanggwan* 堂上官, encompassing thirty to fifty officials of the top three bureaucratic ranks who had the right to request a royal audience. Also included in this number were various sinecured elder statesmen. This consensus-based policy-making was a significant hurdle for the king to overcome should he desire to impose his own will on the bureaucracy.

Finally, Korea was relatively isolated from political shocks (such as invasions) and economic shocks (such as extensive foreign trade) on any major scale. Indeed, in nearly five centuries of the dynasty up to 1876, Chosŏn experienced only two periods of major invasion: Japanese from 1592 to 1598 and Manchu from 1627 to 1637. As devastating as these periods of invasions were, it remains that they made up less than twenty years out of almost five hundred. It is this relative stability that allowed Chosŏn to remain an aristocratic agricultural society, in sharp contrast to China and Europe. In China, the Tang 唐 dynasty (618–907) aristocratic-bureaucratic hybrid class was slowly transformed into the Song 宋 dynasty (960–1276) bureaucratic gentry class around the turn of the second millennium, as invasions from the north forced the landed aristocrats to abandon their power bases there and flee south, increasing their dependence on service in the imperial government under an autocratic emperor by the Ming 明 dynasty (1368–1644).[14] A kind of aristocracy did emerge in southern China after the destruction of the northern aristocracy with the fall of Tang, but this was a much more localized aristocracy that did not dominate central office-holding as the Korean *yangban* did. The lack of a dominating aristocracy in China was recognized by *yangban* at the time, with Chief Censor Sang Chin (1494–1564) remarking in 1539 that "at the Ming court there are no aristocrats

[中朝無士族也]."[15] Extensive foreign trade in Song led to the development of wide-spread commercialization and urbanization, two trends notably absent from Chosŏn until the eighteenth century. Even then, their scale did not approach the comparable trends in Song.[16] Where in Europe extensive wars gutted the nobility (though the old noble families were replaced with new blood),[17] the Korean *yangban* class retained remarkable stability over the early modern period.[18]

Still, despite these formidable challenges to centralization and royal despotism, the Chosŏn monarch was never reduced to a figurehead, as were the Japanese emperors or even some kings of Koryŏ. Chosŏn kings had significant resources at their command, and as long as they were adults of sound mind and body, they were the central figures on the political scene, even in periods of bureaucratic dominance.

First, as much as it was a restriction on the king's authority, the need for consensus also limited what the aristocracy could accomplish when it was not united, which was most of the time. Eighteenth-century Korean politics were dominated by four major hereditary factions known collectively as "the Four Colors" 四色 (*sasaek*): the Patriarchs 老論 (*Noron*), the Disciples 少論 (*Soron*), the Southerners 南人 (*Namin*), and the Northerners 北人 (*Pugin*). Despite their names, the factions were not regionally based. Rather, they originated in a combination of policy disputes and personal animosity between important leaders. A distinguishing feature of the late Chosŏn polity was the hereditary nature of the factions. The extreme *yangban* emphasis on family background and lineage meant that factional strife carried down through the centuries. Factional cohesion was maintained through the generations as aristocrats were educated in their faction's own private academies and exclusively married women from other families in their faction. The Patriarchs dominated much of eighteenth-century politics and consequently were the most resistant to fundamental change and held most strongly to an idealized view of Confucianism and particularly to Zhu Xi, the man regarded as the most correct interpreter of the Confucian Way in Chosŏn Korea. In line with their rather quaint adherence to a pure Confucianism, they were also the most anti-Manchu, with their founder Song Si-yŏl (1607–1689) deeply involved in planning King Hyojong's (r. 1649–1659) never-realized "northern expedition" to overthrow the hated Qing Empire. Their sibling rival, the Disciples—the two factions had split from a parent faction a century earlier—were less conservative than the Patriarchs, but not by much. It was the Southerners who were the most pragmatic and reform-minded, often calling on the throne to lead the reform drive, and the least hostile to the Qing. As one might expect, this was largely because the Southerners had been out of high office since 1694, and so had the most to gain from altering the existing system. No one much cared what the Northerners thought by the eighteenth century, as their association with the bloodshed surrounding the overthrow of King Kwanghae in 1623 had tainted them beyond hope of returning to power.[19]

In addition to these vertical cleavages between official factions, there were horizontal cleavages as well. Because the high officials 大臣 (*taesin*) were consulted and gave their assent to policy decisions, they were the king's ally when it came to implementing them in the face of opposition from lower-ranking ministers. Over the course of the dynasty, the critical voice of the Censorate—made up of three separate offices whose duties nevertheless overlapped, leading them to be referred to collectively—became more and more sacrosanct. Younger ministers, having been appointed to the one of the three censorial offices 三司 (*samsa*), were expected to be free to criticize the government. In practice, to avoid accusations of *lèse majesté*, they usually attacked the high officials instead. Thus, the censorial voice acted both to restrict the king and to push the high ministers into defending him and his policies. Early modern absolutism in Korea was just as much about collaboration between the highest *yangban* and the king as about a willful monarch demanding obedience.

Second, the path to political leadership involved success in the state examinations, obtaining royal favor, and the holding of high office, the second of these being the most critical. No official, no matter his position or power base, could remain in power after losing the favor of the king. Cho Kwang-jo 趙光祖 was put to death when he lost the trust of King Chungjong 中宗, despite there being only a few calls for his execution and a great deal of official support for him. Song Si-yŏl 宋時烈, for a time the most powerful official in the country, was executed for opposing King Sukchong's 肅宗 choice of heir. Hong Kuk-yŏng 洪國榮, decried for running the country in place of King Chŏngjo, was exiled when his scheme to put his adopted nephew in the line of succession incensed the king. All these men reached the apex of political power when they had the favor of the king and tumbled into death or exile when they lost it.

Third, the king, though with the advice and recommendation of his ministers, retained the right to appoint and dismiss officials at will. Though he was often criticized for the choices he made in individual cases, this power remained firmly with the throne. To suggest anyone other than the king should control official appointments was treasonous, and any official foolhardy enough to be so brazen would unite the rest of the *yangban* against him. Unlike France, where the crown was often financially disincentivized to dismiss officials, the Korean monarch was not shy about taking back what he had given.

Even the most illustrious of *yangban* families had to legitimate their power through holding office in the central government or risk losing recognition as a leading clan. Failure to produce a high-ranking government official for enough generations relegated a family to second-tier *yangban* or rural elite (sometimes referred to as *hyangban* 鄉班), who "still retained a vestige of prestige from inherited social status" but "whose life style hardly differed from that of commoners."[20] This kind of downward social mobility, though by no means common, was a regular occurrence throughout the dynasty. Thus, the king's bureaucracy was an important source of *yangban* status, one they could not afford to ignore. Therefore, aristocratic resistance in late Chosŏn rarely resulted in open defiance or outright rebellion, since the *yangban* were intimately tied to the state and the king for their very positions and collaborated with him to support their positions in the absolutist, centralized state. Just as the early modern French monarchy "had grown strong over two centuries by co-opting much of the French elite" through their "actual purchase of small pieces of the state, which could then be handed down to descendants,"[21] Chosŏn *yangban* were bound to the state by ties of prestigious office-holding. As Hillay Zmora put it, "[o]nce the state was worth fighting over, there was less point in fighting against it."[22] This is a prime example of how differing social conditions and cultures can nevertheless lead to the same conclusion by different paths. Aristocrats' gaining a share in the state gives them a stake in preserving absolute monarchy.

Finally, though the *yangban* as a class were wealthy, the royal family remained the wealthiest individual family, and the aristocrats were never able to significantly restrain the king's use of the royal treasury. Short of insisting that the king ought to be frugal, there was nothing the *yangban* could do to halt the king's spending.

As a practical matter, then, the king was only the most powerful political figure in the realm, not the only one with any power. Indeed, his formidable might was only possible because he was locked in a dependent embrace with the *yangban* scholar-aristocrats. These men, bolstered by prestigious lineage—some boasted illustrious ancestors in Koryŏ and even the ancient Silla kingdom who outshone the royal ancestors—and extensive landholdings, worked with him because they saw a powerful, independent king in a position to dispassionately arbitrate disputes was the best way to uphold their privileges. No matter how serious factional disputes became, the aristocrats would close ranks to defend against any attempt to reduce their land- or slave-holdings or to eliminate either their immunity to military and corvée labor service or their monopoly on office-holding. Like their European counterparts, the *yangban* were happy with absolute monarchy so long as its power was not used to strike at their property rights.[23] For this reason, cadastral surveys carried out in an attempt to equalize the tax burden and reduce aristocratic tax dodging in Spain, in Joseph II's Austria, and in Chŏngjo's Korea all failed.[24] Indeed, as the dynasty went on, the *yangban* further restricted access to the highest levels of power, even as the military examinations and sale of degrees permitted the lowest ranks of *yangban* to swell, prompting Eugene Park to remark that late Chosŏn social status was "rigid at its extremes but fluid in the middle."[25] The most powerful *yangban* families continued to marry each other and block lesser *yangban* from the corridors of power, whatever degrees they bought, just as "the older nobility [in France] closed the doors to many offices to anyone who could not demonstrate 'four quarters' noble descent, that is from all four grandparents" in order to shut out commoners who had bought their titles.[26] Reflecting early modern trends throughout Eurasia, the development of the Korean state "played a critical part in the tendency towards the concentration of power and wealth in the hands of an ever smaller number of prominent nobles," who perpetuated their power in part by marrying almost exclusively within their own narrow circle.[27] Whether kings pushed for centralization to bolster their own power or whether their efforts to expand their authority bolsters other centralizing forces, the early modern period saw both trends in operation at both ends of Eurasia.

As only *yangban* were effectively able to take the examinations, the king had no alternative but to staff his bureaucracies with them, all the more so because he was usually expected to select from a list of candidates submitted by the Minister of Personnel. Like "French families [who] zealously guarded their 'survivance' and might give the king little room for maneuver in appointments,"[28] the *yangban* jealously guarded their privilege of office-holding, blocking their own sons by consorts and men from the northern provinces. In a society in which family descent and Confucian learning were vital, no Chosŏn king could emulate the Ming example by making political use of eunuchs, since they lacked opportunities for education and any semblance of prestige in Korean society. Confucian scholars' hold on high politics in Chosŏn made it likewise impossible for the dynasty to emulate King Kongmin's 恭愍 (r. 1351-1374) employment of the Buddhist monk Sin Ton during the late Koryŏ period. Adoption was practiced, but only among collateral family lines; adopting a son from a completely unrelated family was unacceptable among *yangban* families by the late Chosŏn. Commoners were effectively banned from taking the examinations, and kings struggled even to bring lesser *yangban* into the government. King Chŏngjo in the eighteenth century and the Taewŏn'gun in the nineteenth century had some success in bringing in *yangban* from the northern provinces—traditionally regarded as not even true *yangban* by the illustrious families in the capital—but these attempts were strongly resisted and did not continue when the reins of power passed to a new ruler. Indeed, a key *yangban* advantage was simply their ability to perpetuate themselves as a class. The throne's power waxed with strong monarchs but waned again with weak ones; as kings came and went, the *yangban* class remained, weathering the storm of strong rulers until one came along that they could dominate.

In addition to their lineage prestige, landholding, education, and monopoly of the bureaucracy, the higher officials controlled the careers of lower officials through the processes of review of current performance and recommendation to higher office. Through these twin pillars, high officials could ensure that lower officials would be careful of who and how they criticized from their otherwise inviolate censorial offices. Thus, any maverick official who made a strong challenge to *yangban* privilege in the name of reform for the sake of better government risked not only his own career but those of his brothers, sons, nephews, and even cousins.[29]

Like Christianity in Europe, the dominant ideology of Confucianism was a two-edged sword, whose contradictory tendencies contributed to the balance of royal/bureaucratic and aristocratic forces in Korea. For the *yangban*, the Confucian virtue *hyo* 孝 (filial piety) represents a source of loyalty outside the state (such as justifying private inheritance and control of land), and it helped to perpetuate factional loyalties down through the generations. The emphasis on bureaucracy and the right to remonstrate restrict the ruler's ability to curtail *yangban* privilege, and the notion of a ruling class made up of virtuous men justified inequalities of status and wealth.

For the monarch, Confucianism is powerful because it is predicated on there being a king. The educated elite serve him, offering advice while he does the actual ruling. Through emphasis on the Confucian virtue *ch'ung* 忠 (loyalty), he dispatches his officials to carry out his instructions. The Confucian bureaucracy gives him sole right of appointment over key offices, both in the capital and in the provinces. While reformers like Chŏng To-jŏn 鄭道傳 envisioned a figurehead monarch with actual power in the hands of a prime minister, the Confucian stigma against ministers usurping the monarch's power had roots both wide (appearing many times in many Confucian texts and dynastic histories) and deep (extending back to the earliest Chinese classics). As long as the king was an adult of sound mind, he could not be replaced as the locus of power. And while the Korean king in the Confucian worldview was subservient to the Son of Heaven, the emperor of China, he was the final arbiter in his country. The Chinese emperor may have been theoretical true master of the world, but in practice Chinese rulers did not interfere in domestic Chosŏn affairs—even to the point of not intervening in succession struggles.[30] By the eighteenth century, Confucianism no longer weakened even the ideological basis for absolute monarchy in Chosŏn, because China was governed as part of the Manchu Qing Empire (1644-1912). The Korean elite—with some notable exceptions, who were grouped together under the term *Northern Learning* 北學 (*pukhak*)—regarded the Manchus as uncultured barbarians who lacked the moral worth and Confucian refinement necessary to rule the Middle Kingdom. The Manchus had to subjugate Korea through repeated invasion to force it to accept Manchu suzerainty, and the elite continued to imply a lack of recognition of Qing in secret. The government maintained a shrine to the emperors of Ming, and private letters continued to be dated according to the reign of the last Ming emperor. Both of these actions were treasonous in traditional East Asia, and they were carefully hidden from Qing ambassadors. King Hyojong— held hostage as crown prince by the Qing in their capital to ensure the loyalty of his father—even planned a military expedition to liberate China from the Manchus, though this foolhardy mission never got beyond the planning stage. Thus, the eighteenth-century Korean elite regarded the king of Korea as the last legitimate authority remaining in the world. The Eastern Kingdom had no choice but to bow to the superior military might of the Qing as a practical matter of survival, but it remained the "Little Civilization Center" 小中華 (*So chunghwa*), the last bastion of civilization.

THE PRINCE SADO AFFAIR AND LEGITIMACY

> I have just returned to the palace. Not only am I exhausted, but today I made a sacrifice, and it is all the more difficult now to stay focused due to my longing for my father.
>
> [承慰。此中今始還內。憊甚之外。此朔此享。孺慕尤難抑耳。]
>
> —Chŏngjo to in a letter to Sim Hwan-ji, June 26, 1800[31]

Chŏngjo was the son of Crown Prince Sado 思悼世子, the son of King Yŏngjo, and Lady Hyegyŏng 惠慶宮 洪氏 of the P'ungsan 豊山 Hong 洪 clan, Sado's legitimate wife. As the grandson of the king and the only son of a legitimate wife, Chŏngjo's own legitimacy ordinarily would have been unquestionable. But the tragedy of Prince Sado's death made the issue more complicated. Chŏngjo's relationship with his father's memory and his mother's clan are thus complex and contradictory, illustrating the intricate labyrinth of Chosŏn politics in which the public and the private are fused—for no one more so than the king—and the slightest misstep could prove fatal.

While neither Yŏngjo nor Chŏngjo ever faced a plot that came close to overthrowing him—due in no small part to the lack of a rival with a credible claim—both kings struggled with legitimacy. Yŏngjo was the son of a palace servant and ascended to the throne after the brief reign of his brother. While the rules for royal sons of concubines were less strict than those for *yangban*— the son of a *yangban* by a concubine was, in many ways, not even considered *yangban* at all—it was still a touchy subject, for the son of a concubine would take the throne only if there were no legitimate sons available.[32] Yŏngjo also had to deal with rumors that he had poisoned his own brother to become king himself. The rebellion he faced early in his reign was quickly put down and he himself was never in serious danger, but the rebellion profoundly affected the way he conducted himself as king.[33]

In 1762, Yŏngjo ordered Sado to enter a rice chest, which was then sealed, and Sado died eight days later. The reasons for this are not clear, with contradictory accounts claiming that Sado was provoked to treasonous conduct by extremist Disciples or that Sado's own mental illness meant that he had to be eliminated to secure the dynasty.[34] While it is impossible to make a definitive statement on the matter, the latter account seems better supported by reason and the available historical evidence. First, it is buttressed by a firsthand eyewitness who was not herself directly involved in court intrigue and had no direct connection to any of the factions—Sado's wife, Lady Hyegyŏng.[35] Her 1805 account also fills in gaps about the execution of Sado, where the official records are conspicuously elusive. It is not merely that the record is silent but that it elides and obscures the events, not least because Chŏngjo requested and received Yŏngjo's permission to excise parts of the official record that he (Chŏngjo) deemed injurious to his father's memory. Lady Hyegyŏng's account is, moreover, supported by its damning portrayal of Sado himself, particularly the final memoir that exposes the symptoms of his madness. It is impossible to know, but it is tempting to speculate that these are exactly the sorts of things that Chŏngjo had expunged from the official record. In any case, that Lady Hyegyŏng includes them lends significant credibility to her account, since Sado's madness is no better than—and in fact could be judged *worse* than—his intriguing with an extremist faction. It is hard to see any benefit to Lady Hyegyŏng herself, her natal family, or to her grandson Sunjo that could be gained by manufacturing such an account of madness. Indeed, if she were to lie about Sado's death, it would have been much more culturally and politically acceptable at the time simply to blame the deceit of the extremist Disciples who supposedly conspired with Sado, especially since her own family were Patriarchs and so had no reason to elide Disciple misconduct. Second, as the only surviving son of Yŏngjo, it is difficult to conceive of Sado's intriguing against his father for the throne as a rational political calculation. Unlike the constantly warring sons of Henry II, Sado had no rival, nor did he come from a culture emphasizing martial prowess as a quality of kingship. When Sado lamented to his wife that the birth of Chŏngjo meant his father no longer needed him as heir, this is not the reasonable conclusion of a sane man. After all, there had been in the history of the dynasty—all 350 years of it to that point—not a single instance of a son being passed over in favor of his own son in the succession. Though Haboush believes Sado's claim to be a possibility,[36] Sado, as the sole legitimate adult son of the reigning monarch, could not have been displaced as heir were he of sound mind and body in late Chosŏn, without sparking a rebellion, if not a dynastic war—exactly the sort of thing Yŏngjo spent his entire reign trying to avoid. Indeed, Yŏngjo was sure to have Sado killed rather than allowing him to remain in the capital or even to be exiled, for a living Sado would have been a constant threat around whom enemies of the king could rally. With benefit of hindsight, we historians know that Yŏngjo lived for another fourteen years after Sado's death, but Yŏngjo himself did not know this, so, for him, passing over Sado would mean in all likelihood giving the throne to a child (Yŏngjo was sixty-seven years old when Sado died), making it extremely unlikely either that Yŏngjo would have considered it or that his officials would have accepted it. Finally, Yŏngjo spent virtually the entirety of his reign struggling against calls that he side with one faction or another and conduct bloody purges against others. That he would chose to murder his own son merely because he was involved with a particular faction beggars the imagination.

Whatever the reason, what is pertinent for us is that, in addition to the horror and grief felt by a parent who made the decision to end the life of his child, Yŏngjo was profoundly disturbed by the possible implications of Sado's execution on the dynasty. Under Chosŏn law, a criminal's family was punished along with him, including his sons, and they all shared the status of a convicted criminal. Considering the moral dimensions of a Confucian kingship, the son of a criminal ascending the throne was unthinkable. Thus, Sado was not officially convicted of any crime, and he was not technically executed. Rather, he was ordered to enter a rice chest, which was then sealed, and eight days later he died. But Yŏngjo still was not confident in the succession, so two years later he had Chŏngjo adopted by Sado's deceased elder brother, known to history as Crown Prince Hyojang 孝章世子. (This sort of posthumous adoption was not unusual among elite lineages in late Chosŏn.)

All of this legalistic jiggery-pokery had one ultimate goal: to avoid any taint on the legitimacy of Chŏngjo's accession. To a large extent, it was successful; as noted, no serious challenge to Chŏngjo's rule ever emerged. That does not mean, however, that Chŏngjo was completely free of legitimacy issues. Indeed, he addressed the matter on the very day of his succession in 1776.

> The King met with the high officials outside the gates of the Funereal Palace. The King said, "Alas! I am the son of Crown Prince Sado, but because the Late King took the royal succession seriously, he ordered that I become the heir of Crown Prince Hyojang, alas! Some time ago there was a memorial sent up to the Late King in which it was pointed out that I cannot have sprung from two different roots. Although the regulations governing rites must be strictly observed, feelings likewise cannot be suppressed. The regulations for this sacrificial offering of food ordain that this should be a ritual for the sacrifice to great men and should not be the same as those to the royal ancestors. Lady Hyegyŏng also properly receives gifts outside the capital but cannot be treated as the Queen Dowager,[37] so I want the high officials to discuss and inform me of the proper procedures. As soon as I hand this down, if any fiendish cliques attempt to use it is a pretext to have a debate over my father's having been given a posthumous title, it was the Late King's wish that I decide according to the law and inform his spirit of the decision."[38]

[召見大臣于殯殿門外。下綸音曰嗚呼。人思悼世子之子也。大王爲宗統之重。命予嗣孝章世子。嗚呼。前日上章於先大王者。大可見不貳本之予意也。禮雖不可不嚴。情亦不可不伸。饗祀之節。宜從祭以大夫之禮。而不可與太廟同。惠慶宮亦當有京外貢獻之儀。不可與大妃等。其令所司。議于大臣。講定節目以聞。旣下此敎。怪鬼不逞之徒。藉此而有追崇之論。則先大王遺敎在焉。當以當律論。以告先王之靈。]

Here we see the King express the fundamental contradiction between the roles he was assigned publicly (as ruler) and privately (as son) and his manipulation of views of his private life in the service of his public (political) goals. He could not title his mother Queen Dowager because his father had been effectively cut out of the line of succession by the adoption. He could perform a ritual appropriate for a great man for his father, but he could not perform for him a ritual that implied he was part of the ancestral line of Chosŏn kings.

Still, the King paid great attention to honoring his birth parents as part of his moral legitimacy, and much effort went into finding the most laudatory titles that ritual precedent would allow him to bestow on them. Ten days after his succession, Chŏngjo likewise lamented his inability to title his father as posthumous king, as would have been ritually permitted (indeed, demanded), but for his adoption, even as he ordered that his father's tomb be administered by the very same directorate he had established to deal with his adopted father Hyojang as an "uncrowned king," though Sado was no longer in the royal line.[39] However, he could not bestow these honors on his father until the day *after* he had properly honored his adopted father by bestowing on him the title appropriate for the legal father of a reigning king, which he did on the eighteenth of April.[40]

It is telling that when Chŏngjo re-interred Sado's remains in a new tomb, the site he chose for the tomb was originally intended for King Hyojong.[41] The King made frequent trips to his father's tomb throughout his reign. As with all royal processions, these were lavish spectacles. Equal spectacle was provided by Chŏngjo's displays of filial affection in front of his officials, such as when he threw himself to the ground crying and "dug up handfuls of earth until his fingernails were torn [手撮莎土。至損爪甲]."[42] While these displays were undoubtedly the result of deep personal feelings, Chŏngjo could scarcely have been unaware of their political meaning as well. For the Chosŏn monarch, there was no distinction between public and private, no moment—save perhaps those in his bedchamber—where he was not observed, recorded, and monitored. Like Louis in Versailles, his every gesture, no matter how personally motivated, carried political weight as well, and the King was willing to use this tool in his arsenal to cow his officials. I include but one of many such occasions here as an example of Chŏngjo's political theater.

The King went to the Garden of Perpetual Blessings to perform the rites there. When the royal carriage arrived at the Peaceful Repose Hill, [his] breathing became labored. The palanquins all stopped, and liquid and pill medicines were presented to him. He then went into the Sacrificial Hall.

. . .

When the time arrived, the King mourned his father and did homage to his father's spirit tablet. Upon reaching the garden, the King entered the *on'ga*[43] and, grabbing and pulling at the grass covering the tomb, he wailed and beat his breast. Those in charge of the palace clinic, the officials of the Royal Library, the Royal Secretaries, and the various high officials repeatedly requested that he stop, but the King did not listen to any of them. By that point, much time had passed, and the King's breathing symptoms had returned more severely, such that even his crying made no sound, as if something were caught in his throat. Those ranked below the high officials came forward with a memorial:

"We your servants must take this step which is such that it might be punished with death." Following this, they took the royal person by the arms and helped him to stand. From the rest lodge, he rode in the palanquin and entered the Sacrificial Hall. After a moment, his breathing became settled and he returned to the palace.[44]

[詣永祐園。行啓園禮。駕至安樂峴。膈氣添劇。駐輦連進湯丸。入齋室。

...

時至上具緦服。詣版位。及啓園。上詣甕家內。攀撫莎草。號擗踴節。藥院提調閣臣承旨諸大臣。迭請止哭。上皆不聽。時更漏已深。膈候復劇。哭不能成聲。連有嘔吐之候。大臣以下齊進奏曰臣等不得不犯此死罪。遂扶掖聖躬而起。至小次乘便輿入齋室。少頃氣定還宮。]

Another entry in the *Veritable Records* describes the King "wailing and pouring out his heart without ceasing [哭盡哀不止]" until his officials physically dragged him away,[45] because as he noted, "I cannot restrain what is in my heart [心懷自不抑制]."[46] His officials, of course, are no strangers to this sort of manipulation. Hence, their solemn declaration that they must assist the king, even though their actions (in this case, touching the royal person without permission) "might be punished with death." Ch'oe Seong-hwan argues that the King used sympathy for this tragedy to make it harder for the factions to oppose him and that it served as his trump card to force the opponents to bend to his will.[47]

Chŏngjo was fortunate enough to ascend the throne as an adult, with the full support of his predecessor and with no serious contender. However, as is often the case with the accession of a new monarch, the King and his supporters immediately moved to secure the throne. The death of Sado had profound repercussions for Chŏngjo's reign. Yŏngjo, the king who spent his entire fifty-year-reign trying to contain factionalism, by the act of executing his son created two new factions: the Intransigents 僻派 (*pyŏkp'a*), who supported Yŏngjo's decision to end his son's life and initially clustered around Kim Kwi-ju 金龜柱 and his Kyŏngju Kim clan, and the Expedients 時派 (*sip'a*), defenders of Sado, who were generally regarded as supportive of Chŏngjo and initially rallied around Chŏngjo's maternal grandfather Hong Pong-han 洪鳳漢. Though these new factions cut across existing factional lines, the Intransigents were strongest in the Patriarchs faction while the Expedients were concentrated in the Disciples and Southerner factions.[48] There was presumably great fear among the Intransigents that the son of Sado would, upon his accession to the throne, wreak vengeance on those who advocated his father's execution. Chŏngjo, however, astutely refused to follow the example of King Yŏnsan, who in 1504 had set off a round of bloody violence to avenge the death of his mother. Rather, he emulated Yŏngjo's refusal to purge the Disciples who had opposed Yŏngjo's own succession. Chŏngjo resolved instead to continue his grandfather's Policy of Impartiality of minimal bloodshed and factional violence, though as we will see, his conception of that policy was in reality distinct from Yŏngjo's. This is not to say some officials did not attempt to use vengeance as a tool to manipulate him. But Chŏngjo would not be moved, for his ultimate goal was to carve out a space for independent action of the throne, and he was to make it clear again and again that he would be beholden to no one: not to the Expedients faction, not to his mother's clan, not even to graduates of his own royal selection system or to his key supporters like Ch'ae Che-gong and Hong Kuk-yŏng.

So despite his understandable bitterness with the Intransigents, he did not move against them en masse, nor did he sweep the Expedients into power. Indeed, relatively few men suffered immediately. People like Kim Sang-no 金尙魯, Hong Kye-hŭi 洪啓禧, and Mun Sŏng-guk 文聖國 were posthumously stripped of office for their support of Sado's execution, and their families were banished or enslaved or both.[49] Yet the sons were not killed, and the King refused demands that other men be punished simply for being connected to Kim or Hong.[50] He also initially rejected calls to execute Mun Sŏng-guk's aunt, Lady Mun 淑儀文氏, presumably due to her position as Yŏngjo's consort.[51]

King Chŏngjo's father died inside a sealed rice chest, a shadow under which he labored to rule the country during his twenty-four-year reign. Only a child at the time, he probably did not understand his father's madness or the heart-breaking decision Yŏngjo was forced to make to protect the dynasty and the state. Instead, he believed Sado was a victim of factional intrigue and political infighting.[52] His grandfather Yŏngjo was misled by scheming ministers to make a tragic mistake. Chŏngjo was determined to avoid a similar fate. He set out to establish himself as the supreme authority and final arbiter in the land. Against the background of early modern Korea, he sought every available tool to exercise, and even expand, the full power of the eighteenth-century Chosŏn monarchy, including the development of a more inclusive political system by bringing previously excluded men into the government, the loosening of restrictions on Chosŏn's expanding commercial trade through the Commercial Equalization Law 辛亥通共 (sinhae t'onggong), and putting more men on the tax rolls through the elimination of hereditary slavery. But all of this had to be justified according to the dominant Confucian norms of the Korean ruling class. It is in the ideological realm that Chŏngjo's struggle begins.

3

THE POLITICS OF CONFUCIANISM

AS ANDREW LOSSKY POINTS OUT IN HIS DISCUSSION OF THE EARLY MODERN
French monarchy, there was no clear separation of church and state in
seventeenth-century France. Rather, the lack of attention to Roman Catholicism
in examinations of royal power reflects twentieth-century ideas of separation.[1]
In the same vein, Confucianism was inextricably linked with politics in Chosŏn
Korea, at no time more so than the eighteenth century. Indeed, the lack of any
Confucian institution or leadership analogous to the Roman Church and the
pope meant that Confucianism was even more entwined with the state. In addition to enhancing royal power through structural innovation, Chŏngjo enlisted
his extensive Confucian education to further a royalist political philosophy
to combat the minister-centered thought of the entrenched aristocracy. This
chapter examines how Chŏngjo attempted to redefine the sage-king concept
away from the standard ideal in Korean Confucianism of a passive, even aloof
king, who need only determine who the virtuous men were and then hand the
reins of government over to them, intervening only as necessary to prevent
injustice perpetrated by one aristocratic clique on another. Instead, Chŏngjo
sought to formulate the sage-king as an active ruler who instructed his ministers rather than received instruction from them, was directly involved in the
administration of the state, and exercised discretion when and how he, in his
sagely wisdom, deemed fit. For Chŏngjo, that the king was above factions
was due to his position at the center of political world, the source from which
legitimate power flowed, not a result of his being uninvolved in the dangerous
game of politics.

An alleged Confucian emphasis on obedience to authority has been
claimed at least since Weber, and "oriental despotism" continues to be invoked
today, for example, to explain economic success without democracy in supposedly "Confucian" Singapore and China.[2] Those opposed to the simplistic view of
Confucianism as unthinkingly supportive of authority point to contrary strains

of Confucian thought, notably Mencius's dictum that a "true king" cannot be overthrown and the claim that anyone can be a moral person.[3] Like many ancient systems of thought that have been interpreted and reinterpreted for millennia, Confucianism contains strands of argument that can be harnessed for opposing viewpoints, in this case for both pro- and anti-autocratic thought, and it is not incompatible with a functioning autocratic system, as is evidenced by works on Chinese political history with titles like Pei Huang's *Autocracy at Work*. Chŏngjo's challenge, then, was to argue for the supremacy of the proroyal strains of Confucianism against the formidable opposition of the highly educated *yangban* aristocracy.

When it comes to royal power, Confucianism is a two-edged sword. On the one hand, it is predicated on there being a king who necessarily rules both de jure and de facto. The Confucian virtue of loyalty is paramount, with the king retaining the sole right to appoint and dismiss officials. On the other hand, the privilege of learned men to remonstrate and the steep requirements for service in the bureaucracy—rigorous education and illustrious family background—restricted the ruler's ability to curtail aristocratic privilege. Further, the *yangban* could justify their grossly unequal wealth and high status by portraying them as rewards for virtuous men like themselves. As in France, the "sacred basis" of his position "binds the king as much as it frees him"; Confucianism and Catholicism both empowered the ruler and set limits on his power.[4] Further, the theoretical subservience of the Korean king to the Son of Heaven—while rarely of practical relevance, as the Chinese emperor did not intervene in Chosŏn's domestic affairs—weakened the ideological basis for absolute monarchy in the first half of the Chosŏn period. This weakness became less influential following the Manchu conquest of China, which delegitimized the emperor as the political center of civilization in Chosŏn, and Korean intellectuals increasingly began to view their kingdom as the "Little Civilization Center" 小中華 (*So Chunghwa*).[5]

The belief that Confucianism after the early Chosŏn period was a metaphysical preoccupation with little relationship to the execution of policy forms one of the bases of the modern scholarly dichotomy dividing mainstream Confucianism, rigidly conservative and concerned with esoteric matters of ritual and philosophical navel-gazing, from the "School of Practical Learning" 實學 (*Sirhak*), a radical new school of thought that sought concrete solutions to real problems. Yet more recent scholarship has questioned the usefulness of this distinction, pointing out both the continuity of *Sirhak* scholarship with earlier strands of practical-oriented Confucianism and the connection between seemingly esoteric debates and practical matters.[6] Thus, Confucianism has become prominent in the study of Chosŏn politics, with scholars noting that ideology and political reality intertwined to form a complex relationship. Still, even if *Sirhak* was not distinct from Confucianism or even a distinct school within it, by the eighteenth century it was recognized that practical administration had been neglected in favor of metaphysics. Chŏngjo himself lamented this state of affairs. His view of "learning" as embodied in the classics and "governing" as embodied in the dynastic histories can be compared to the division between emphasizing practical matters and emphasizing more theoretical issues. In a discussion with Royal Library officials, he expressed his dismay at the failure of some to combine both of these. During the Three Dynasties,[7] the King said, the study of both history and statecraft were valued, and classical texts discussed them together. He pointed to the example of the *Book of Documents*, which discussed statecraft in chapters that dealt with the importance of scholarship, and vice versa. Scholarship was not considered apart from promulgating laws. It was only upon reaching the Qin and Han dynasties[8] that men began to study the one to the neglect of the other. As a result, "some were able to get the basics right but were unable to make use of them, while others pursued the final results without even mastering the basics [或有體而無用。或循末而舍本]." The histories thereby became divorced from the study of statecraft, leading to intermittent disorder.[9]

The importance placed on education in Chosŏn, coupled with the necessity of ruling in line with the ancient Chinese classics—or at least appearing to do so—ensured that Chŏngjo took education seriously. Rather than bringing his rule into conformity with the standards of the Chinese antiquity as understood in eighteenth-century Chosŏn, which he consistently claimed (and perhaps even believed) was his actual goal, he in fact reshaped interpretation of the classics to bring contemporary views of ancient Chinese governance into conformity with an absolutist conception of kingship.

EDUCATION AND THE CLASSICS

As part of his effort to exalt his own position, Chŏngjo sought to place the king not only at the political apex but also at the ideological apex by emphasizing the king-as-teacher, thereby unifying practical administration with statecraft theory once again. He balked at the notion of being instructed by his officials in the inferior position of student, for it was the king who was the instructor in his conception of kingship. Thus, he sought to portray himself as a scholar-king who ruled and taught his ministers, whom he deemed subordinate and receptive. Chŏngjo also looked for ways to counteract the minister-centered thought of mainstream Korean Confucianism, which emphasized the self-cultivation aspects of the Confucian canon to the neglect of the aspects that dealt with governance, which Chŏngjo interpreted as loyal ministers who dutifully carried out the orders of their ruler. Chŏngjo's keen mind coupled with the thorough education he received as a prince in the line of succession from early childhood ensured that he was well-equipped to do intellectual battle with his officials.

Scholar-King

Although I am not virtuous, the responsibility of ruler-teacher is held by myself alone.[10]

[予雖否德。君師之責。在予一人。]

—*Chŏngjo sillok*

One of the constraints on the Chosŏn king was the expectation that he would attend the royal lectures. These were meetings with elderly scholars who would educate the ruler in the ways of Confucianism so that he could perfect his virtue and thereby bring order to the state. This meant that the king was in the subordinate position of the student, and that his officials were, in a sense, placed above him. It is thus no surprise that the two strongest kings of early Chosŏn, T'aejong and Sejo, hardly bothered to hold these lectures, while the tyrant Yŏnsan eliminated them entirely, along with other perceived trappings of bureaucratic power.[11] By late Chosŏn, however, the tradition had become established, and officials were quick to complain if the king was lax in attending. Yŏngjo was able to turn the tables on his officials and become the effective teacher during the lectures, thereby reinforcing his own power, though it took him decades of effort to do so.[12] Chŏngjo continued to argue that the king was the teacher, not the student, to avoid ever being in a subordinate position to his own ministers. In a discussion with Royal Library officials, he represented himself as instructor, saying that in the Three Dynasties "the Way of the teacher lay with the ruler, and therefore" the realm[13] was at peace [師道在上。故治隆俗美。而天下歸仁]. After some rote self-deprecation, he asked his officials, "How can I underestimate myself and say that I am not qualified to assume the responsibility of being scholar-king [亦豈可過自菲薄。不以君師之責自居乎]?"[14] This is a rather striking example of Chŏngjo's exaltation of himself, particularly in contrast to his grandfather, who had gone out of his way to be modest. Chŏngjo here

DISCRETION 權

The right way is not unalterably fixed, rather it changes with circumstances and time.

—King Chŏngjo, as quoted by his mother in 1802[22]

One of the constraints on absolute monarchy is the shared understanding of "the way things are done," an understanding partly formed by the example of the ruler's own predecessors. The legitimacy of the Yi family in the thoroughly Confucianized Korea of late Chosŏn rested on the moral character of the dynastic line. There was thus a great reluctance on the part of the Yi monarchs to overturn a predecessor's policy because it implied an imperfection in one's own ancestor.[23] Like European monarchs of the early modern period, they "consciously compared themselves with their ancestors and judged themselves against the record of those who had gone before them," with no desire to change "the essential nature of monarchy."[24] The Confucian emphasis on a past golden age led to the widespread belief that the system of that age had only to be reproduced in the present, and then no further change need be made. Even the most radical reformers in Chosŏn argued not for innovation but for the adoption of the land distribution system that supposedly prevailed in the early Zhou Dynasty around 1000 BC. When third-century BC Chinese philosopher Han Feizi complained that Confucians did not adjust to contemporary circumstances[25] he was not entirely incorrect. Yet conditions did change, and Confucian reformers in Korea had recognized that the system of the Zhou could not be transplanted fully intact into their Eastern Kingdom, since the Korean peninsula was not that cradle of Chinese civilization, the Yellow River basin. Likewise, some alteration of past decisions had to be accepted in order for the political system to continue to function at all. The monarch had a certain freedom of action to make adjustments in accordance with changing circumstances, particularly in times of crisis. In Europe, early modern kings had a loose collection of "broad, often arbitrary powers" known as the royal prerogative.[26] In East Asia, it was known as the king's discretion 權 (kwŏn, literally "weighing"), which had roots going back at least to Mencius. When asked what the gentleman should do if his sister-in-law is drowning, Mencius replied, "Men and women's not allowing their hands to touch in giving and receiving is proper etiquette. Using your hand to rescue your sister-in-law is discretion [男女授受不親禮也。嫂溺援之以手者權也]."[27] Thus, for Mencius, only a fool would hold so rigidly to the rites—which guarded against improper sexual relations by forbidding the excessive intimacy of physical contact between unrelated men and women—that he would sooner let someone die than behave contrary to them. Every situation was different, and so inflexibly adhering to the letter of the rites was just as mistaken as never following them. Creative and flexible application of the rites in pursuing the larger goal of virtue was required, not blind obedience. If one way of conceiving absolute monarchy in Europe was that its "behavior might be guided by laws, but was not bound by them," it brings into focus how Chŏngjo repeatedly "sacrificed the law" (just as the Hongwu Emperor did), as when he pardoned an accused man based on his own interpretation of morality, remarking "there is no need to cite" the *Great Code* to justify this decision.[28]

What King Chŏngjo sought to do was expand the throne's freedom of action. One of the ways he did this was by subtly altering a predecessor's policy while claiming to uphold it. Chŏng Ch'ang-sun, a Disciple appointed as royal secretary immediately upon Chŏngjo's accession, defended the King's use of discretion by claiming that it was in keeping both with Yŏngjo's policies and with the policies of the sage-kings of Chinese antiquity. Chŏng invoked the Imperial Pivot metaphor, one of Chŏngjo's favorites, to support Yŏngjo's Policy of Impartiality of ending political infighting and eliminating factionalism. The ancient sage-kings did this "not to monopolize power [古聖王建中之治。罔俾專美]," and their "use of discretion in a timely manner" was so beneficial that it could not be questioned (時權宜之政。 而若論其導率之效。焉可誣).[29]

Chŏngjo used the precedent of the ruler's discretion to justify his attempts to go outside of established state mechanisms, since these mechanisms often acted as a barrier that could obstruct royal initiatives. He had no place for the scholar-officials whose view of kingship entailed merely a morally perfect king who brings harmony without action. The kingship he envisioned—and carried out—was activist. In response to the charge leveled at him by Sim Hwan-ji, then serving in the Royal Library, that he was not listening to his officials, the King responded by imbuing his sole use of discretion with cosmic significance: "I think of myself as inwardly a sage and outwardly the king. The matter of my joining discretion with immutable principles is just like how the Sun, the Moon, and the stars shine high in the sky and illuminate the road [自以爲內聖外王。權而合經事。如日月星辰高照耀道]."[30] Likewise, those officials who supported increased royal power were often close to the King, like Hong Yang-bo, who wrote in favor of employing discretion in his "Discussion of Discretion in the Classics" 經權論. Confucius himself, Hong noted, sanctioned discretion as the sage's response to an ever-changing world.[31] Likewise, though Chŏngjo refused to be beholden to any faction, he did appreciate the proroyal bent of many Southerners such as Tasan, who wrote extensively on the centrality of the king in politics. Tasan pointed out that the "Great Plan" section of the *Book of Documents* has the ruler in charge of the distribution of resources for the people's benefit, and therefore all land and wealth in the land belongs to the ruler. Using the same metaphor of the Imperial Pivot that Chŏngjo himself used extensively,[32] Tasan reasoned that the ruler was the metaphysical center of the state just as the North Star was the metaphysical center of Heaven. He was therefore the source of all political power, and his discretion controlled his relationships with the ministers of state. Further, Tasan argued, anyone attempting to block the royal use of discretion was directly blocking the king's ability to rule justly for the people's benefit.

> If there is anyone coming between the king and the people, usurping his use of discretion to accumulate [blessings] in a timely manner and throttling his grace which he bestows upon them, then the king cannot establish the Pivot and the people will not be equally cared for.[33]
>
> [王與民之間。有物梗之竊。其斂時之權。阻其敷錫之恩。則皇不能建極。民不能均受.]

He then went on to explain how the king, by setting himself up as this Pivot, made possible the propagation of the "five blessings," which is otherwise not possible, that even "life and death, existence and destruction, are beholden to the king [生死存亡。唯辟是順]," and that his discretion determines whether or not one dies a natural death.[34]

Tasan explicitly connected the king's exclusive use of discretion with the stability of the state and the welfare of the common people, tying it to the Great Plan that commanded so much attention from Chosŏn scholars. His view that the king's position and his exclusive use of discretion as central to maintaining good order stands in stark contrast to the view of the Patriarchs faction, who criticized Chŏngjo for taking too much of the responsibility to govern on himself. One who articulated this criticism was Yi Pyŏng-mo, a member of the Intransigent branch of the Patriarchs. Yi, serving as councilor of the left in 1798, admonished the King for his refusal to treat his half-brother Prince Ŭnŏn more harshly. Yi directly challenged Chŏngjo's employment of discretion.

> Your Majesty has great self-confidence, which arises from your refusal to back down, particularly when you refer to the ability to take advantage of this word "discretion." I your servant do not presume to know for sure, but has there ever been a time that the sages of old used royal discretion the way Your Majesty does on a yearly basis?[35]

[殿下自信之篤，終始不撓。特權之一字。視作參倚之資。而臣不敢知從古聖人之權。
亦嘗有以一事而歲以爲例如殿下之爲者乎。]

Fifteen years earlier, Chŏng Chon-gyŏm, despite being an Expedient (and
therefore supposedly a supporter of Chŏngjo, again complicating our understanding of the factions as adhering rigidly to certain positions) took the King
to task for arrogating too much authority to himself in a memorial criticizing
Chŏngjo's employment of men, while also putting forward a fair representation
of the typical *yangban* view of kingship that Southerners like Tasan opposed.

> It was said, "When the ruler's will is fixed, the order of the realm is
> fixed."[36] None of the Sage Kings of old refrained from working hard
> at governing, yet they never were sullied by it. A sullied mind is the
> result of focusing too much effort on insignificant matters. Instead,
> they appointed the worthy and employed the able, employing them
> each effectively in his office. *They merely gave them guidance, and that
> is all.* The cleverness of a single person has limits, and the affairs of the
> realm are of the utmost complexity. If one wishes to use the cleverness
> of one person to exhaust the affairs of the realm, then on occasion that
> cleverness will fall short of the mark. The best way to govern is not to
> trust your own cleverness but to see clearly through the eyes of the
> people around you and thereby reach your goals through the clever-
> ness of the people around you. Truly, *it is in employing good people that
> you can succeed.* It is not a disaster that one has not completely ordered
> the Way. It is only a disaster not to have established a Sagely will. If
> you remain steadfast and do not sometimes change direction, then the
> Two Emperors will become three and the Three Kings become four.[37]

[此所謂君志定。而天下之治定者也。古之聖王。莫不勤於爲政。而亦未嘗以弊。弊
精神。躬親庶務爲勤。任賢使能。使之各效其職。統攬之董飭之而已。一人之聰明
有限。天下之事物至繁。以一人之聰明。欲窮天下之事物。則聰明有時乎不及。不任
一己之聰明。以明四目達四聰。取人爲善者。實以此也。不患治道之不成。惟患聖志
之不立。期以悠久。毋或退轉。則將見二帝可三，三王可四。]

By "remain steadfast," Chŏng was arguing that the King not deviate from established precedent ("change direction"), in effect arguing against Chŏngjo's use of
discretion. That is, he implied that by not taking action outside of established
convention, Chŏngjo would become the equal of Emperors Yao and Shun and
Kings Yu, Tang, and Wen, the greatest rulers of Chinese antiquity, who reput-
edly created paradise in the realm simply by perfecting their own virtue. He

賢。體不可以不順。臣不可以不忠]." Here Chŏngjo is using a body-based metaphor to argue forcefully for his conception of the king as final decision-maker.[52]

Part of the challenge for Chŏngjo was the general suspicion of reform of any kind among the *yangban* class. Even when there was general agreement that there was a problem and that urgent action was needed, the *yangban* consistently refused to make radical changes and often watered down or rolled back even minor reforms. The case for reform was not helped by the acceptance of the Cheng-Zhu strain of Neo-Confucianism as the basis for society in Korea, because its discourse sided with the conservative Sima Guang against the reforms of Wang Anshi. Because of Wang's fall from power in China in 1085 and the perceived failure of his reforms during the Song dynasty, officials opposed to change could cite Wang as evidence that reform was dangerous to the stability of the state. Chŏngjo could not ignore the ideological basis of resistance to reform, and so he could not ignore Wang Anshi. Because of the immense prestige surrounding Wang's rival and paragon of antireformers, Sima Guang, the King could not simply declare Sima wrong and vindicate Wang. Instead, on June 1, 1791, he tried to justify taking what was good from Wang's reform effort, all the while praising Sima. That day, the *Doctrine of the Mean* was the subject of discussion. After discussing whether the classic teaches that action proceeds knowledge or vice versa, the King moved the discussion to Wang Anshi's reforms, the New Law 新法 (*xinfa*). Although Sima, Chŏngjo stressed, "did not lack a pure nature," he might have gone too far when he eliminated *all* of Wang's reforms, since some of them were positive and removing them made "military affairs worse off and national power left weakened [使戎政不振。國勢益弱也]." Emperor Shenzong had had the right idea by appointing the reform-minded Wang to office, even if the latter did take things to an extreme. Chŏngjo defended Shenzong's employment of Wang Anshi in order to carry out needed reforms and criticized the sudden reversal of all of Wang's policies as throwing out the good along with the bad. Officials responded by unfavorably comparing Wang to Sima, but the King complained that "when it comes to his talent as a Confucian, Wang Anshi certainly was not the inferior of Sima Guang [若其需世之才。則王安石必不讓於司馬光矣]." Yi Ŭi-bong protested that Shenzong should have selected Sima Guang, who could have brought the glory days of the Three Dynasties back again, but Chŏngjo's old ally Ch'ae Che-gong disputed Yi's claim that Sima could have done so. He argued that because implementing effective reforms is a challenge while holding to the status quo is easy, Sima's success was not comparable to the difficulties Wang faced, and Chŏngjo readily agreed with this.

Ch'ae Che-gong said, "... Changing the old laws is of the utmost difficulty while abolishing the New Law was of the utmost simplicity, so how can anyone think this means Sima Guang was more able than Wang Anshi?"

The King said, "It is as you say. Although the Confucian ministers say they were not made use of because of Shenzong, at that time the situation of the realm could not but bring about great disturbances. Therefore he calmed his mind and planned how to bring about order with certainty and without wavering. I believe that after Emperor Wu of Han, only Shenzong had the correct idea of what to do in all matters. At the founding of the [Chosŏn] state, the *History of Song* had not yet been published.[53] When deciding which section the names of various scholars should go in, some said, 'Wang Anshi should certainly be in the "Flatterers" chapter,' and others said, 'It is appropriate to list him in the "Illustrious Ministers" chapter.' In the end he was included in the *Record of Illustrious Ministers* and in the *History of Song*. Zhu Xi is also recognized as an illustrious minister, so is this not something that is very difficult to obtain?"[54]

[濟恭曰 ... 故天下至今稱之。誠好八字矣。變舊法至難。罷新法至易。有何才幹之的勝於安石者乎。上曰然。儒臣雖以宋神宗謂之用非其人。當其時天下之勢。不得不大振刷。故銳意圖治。堅定不貳。予則以爲漢武帝後。惟神宗頗有事事之志矣。國初宋史之未及出來也。諸名碩預度之。或曰安石必入佞幸傳。或曰當入名臣傳。及得名臣錄。則果編入其中。而宋史亦然。朱子旣以名臣許之。豈非難得之人乎。]

Chŏngjo supported Ch'ae's point by noting that in the end later scholars recognized Wang Anshi as an outstanding official, ranking him in a category that included Zhu Xi himself. Reform, then, was not something that was always to be avoided.

Chŏngjo astutely recognized that the concept of discretion, with its long-established history and grounding in the classics, gave him an opening to expand the King's freedom of action. Southerners and other supporters of Chŏngjo tended to support his readings, while the Intransigents and other opponents argued against it. Yet the opponents could not convincingly argue that the king was not permitted to employ discretion at all—though some like Chŏng Chon-gyŏm certainly tried. More reasonable were the complaints of men like Yi Pyŏng-mo, who conceded that discretion was necessary but criticized Chŏngjo for employing it too often, in trivial matters where it was not needed. Again, it was not the *existence* of the king's power that was in dispute but the appropriateness of its *application* according to existing norms and understandings of how the king could use and misuse his powers. But how far a power extends and when it is legitimate to use it are thorny questions. At both ends of Eurasia, the early modern period saw "a series of quite similar confrontations between [rulers] and nobles over the relative scope of their authority, the nature of their rights and obligations."[55] Chŏngjo was comparatively successful in having his way—constructing the Illustrious Fortress, appointing members of the Southerner faction to high posts, establishing the Royal Library and making it a key player in government—as long as he was willing to expend both his intellectual energy in defending it publicly and his political capital in promoting it privately.

Chŏngjo was a master of the Confucian canon who deployed that mastery to produce ideological justification for a stronger throne. He portrayed himself as a scholar-king who sat above his ministers and taught rather than a student who sat below them and was taught, and he pushed interpretations of the Chinese classics toward a ruler-centered view over the minister-centered view of mainstream Chosŏn Confucianism. When it came to his freedom of action, Chŏngjo argued that as a sage-king he had the power to act out of accordance with precedent when necessary and, moreover, that only a sage-king such as he could determine when doing so was, in fact, necessary. In effect, he claimed that only he could determine the limits of his own power, at least when waxing into perhaps rhetorical excess. These ideological justifications were the intellectual framework for his concrete reforms: the Royal Library, the royal selection system, and the employment of men from groups that were marginalized from political power in Late Chosŏn. Ideology is all well and good, but Chŏngjo also knew how to play politics: how to gain support, how to defeat or convert opposition, and how to make deals. It is to the shady world of politics that we now turn.

4

POWER AND FACTIONS

Morality refers to the common good of the realm. It does not permit favoring one thing at the expense of everything else. In the world there are sometimes opportunities to take advantage of someone else. Those who cling to their own selfish interests and take advantage of others are the extreme of inhumanity.

[義理天下之公也。不當偏主。世或有乘機藉重。挾已私而傾奪人者。其亦不仁之甚矣。]

—Chŏngjo, "Royal Instructions"

THE REALITY OF CHOSŎN FACTIONALISM IN THE EIGHTEENTH CENTURY coexisted uneasily with the Confucian notion that virtuous men could not legitimately disagree about the right way to govern, because there was only one correct way: Cheng-Zhu Neo-Confucianism.[1] Neither the king nor the scholar-officials were unaware of this tension, and factionalism was long recognized as a hindrance to the smooth and effective operation of the state. This chapter discusses how King Chŏngjo dealt with the limitations on his choice of government officials and the fractious factionalism of those officials. After settling the initial difficulties of establishing his position as king, Chŏngjo addressed these issues in two key ways.

First, the King made efforts to unite the three major factions behind his own leadership by portraying himself as superior to them. On the surface, this was simply a continuation of his predecessor's Policy of Impartiality 蕩平策 (*t'angp'yŏngch'aek*), an attempt to placate the factions by allocating offices equally ("impartially") among them, in accordance with the monarch's role for early modern aristocrats as a disinterested arbitrator. After all, that the king was above any minister had been accepted in Chosŏn since the beginning of the dynasty, and if the *yangban* were reluctant to implement policies that eroded their own positions, they reacted with swift and terrible vengeance on any minister who seemed to be usurping the king's place at the top. However,

Chŏngjo's implementation of this policy was quite different both in theory and in practice, because he faced a changed political landscape. Yŏngjo's Policy of Impartiality was largely an attempt to get the rival descendants of the Westerner faction 西人 (Sŏin), the Patriarchs and the Disciples, to work together.[2] This task was made more difficult with the appearance of the two new factions in the wake of Sado's execution, the Intransigents and the Expedients. Yŏngjo was able to keep these two groups in check by demanding silence on the Sado issue, but Chŏngjo's reign was more complicated. As the son of Sado, it was expected that he would deal with that issue, and so the Intransigents/Expedients divide moved to the fore during his reign. He also brought Southerners into the government for the first time since 1694, complicating the balance between the Patriarchs and the Disciples that Yŏngjo had labored to maintain. Thus, a tit-for-tat Policy of Impartiality was unsuitable for the last quarter of the eighteenth century.

Forever in his father's shadow, Chŏngjo's solution was to free himself from factional considerations altogether. He argued that, as king, he was the only one in a position to make an unbiased judgment, since officials' advice would be in lockstep with factional considerations and would not offer a genuine evaluation of the situation. As I have noted, it is questionable whether officials really so unthinkingly lined up behind their factional leaders, as Chŏngjo's letters demanding that Sim Hwan-ji rein in members of his faction seem to make clear. He explains his reasoning in a discussion with the Royal Library officials on how to decide official appointments.

> After they divided into factions, the scholars have nothing to say that is relevant to the common good. I hear from Mr. X that a certain person is truly worthy, and from Mr. Y I hear that he is not. When I ask those in the east, I am told that a given matter is ultimately correct, but asking those in the west, I am told it is not. So how am I to make decisions? All I should do is broaden my vision and make my heart impartial. When I examine something via the principle of impartiality, although I am not always on target, I am also not far off the mark.[3]
>
> [分黨以後。士無公議。聽於甲則某人實賢。而乙則否之。問諸東則其事極是。而西則非之。是將惡乎決哉。予只當恢著眼平著心。一以公理觀之。雖或不中。亦不遠矣。]

The implication here is clear: Because he receives contradictory advice from ministers, he relies on his own judgment. Thus, rather than balancing factions, Chŏngjo claimed to choose men without regard to faction and then to work with whoever he got. As revealed through his letters to Sim Hwan-ji from 1797 right up until his death in 1800, Chŏngjo was adept at building support by appearing to be all things to all people while in reality manipulating them for his own ends, to the point that even his own mother doubted his word.[4] Avoiding the charge leveled at Yŏngjo—that the Policy of Impartiality just created a new faction of pro-Policy royal toadies—Chŏngjo tried to convince all the factions that he was really on their side and that supporting him would further their own goals. So he was perfectly happy to criticize the Manchus as barbarians to anti-Qing Patriarchs like Sim Hwan-ji while using Qing technology to build the Illustrious Fortress and employing Qing Evidential Learning techniques to justify his king-centered philosophy. Similarly, he disavowed one of his key supporters, Sŏ Yong-bo 徐龍輔, in a letter to Sim while continuing to bolster Sŏ's career and to draw on his support.[5]

In this, Chŏngjo was not entirely honest, but neither was he completely unfair; he was willing to give something minor in exchange for support on an issue that was, for him, major. Thus, he was able, for example, to drive a wedge that split three leading Intransigents, his nominal opponents, so that he could gain support from one of them on this issue and from another of them on that issue. So much the better if, all the while, all three of them believed he actually agreed with them. Thus, Kim Chong-su 金鍾秀 opposed Chŏngjo's military reorganization while supporting the Policy of Impartiality, Sim Hwan-ji was an enemy of the Southerners who supported the construction of the Illustrious Fortress, and Yi Pyŏng-mo 李秉模 opposed the Illustrious Fortress and the reforms associated with it but supported the abolition of hereditary slavery.[6] In his letters to Sim Hwan-ji, Chŏngjo reveals his willingness to exploit the existing rift between these men—an important indicator of major differences of opinion within factions—by reassuring Sim: "I know without asking that Yi Pyŏng-mo has evil intentions towards Your Lordship [秉也之向卿有惡意。不問可知]." Though we currently lack any extant letters to Yi, one can easily imagine the King telling him the very same thing about Sim. He also joked with Sim that Yi's list of successful examination passers seemed to have been drawn up while Yi was drunk and wryly noted that Kim Chong-su was hated by everyone.[7] That Chŏngjo was able to manipulate these three men in such ways lends further support to current research revealing that the factions were not quite as rigid as once thought, and there was no guarantee that every prominent member of a given faction would follow lockstep with his faction's policies.

EARLY SETBACKS: HONGS AND PRINCES

The early years of Chŏngjo's reign saw the young king push back against those who would dominate him. The men who allegedly brought about the death of Sado had to be posthumously dealt with. The King also eliminated a number of men who spoke out against his regency in 1775 and its supporters, including a key member of his mother's family, so that the Hong clan would have no illusions that its support for his accession would translate into domination over his reign. He brought in a number of men who had served him well while he was crown prince, the core group on which he would construct his power base.

However, not everything went smoothly. The instrument he used to free himself from his mother's clan in turn sought to take that clan's imagined place as Chŏngjo's puppeteer, and while the King in his youth was slow to respond to his close friend's machinations, his conviction that the throne must be controlled by no outside force eventually ended that friend's life.

The Trouble with Hong Kuk-yŏng

Hong Kuk-yŏng (1748–1781) passed the *munkwa* examination in 1771 and found himself fortunately appointed as one of the crown prince's tutors, though he was only four years older than his royal student. He was a member of the Expedients branch of the Patriarchs and worked closely with Kim Chong-su, at least until Kim, with his considerable political acumen, detected the shift in the political climate and turned against him. Hong, along with Sŏ Myŏng-sŏn 徐命善 and Chŏng Min-si 鄭民始, were with Chŏngjo from his time as crown prince, and they would largely remain his loyal supporters until the end of their lives. Hong, though, overstepped the bounds of Chosŏn propriety, and so he reached the end of his life rather earlier than Sŏ and Chŏng. His fall serves as a fine example of aristocrats upholding the king's role as impartial arbiter, shoring up his power in the face of an excessive aristocratic challenge that jeopardized the early modern collaboration between crown and noble.

An implacable foe of Chŏngjo's maternal family, Hong is unsurprisingly painted in damning colors by Lady Hyegyŏng, and she has little positive to say about his relationship with Chŏngjo. Yet whatever his motives were, his actions supported Chŏngjo in the early years of his reign, when the King was most vulnerable to whatever challenger might emerge. Hong denounced opponents of Chŏngjo's regency, Chŏng Hu-gyŏm 鄭厚謙, Hong In-han 洪麟漢, and Hong Pong-han's rival Kim Kwi-ju. Chŏng and Hong were executed, and Kim was banished. Hong Kuk-yŏng, in the meantime, quickly rose to relatively high offices in the Ministry of Personnel and the Office of Inspector-General 司憲 府 (*sahŏnbu*) despite being barely over thirty years old.

Not satisfied with this fairly rapid rise, Hong concocted a scheme to become a royal uncle. He convinced Chŏngjo to take his sister as his second wife in 1778. Marrying a relative to the king was not particularly unusual, but having his sister titled "Wŏnbin" 元嬪洪氏 or "First Consort" was a provocative act when Chŏngjo's primary wife remained both alive and childless. Lady Hyegyŏng claims Hong purposefully attempted to prevent Chŏngjo from having intimate relations with his wife as part of his scheme, though she presents no evidence for this other than Hong's evil character.[8] It is more parsimonious, given the present state of evidence, that Chŏngjo, meeting constantly with Royal Library officials, holding audiences, instructing royal selection system students, reading dozens of memorials and petitions every day, and conducting a host of other ritual and official duties, perhaps did not place sufficient weight on conjugal relations to make sufficient time for the vital task of producing an heir as soon as possible, considering the vital importance of an adult king for early modern absolutism.[9] Such natural proclivities, if indeed he had them, would have exacerbated Chosŏn court regulation of royal conjugal relations that already encouraged such activity only on auspicious days so as to ensure the fitness of potential heirs.[10] Here was an area that Chŏngjo, if he truly desired to perpetuate a strong monarchy, should have paid more time and attention, revealing the fundamental contradiction at the heart of his project: It was nearly impossible both to maximize his own authority while also institutionalizing a strengthened kingship in an early modern world where power primarily remained in people, despite the increasing importance of institutions.

The next year, Hong's plans were thrown into disarray when Wŏnbin died, but rather than being deterred, Hong made even bolder and more dangerous moves. He labored to have Wŏnbin treated as a queen in death while attempting to displace Chŏngjo's primary wife, Queen Hyoŭi. For the former, the *Veritable Records* claims that Wŏnbin's funeral was so lavish the officials would have spoken against it but for fear of Hong's power—though whether they were actually so afraid, or were instead desperately covering for silently acquiescing to Hong's rise, it is impossible to know—and Lady Hyegyŏng tells us the funeral was held in the same place as that of Yŏngjo's first queen. Hong had the court mourn his sister and dismissed from office a high official who did not participate in the incense burning ritual for her. For the latter, he brutally interrogated Hyoŭi's ladies-in-waiting in a failed attempt to implicate the Queen in Wŏnbin's death.

At the same time, his close ally Song Tŏk-sang, almost certainly at Hong's behest, sent a memorial with the veiled suggestion that Chŏngjo adopt an heir. This was tantamount to suggesting that the line of succession be transferred to a collateral line, a treasonous act for which Song's illustrious ancestor Song Si-yŏl had been executed. Song Si-yŏl had argued a century earlier that the recently deceased king should not be mourned with the heaviest mourning because he was not the eldest son. The reigning king, Hyŏnjong, thought Song's argument implied the line of succession should have bypassed his father and that, consequently, Hyŏnjong himself was not the legitimate king, and Song was executed for treason, though later generations came to admire Song's martyrdom. When Hong Kuk-yŏng fell from power, Song Tŏk-sang tried to downplay his connection to Hong, but he could not downplay this memorial and was banished, despite Chŏngjo's professed reluctance to punish a descendent of Song Si-yŏl.[11]

As if suggesting a shift in the succession to a collateral line were not enough, Hong then had the son of Chŏngjo's half-brother Prince Ŭnŏn posthumously adopted by Wŏnbin, strengthening the child's claim to the throne as long as Chŏngjo remained without a son. The *Veritable Records* say that Hong raised the child himself. The boy received the title "Prince of Great Abundance" 完豊君 (*Wanp'unggun*),[12] and the *Veritable Records* again claims official dismay at these actions and that fear of Hong muzzled any dissent. On top of that, according to Lady Hyegyŏng, Hong had the boy publicly escorted by royal eunuchs as if he were Chŏngjo's heir.[13]

Finally, in 1780, Chŏngjo had had enough. He dismissed Hong from all of his offices and revoked the boy's princely title. Once Hong was out of office, the official torrent against him was unleashed. Kim Chong-su, either because he recognized the tide had turned against Hong or because he genuinely believed Hong had gone too far with his schemes, did an about-face and vehemently denounced him. Lady Hyegyŏng could not understand why Chŏngjo tolerated Kim's reversal.

> Later, Chong-su sent a memorial to the throne attacking Kuk-yŏng, but he did this under pressure from the King. I said to my son, "Chong-su acted as if he were Kuk-yŏng's own son. Now he recriminates against him mercilessly. How can this be?" The King answered, "It isn't his intention, but if he wants to survive, what choice does he have?" I said, "He must be a nine-tailed fox who is capable of a thousand changes and ten thousand transformations." "It is an apt description of him," the King answered laughingly. This shows that my son was not unaware of Chong-su's true character.
>
> . . .

But despite his knowledge of Chong-su's character, the late King remained constant to him to the end. Because of his frugal habits and his uncorrupted tenure in office, Chong-su did not alienate people. The King felt that, under the circumstances, he could maintain his old affection for him. But Chong-su's so-called frugality and incorruptibility were all posture.[14]

Undoubtedly she was correct that Chŏngjo knew Kim's character, but she did not see that Chŏngjo could make use of a man who appeared incorruptible but was in fact a realist. As we will see later, the King would even help officials to appear uncompromising while actually compromising with them in secret.

Chŏngjo initially resisted calls to punish Hong further, but he eventually conceded to banishment, and Hong, perhaps a little too conveniently, died in exile the following year, at age thirty-four. In another instance of Chŏngjo's dual public and private roles, he was likely genuinely reluctant to banish his old friend, but he was also astute enough to know that, regardless of Hong's actions, he had to defend him; suddenly and immediately executing or banishing a close associate, without showing any reluctance to do so, would have appeared inhumane and might have created sympathy for Hong. As it was, no one, including his fellow Patriarchs, mourned Hong's passing, and his name would be referenced for the rest of Chŏngjo's reign as the worst kind of traitor, even by the King's most consistent opponents, the Intransigents. The throne's independence was preserved, not in spite of official opposition to it but rather allied with official dedication to it. The King also undoubtedly learned the dangers of relying too heavily on one person. From this point forward, no one would gain that level of trust from him.

The P'ungsan Hong Clan and Royal Relatives

Chŏngjo's relationship with his mother's family was complicated. Though he doted on Lady Hyegyŏng herself throughout his life, her family members were not thereby given a pass. Chŏngjo's relationship with his deceased maternal grandfather Hong Pong-han is a case in point. On the one hand, though Lady Hyegyŏng is vehement that the execution of Sado was not Hong Pong-han's idea and that he did not provide the rice chest in which Sado was sealed, it is clear that Hong acquiesced to the killing of Sado.[15] Despite this, Hong was just as dedicated as Yŏngjo to preserving the legitimacy of Chŏngjo and was a key member of the Expedients faction that protected Chŏngjo while he was crown prince. Undoubtedly a posthumous punishment of Hong would have devastated Lady Hyegyŏng, but Chŏngjo did not shy from executing her uncle for treason, so it is likely that Chŏngjo defended the deceased Hong Pong-han against incessant criticism because he was reluctant to accept attacks on his own grandfather.

But if Chŏngjo was careful to protect those who had a direct blood relationship to the throne from any diminution of their virtue, Lady Hyegyŏng's uncle Hong In-han had no such protection. The controversy here revolved around a remark Hong made during Yŏngjo's last full year on the throne (1775), when the ailing Yŏngjo desired to establish Chŏngjo as regent. This type of regency—an ill or elderly king appointing the heir apparent as regent to relieve himself of much of the burden of governing—did not have a positive history in Chosŏn Korea. Despite the early Chosŏn precedent for abdication—the first three monarchs of the dynasty all having done so—Sejo's usurpation of the throne in 1455 seem to have eliminated abdication as a viable option for succeeding kings. Sejo forced his own fourteen-year-old nephew to abdicate and took the throne himself; the youth was murdered two years later on Sejo's orders.

This bloody affair left the regency of an adult heir apparent as the alternative. But Yŏngjo's regency for his brother Kyŏngjong 景宗 (r. 1720–1724)—and the Patriarchs' quick acceptance of it—had been the cause of a purge of the Patriarchs under Kyŏngjong, and their desire for revenge on their Disciple rivals when "their" king took the throne was a constant thorn in Yŏngjo's side early in his reign. Further, Sado's regency for Yŏngjo was regarded as an unmitigated disaster.[16] So when Yŏngjo proposed a regency for Chŏngjo in 1775, there was little enthusiasm for it despite Yŏngjo's evident age and ill health, and not just because the king's officials were expected to show reluctance at the thought of a legitimate authority apart from the reigning king. Still, the officials did not outright oppose the regency, either, lest they impugn the majesty of the heir apparent. Regency was a thorny topic in eighteenth-century Chosŏn, one that put officials in a difficult bind: Accept the king's proposal too readily, and risk being viewed as questioning the king's place at the top of the political pyramid; reject it too strongly, and risk impugning the crown prince's ability to rule.

Yet according to the *Veritable Records*, Hong In-han did oppose the regency. Chŏng Hu-gyŏm was executed for this, and Hong's relationship to Lady Hyegyŏng would not protect him from the same fate. When the regency was proposed, on December 22, 1775, Hong said that "The Crown Prince [Chŏngjo] need not know anything of the Patriarchs or Disciples, nor need he know who the Minister of Personnel or the Minister of War is, much less the affairs of the court [東宮不必知老論少論。不必知吏判兵判。至於朝廷事。 尤不必知矣]." By stating that the crown prince "need not know" about state matters, Hong appeared to question Chŏngjo's ability to handle such matters. Lady Hyegyŏng claims that Hong merely misspoke, a "slip of the tongue," she calls it.[17] Indeed, the line between acceptable criticism and *lèse-majesté* in Chosŏn Korea was never clearly established, so officials had to be very careful how they phrased their opinions, lest they be accused of slighting the king.[18] Still, even in this reading it was a foolhardy statement, for it is well-nigh impossible not to view its meaning—not merely its phrasing, but the underlying meaning—as accusing the crown prince of lacking the ability to govern the state. Such a statement was bound to get Hong in trouble, and so it did. Presumably despite the desperate pleas of Lady Hyegyŏng, Chŏngjo ordered Hong to take poison on August 18, 1776, after repeated official demands, with Chief State Councilor Kim Yang-t'aek remarking that allowing Hong the dignity of suicide made the death sentence too light a punishment. The next day, the King refused a request to make Hong's children slaves.[19]

For those who were blood relatives of the royal house, however, Chŏngjo was reluctant to mete out harsh punishment, especially death. He justified his leniency in deviating from the strict punishments required by law as falling under the purview of royal discretion. In the tried-and-true manner of legal argumentation in Chosŏn Korea, he cited a precedent from Chinese antiquity, namely the Duke of Zhou's tailoring of punishments to individuals in the ancient *Book of Documents*.[20] Early in his reign, before his power base was secure, the King struggled to protect royal relatives. Princess Hwawan 和緩翁主, the sister of Sado and Chŏngjo's aunt, was accused of opposing the regency along with Hong In-han and her adopted son Chŏng Hu-gyŏm. Since Chŏng was not Hwawan's natural son, he was quickly executed, as was Hong In-han, but the King stubbornly resisted the Intransigents' demands to send Hwawan to the grave along with him. Still, he was forced to strip Hwawan of her title and banish her from the capital. Over the course of his reign, as his position strengthened, Chŏngjo progressively lightened her sentence. Initially she was banished to Cheju Island. She was then allowed to move first to P'aju and, later, to the outskirts of the capital, and she was finally pardoned entirely and her title restored in April of 1799, despite continuous official protests from the Intransigents over the course of that month.[21] Strikingly, the King declared this to be in keeping with the intentions of Prince Sado. Further, as will be discussed in the next section, the King had at least one Intransigent leader's support for this action, though that support was not publicly expressed.

Chŏngjo's half-brother Prince Ŭnjŏn 恩全君, Prince Sado's son by a concubine, was not so fortunate. As noted, Hong Kuk-yŏng was an enemy of Lady Hyegyŏng's branch of the Hong family and thus pressed for the elimination of that branch and its supporters—including both Chŏng Hu-gyŏm and Hong In-han—immediately upon Chŏngjo's accession. Prince Ŭnjŏn was implicated in the course of these interrogations, when it was claimed that Lady Hyegyŏng's family was laying the groundwork for the installation of Ŭnjŏn as king. A number of executions were ordered, but Chŏngjo demurred at the demands for Ŭnjŏn's death. However, barely a year on the throne and faced with repeated calls for his half-brother's execution for treason, the King was forced to relent, and Ŭnjŏn was forced to commit suicide.[22]

Nine years later, however, a stronger Chŏngjo had much greater success in protecting another half-brother, Prince Ŭnŏn 恩彦君, the older son of Sado by his consort Lady Im, when he was accused of poisoning Chŏngjo's son. The Intransigents, along with Queen Chŏngsun, accused Ŭnŏn of poisoning not only the boy but a number of others who had recently taken ill and died, including Ŭnŏn's own son Prince Sanggye. This time, not only was Ŭnŏn not killed, he did not even lose his title. He was merely exiled to Kangwha Island, one of the mildest punishments in terms of exile. Even after he escaped from exile and was recaptured, Chŏngjo refused to have him executed or even to increase his punishment; Ŭnŏn was simply returned to Kangwha. Chŏngjo also continued to see him in spite of his exile.[23] Ŭnŏn did not meet his fate until after Chŏngjo's death, when the Intransigents executed him in 1801 for the heinous crime of having a Catholic wife.[24] The eighteenth century saw the first Korean converts to Roman Catholicism, the result of the spread of Catholic writings and conversations with Chinese converts and missionaries in Beijing rather than active proselytizing on the peninsula. Catholicism was banned in Chosŏn, but Chŏngjo did not strongly enforce the ban. His close ally Ch'ae Che-gong argued that as heterodox writings were destroyed, the religion would "sort itself out [自然寢息矣]" without the need for meting out punishments. It is impossible to know, but one might suppose Chŏngjo refrained from persecuting the religion in part because Catholicism tended to be more prevalent among opponents of the Patriarchs faction, or dissident elements with it.[25] The vigorous persecution against such elements carried out less than a year after his death, the Catholic Purge of 1801 辛酉迫害 (sinyu pakhae)—the first in Korea—lends support to this contention.

As prominent as Lady Hyegyŏng's family became, there remained the four major factions, the so-called Four Colors, with which Chŏngjo had to deal. The King inherited the Policy of Impartiality, Yŏngjo's central vehicle in his fifty-year struggle with bureaucratic factionalism. In his familiar way, Chŏngjo claimed only to be continuing the Policy his grandfather had bequeathed him, but the reality turns out to paint a more complicated, and interesting, picture.

THE POLICY OF IMPARTIALITY

The one who insists on impartiality must say "mutual agreement" as a strategy. Nevertheless, what brings harm to impartiality is also those two words, "mutual agreement."[26]

[主蕩平者。必曰互對一著。然害蕩平者。又是互對二字。]

—Chŏngjo, "Political Matters"

The Policy of Impartiality originated with Chŏngjo's great-grandfather Sukchong 肅宗 (r. 1674–1720) as an attempt to control factionalism. His version of the policy amounted to playing the factions against each other by alternately putting one faction in power and then purging it in favor of a rival faction. Chŏngjo himself explains this in his veiled criticism of Sukchong, who despite his "sagely intention" could not control factionalism, in a discussion of the crimes of one Kim Ha-jae, an Intransigent executed for *lèse-majesté* in 1784.[27]

> In the reign of Sukchong, the custom of factionalism gradually worsened, and there were none who could bring it under control. Sukchong sagely favored first this faction and appointed its members and then that faction and appointed its members, and back again. My predecessor's court at first faced conflict, and untangling the mess [created by Sukchong's policy] was certainly difficult.[28]
>
> [曾在肅廟朝。黨習漸痼。莫可收拾。聖意或謂此勝於彼。而專用之。或謂彼勝於此。而更進之。逮我先朝之初。戈戟相尋。膠固難解。]

Yŏngjo, in contrast, strove to avoid the bloody purges associated with this policy and tried to contain factionalism. At first, Yŏngjo even rejected the Policy of Impartiality altogether and tried to work within factional politics as they existed under Sukchong,[29] but before long he did adopt his own version of the Policy. Under Yŏngjo, this was essentially refusing to give one faction the right to take vengeance on another and trying to force the Patriarchs and Disciples to work together, while avoiding the appearance of favoring either of them by rewarding or punishing a member of each faction commensurate with one another. Yŏngjo applied the Policy sporadically, especially early on. Facing a Disciple-dominated government upon his succession, he turned them out almost immediately, replacing them with the Patriarchs who had suffered for their support for his regency. Two years later, it was the Patriarchs' turn to be unceremoniously dumped and forced to watch their hated rivals return to power. Despite the supposed faction-balancing of his Policy of Impartiality, Yŏngjo thus revealed his willingness to fall back on Sukchong's purge-and-replace factional politicking when he deemed it politically advantageous, though with markedly fewer executions. Since he could not get the Patriarchs and Disciples to work together, he then tried creating an Impartial faction of moderates and the nonaligned, until the 1728 rebellion revealed the unworkability of that idea.[30] The revolving door of purge-and-replace politics was nearly Yŏngjo's downfall, when his 1727 change of administration put extremist Disciples in command of major capital military units that formed the rebels' main threat to the court when Yŏngjo's enemies rose against him the next year (though it did throw off the rebels' timetable and force them to move earlier than planned). Thus, Yŏngjo's inconsistent application of the Policy only exacerbated factional issues, as each faction, on seeing its rivals fall and itself restored to power, balked at the king's expectation that they then cooperate with those rivals.[31]

Yŏngjo's Policy of Impartiality was thus, at best, only fitfully effective, and it required suppression of the censorial voice—Chosŏn Korea's equivalent of "free speech"—in order to achieve even that partial success.[32] While that success did mark Yŏngjo's increasing power, it gave rise to criticism that supporters of the policy were in effect forming yet another faction, even after Yŏngjo himself abandoned the attempt to create an Impartiality group. Indeed, Chŏngjo himself tells us he heard this criticism as well soon after taking the throne, during a discussion of factionalism that ended with a (totally ineffective) official ban on factional disputes: "Alas! [The Policy of] Impartiality will soon be rid of factions, so that I will forget their names. Yet it is said that the Impartiality faction is worse than the old factions, and unfortunately that is not far off the mark [噫. 蕩平卽祛偏黨. 無物我之名. 而世傳'蕩平之黨. 甚於舊黨之說. 不幸近之]."[33]

While Chŏngjo's Policy of Impartiality built on that of Yŏngjo, there were important differences, primarily a matter of practicality.[34] Chŏngjo sought to employ able men and to build a coalition of men centered on himself within the existing factions to reduce tensions between them, as opposed to Yŏngjo's efforts to use moderates unaffiliated with the existing factions and to placate them through balancing their representation in the government.[35] Chŏngjo's Policy sought to equate the king with the state, who alone transcended factions.[36] The King cultivated relationships with the down-and-out Southerners and even the Intransigent Patriarchs, who with few exceptions opposed the Policy, and he subtly criticized Yŏngjo for having a formal Policy of Impartiality that lacked substance, with the result that he merely mediated between the various factions such that the situation had not changed much.[37] Instead, in a letter to

Sim Hwan-ji in 1797, Chŏngjo defended his prerogative to choose officials as he saw fit, regardless of faction or family lineage.

> Are there not loyal and sincere men hidden in small villages? It is just that we have yet to see them. The six-month evaluation is not far off, so we need to think of a way to search widely for talented men. If we select men without distinguishing high and low ancestral lineage or Easterner and Westerner faction, instead choosing men of good repute and giving them well-paying official posts, would this not be better than dividing offices between the Shi and Dou clans?[38]
>
> [豈無十室之忠信。特未之聞耳。大政不遠。須思廣探之方。即無論地閥之高庳。色目之東西。惟人望是取。使之需祿。則豈不大勝於石竇內分排青黃之政耶。]

Here, Chŏngjo was also criticizing monopolization of power among a small number of clans by equating it with the monopolization of office by the Shi and Dou clans in China in the fifth and sixth centuries. The reference to giving officials stipends implies that men of little economic means could also be recruited, since they would have funds to support themselves. Thus, Chŏngjo is suggesting, if not a radical notion of recruiting men from all classes, at least reaching comparatively much wider and deeper into the state's pool of talent than the twenty or so monstrously wealthy *yangban* clans based in the capital who dominated office-holding at this time.

Further, while Chŏngjo worked closely with Ch'ae Che-gong and the Southerners, he had no intention of instituting a Southerner-dominated government, for he would be beholden to no faction. Still, Southerners became a force in the central government for the first time since 1694. Ch'ae Che-gong served on the State Council, the highest organ in the state, and Chŏngjo made efforts to get the Southerners greater representation at all levels. In another letter to Sim Hwan-ji, Chŏngjo urged Sim to accept the appointment of a Southerner without complaint.[39] Earlier that year, Chŏngjo complained in another letter about bias against the Southerners and also protected a loyal supporter from that faction, Tasan.

> As for the administration of the Third Minister of Personnel, he is too biased. Will he not broach the subject of putting forward Southerner or Disciple candidates for even the lowliest offices? As for not sending Tasan to the military side, surely there are no good intentions there. Because of one or two incidents, the grudges and remorse of half a lifetime grow worse day by day. Can I ignore this? Vice-Minister Hong

Myŏng-ho will come in, so how can I send [Tasan] to the military in this political climate? Would you read and copy the Third Minister's resignation memorial? It is truly worth reading.[40]

[三銓之政。猶言其太偏。并與虛閒之殿未擬少午。不爲擧論。豈成說耶。丁也之不爲
送西。大非勸善之意。一事二事。半世之怨憾日甚。此等處。何不留意耶。亞銓當入來
矣。今政則使之送西如何。此三銓辭疏。須卽謄見如何。儘有可觀耳。]

While he claimed to be but continuing Yŏngjo's marvelous Policy of Impartiality, in reality Chŏngjo was expanding the Policy such that he could choose freely among factions rather than being expected either to choose one faction as the "right" one and hand the government over to its members (as each faction wanted for itself) or to maintain a balanced system that gave rival factions an "equal" say in the government, as Yŏngjo had tried to do.

Playing Both Sides: Ch'ae Che-gong and Sim Hwan-ji

Chŏngjo's masterful manipulation of politics can be seen in his treatment of two of the most powerful men of the last ten years of his reign: Ch'ae Che-gong, head of the Southerner faction, and Sim Hwan-ji, a leader of the Intransigent Patriarchs. Conventionally Ch'ae has been regarded as Chŏngjo's friend and Sim as his enemy, and while the general tenor of the relationships does follow these broad contours, things get much messier in the details. What the sources reveal is that Chŏngjo was adept at making men who held widely divergent views believe that he shared those views, while actually pursuing his own goals.

Ch'ae Che-gong passed the *munkwa* in 1743 at the relatively young age of twenty-three, and spent his first two decades in government serving in fairly minor posts. He had the good fortune of being out of office for the Sado affair, so he was not tainted by association with that tragedy, though he did refuse to carry out a royal order to depose Sado as crown prince in 1758. Eventually, in 1771, his career received a significant boost when he was placed in charge of Chŏngjo's education. It was during this time that he cultivated his relationship with the future king, and he would remain a staunch supporter of him until his death in 1799. In return, Chŏngjo promoted him to high posts that no Southerner had held since their fall from power a century before, including positions on the State Council. Naturally, the Patriarchs were not about to allow the return of their old enemies to a position of even shared prominence without complaint. The King had to push through Ch'ae's appointment as troop commander of P'yŏngan Province over official opposition, even to the point of dismissing officials who protested too vociferously. This office was granted to Ch'ae by a "special appointment" 特旨 (t'ŭkchi) that did not follow the regular procedure. That procedure called for the Ministry of Personnel to present to the throne a list of three candidates for a given post, from which the king selected one. But here, Chŏngjo simply appointed the man he wanted without consulting the Ministry. He did the very same thing again two years later when he appointed Ch'ae Councilor of the Right, and received an even more outraged response from his ministers; despite dismissing officials for opposing the appointment the very next day, six months later, protesting memorials were still coming in.[41] It is also true that Chŏngjo valued Ch'ae's advice. To take one example, he refused to appoint an official based solely on Ch'ae's criticism.[42]

But Ch'ae was not always in agreement with the King, nor was Chŏngjo's support unequivocal. For example, in 1790, Ch'ae, then serving as Councilor of the Left 左議政, suggested the King may have made a "mistake" in recalling the former governor of Kangwha Island to the capital. Chŏngjo refused to change his decision and ordered Ch'ae not to speak of it again. Further, Ch'ae's call in 1792 for a purge of the Intransigents in response to the Joint Memorial by the Scholars of Kyŏngsang Province[43] demanding justice for Sado was likewise refused, and a year later he was dismissed from his post on the State Council for quarrelling with another of Chŏngjo's supporters, Kim Chong-su, who also lost his own State Council post.[44]

Considering the royal reaction to it, the Joint Memorial was probably orchestrated by Chŏngjo himself to exacerbate the rift between the Expedient and Intransigent branches of the Patriarchs Faction, another ploy to keep the ministers from uniting against him. The Joint Memorial was signed by numerous local notables from Kyŏngsang Province, a stronghold of the Southerner faction. On hearing this bitter and impassioned plea for the King to restore Sado's honor and punish anyone who impugned it, Chŏngjo engaged in a bit of political theater.

> When Yi U had read out the entire memorial, the King choked up and made no sound, desiring to speak but unable to do so. After a few moments passed, he said, "My thoughts have been so long repressed that I do not know what to say. If I speak as I like, I fear it will harm you who have come from so far to see me.... Do not worry that righteous principle will not be illuminated or that correct punishment will not be meted out."[45]

[堣讀疏訖。上掩抑哽咽不成聲。欲言而不能言。如是者屢。良久曰心旣抑塞。語無次序。欲言則恐有傷於遠儒瞻視矣。... 爾等毋憂義理之不明。刑政之不擧。]

Getting choked up, the King confesses that he cannot speak his true thoughts but assures the authors of the memorial that he will do what is right and correct, without giving any indication of exactly what that means. A more evasive nonanswer is difficult to imagine.[46]

However, it was never his intention to purge the Intransigents, even though the memorial provided the perfect opportunity to do so. After all, there were plenty of officials both inside and outside the government that hungered for justice for Sado (not to mention the rewards they would no doubt receive once those who supported Sado's execution were eliminated), and the early 1790s were the height of Southerner power. But Chŏngjo preferred to convert his opponents rather than to crush them, because a living friend could do more for him than a dead enemy. Eliminating the Intransigents en masse threatened to make their enemies believe they would gain positions such that they could control the King. Thus he continued to cultivate his relationship with Kim Chong-su even after Kim switched from Expedient to Intransigent, and no one demonstrates Chŏngjo's capacity to make use of a supposedly intractable foe than Sim Hwan-ji, whom one scholar called "the wall Chŏngjo could not cross."[47]

Sim Hwan-ji passed the *munkwa* in 1771 at the age of 41, though it was not until 1793 that he reached high office. From that year until his death in 1802, he was a leading figure of the Intransigents. Sim had a reputation as uncompromising, and scholars generally considered him Chŏngjo's implacable enemy, one he could not be rid of despite his considerable power, before the recent discovery of Chŏngjo's extant "secret letters" to him from 1796 to 1800. While the letters do not completely overturn this view, they do reveal one reason Chŏngjo was never rid of Sim: The two men could actually work quite well together, so long as the King was able to convince Sim that he was "illuminating principle" and "rectifying affairs" because, after all, "what minister could reject a king's offer to illuminate principle and rectify affairs?"[48]

Derek Beales, writing on Joseph II, remarked that when looking at an absolute monarchy, historians must look at private personal writings together with official public writings,[49] and James B. Collins notes that, to get things done, kings often relied on personal clients rather than official subordinates or regular channels.[50] For these reasons and many others, the "secret letters" are an extraordinary discovery. They were brought to scholarly attention by An Tae-hoe, Kim Moon-sik, and Pak Ch'ŏl-sang when they were invited to examine them by their owner—whose identity they have not revealed—at her home in the Pundang district of Sŏngnam. The anonymous owner claimed she had obtained them from a descendant of Sim Hwan-ji and had kept them in her home for thirty years without knowing just what they were. Upon examining six of the letters, the three scholars quickly realized what they had, and Sungkyunkwan University set about producing a translation, publishing it in 2009.[51] The letters are very informal in their form, and range from 10 to 500 sinographs per letter for a total of about 52,000 in sum. In total, 297 letters were found, an extraordinary number given that, apart from these, there are only about 100 extant royal letters from all Korean kings combined. The letters are contained in their original envelopes, on which someone (whom An Tae-hoe argues was Sim Hwan-ji himself) wrote the date and time they were received.[52]

The letters do not directly name either the sender or recipient, but An and Pak have published explanations of how these can be known as Chŏngjo and Sim, respectively. For the former, An and Pak argue that the handwriting/calligraphy style match known examples of Chŏngjo's from other sources, that many details of the letters are corroborated by the *Veritable Records* and *Records of the Royal Secretariat*, that certain keywords and phrases are used by the king to refer to high officials (*kyŏng* 卿 being one example, a term usually restricted to current or former State Councilors), and that they use the same royal seal, the *Manch'ŏn* 滿川 seal that Chŏngjo began to use early in 1799, that was used for the *Short Letters of Chŏngjo* 正朝簡札帖, currently housed in the National Museum of Korea. In the latter case, An and Pak confirmed the letters were for Sim Hwan-ji by cross-checking references to his titles with the official records and because of references the writer makes to places that Sim lived.[53]

We learn from these letters that much of what is recorded in the *Veritable Records* is political theater, including such examples as Chŏngjo asking Sim Hwan-ji if a man's submitted memorial was "only a formality for my refusal [辭疏。豈慾一番例讓而然耶]," or if he would "stubbornly continue to submit [抑一味固執云耶]" them, cluing us in that memorials' stated purpose and actual purpose need not coincide. A few years later, Chŏngjo asked Sim, "Do you want to return to office immediately, or do you prefer that I beseech you once or twice before you return [欲爲一番辭職後出脚耶。抑一二番敦諭後出仕耶]?"[54]

The letters also reveal that much politicking was going on behind the scenes that the official sources do not speak to. While this has long been suspected, the letters provide strong evidence. For example, it was never guaranteed that the man who submitted a memorial was the sole author of that memorial, or even that he wrote it at all, but now we have King Chŏngjo telling us this matter-of-factly, as if it were a common occurrence, which it undoubtedly was. The scholar-officials of late Chosŏn regularly showed each other and the king drafts of memorials they had yet to submit,[55] edited or wrote memorials for other people,[56] collaborated with each other or even with the king himself in drawing up memorials that they did not necessarily affix their names to,[57] and feigned illness in order to delay taking action.[58] Factional leaders had unofficial control over what lower members of the faction could and could not submit and were held accountable by the king for allowing divisive memorials to come out.[59] Chŏngjo asked Sim to write memorials for him so that he could bring up an issue for discussion without appearing to be the one to do so,[60] showed him drafts of his official responses and communiqués before he presented them in open court or sent them to their recipients,[61] and instructed him to limit the number of memorials his faction sent regarding a particular issue.[62] He also subjected at least some of Sim's memorials to his approval before they were submitted and at times demanded revisions.[63] These revisions could be quite specific. In the following extended quotation, the King directs Sim to ignore his official command and to resign, explaining in great detail exactly what sort of language he wants Sim's resignation memorial to contain:

> Did you pass the evening well? As for the business of supervising the test for the Palace Medical Office, although you are waiting for the royal summons, remain *in defiance of my royal order*. As for the resignation memorial, would you be sure to show me a draft of it first? When you compose the language, say, "Rather, you can never rebuke anyone by saying 'How could this language come out?'" Also, say, "Saying it is defiling; hearing it is contaminating. That the illustrious Royal Library could be shamed this way is unspeakable. Since 1795, have you not read such phrases as 'we extol the Sagely Virtue' or 'we respect the court more than the Sun and Moon' from the Disciples or Expedients? But it is appropriate to praise and encourage that memorial [by one Yi Ŭi-jun], and then Your Lordships can be said to have replied. Is it not less important who wrote the memorial than the accuracy of its contents?" I would like your memorial to generally include this sort of thing. What about also expressing this praise to other people? Show me a draft as soon as you have written it. I will end here.[64]

[夜間安未。醫監試役待牌。一直達召。辭疏則草出後。必爲先示如何。措語則決不可反覆以此言奚爲而至及言之若浼。聽之若汚。名以堂堂內閣。得此羞恥。實欲無言爲言。而乙卯以後。以闡揚聖德及尊朝廷於日月之上等語闖發於章奏者。何嘗見之於時輩與少論耶。然則其疏當極意嘉獎扶植。然後卿等可謂有辭。辭直者。豈不勝人耶。疏中略帶似此意思爲可。對人亦必稱詡。如何如何。疏草待構得。卽示之如何。姑此。]

As if telling Sim the sort of language he wanted was not enough, on another occasion the King even told him *verbatim* what to say, to the point of virtually dictating memorials himself. Here, Chŏngjo instructs Sim on how to compose a memorial requesting posthumous office for one Im Wi, a loyal retainer of Sado.

"Late Royal Secretary Im Wi used to serve Crown Prince Sado as an official when the prince went by carriage to the hot springs. He received the office of Royal Secretary by special favor and did so much more that I dare not try to explicate all of it. After two years he was appointed Magistrate of Hong County, yet from the twenty-fourth day of the fifth [lunar] month he was unable to eat, for he was wailing so, and ten days later he died. His singular loyalty and special integrity could be called a shining star in the dark sky. Though one thousand years pass, later scholars will be moved to tears. So that we might repay him properly, we must bestow upon him by special grace a posthumous office." I would like you to expand upon this.[65]

[故承旨任瑋。以昔年宮官當溫幸時。爲隨駕承旨。偏承異渥。臣不敢畢陳。而及其再明年。出宰洪州。自五月二十四日不食痛哭。仍爲滅性於旬日之內。其孤忠特節。可謂昏衢之一星。千載之下。志士灑泣。其在崇報之道。宜施褒贈之典等語。敷衍措辭爲可。]

Two weeks after this letter was sent, we find in the *Daily Records of the Royal Secretariat* Sim Hwan-ji saying,

Therefore, Royal Secretary Im Wi had moral integrity that stood apart, yet even now he is hidden and is unknown to the world. I your servant am one who has sighed in sadness at this. Im Wi used to serve Crown Prince Sado as an official when the prince went by carriage to the hot springs. He received the office of Royal Secretary by special favor and did so much more that I dare not try to explicate all of it. Two years later he was appointed Magistrate of Ho Township, yet from the twenty-fourth day of the fifth [lunar] month he was wailing such that he was unable to eat, and ten days later he died. His singular loyalty and special integrity could be called a shining star in the dark sky. Though one thousand years pass, later scholars will cry tears of reverence. So that we might repay him properly, it is appropriate that an office of the first rank be bestowed upon him by special royal grace.[66]

[故承旨任瑋。有卓然之節。而至今幽沒。未著于世。臣之所嘗嘅嘆者也。瑋以昔年宮官。當溫幸時。爲隨駕承旨。偏承異渥。臣不敢畢陳,而及其後二年。出宰湖邑。自五月二十四日。痛哭不食。仍以滅性於旬日之內。其孤忠特節。可謂昏衢之一星。千載之下。志士尚爲之灑泣。其在崇報之道。宜贈以一品之職。仍施節惠之典矣。]

Later, Chŏngjo dictates not just part but virtually all of Sim's memorial.

Make the following points in your resignation memorial: "I have no other ability. I did naught but clarify His Majesty's intentions and raise up the virtue of those intentions as my priority. Accordingly, although this is a trivial matter, I intended to make clear your Sagely benevolence so that the common people who have been unaware of it will learn of it and be moved by it. Rumor does not distinguish truth from falsehood. I simply reported to the King all that I know according to principle."

Also, write: "These days it is fashionable to mock clarifying His Majesty's intentions and raising up the virtue of those intentions. His Majesty instructed me saying, 'People say that serving the ruler and exhausting oneself in pursuit of ritual is merely toadying.' Because of this, although everyone blamed me, I did not refuse His Majesty."

Also, write: "Truly if what these memorials to the King say regarding important affairs is true, that there is not a single lawbreaker in the land, it would be a time to celebrate at court that moral order remains intact. But if we had made only halfhearted inquiries and did not inform the King of everything that is going on, that will further endanger moral order, so it is all the more difficult for me to atone."

Also, write: "At present, apart from my acute illness, since there is a law against reckless talk, if I am not punished, everyone would say, 'That man [Sim] takes advantage of his high position close to the king even though he is guilty of crimes.' If this were done, if I am not punished, it would not have the benefit of causing officials who have done wrong to face punishment. Rather, it would hasten the collapse of public order."

When you write the memorial, will you make sure you say all of this? Show me a draft of the memorial as soon as you have written it.[67]

[辭疏名意。則臣無他能。斷斷一心。在於明聖志尊聖德爲主。而雖微事細節。聖恩之關而不揚。小民之愚不知感處。必欲闡揚。無論風傳之虛實。竊附知無不言之義。敢陳淺見爲說。友以爲近俗於明聖志尊聖德。看作嘲訕之資。而聖人有事君盡禮。人以爲諂之訓。雖以此萬口讒臣。臣所不辭爲言。又以爲誠如諸道狀辭。無一犯者。爲朝廷賀紀綱之不挫。而萬一草草行査。泛泛封啓。則緣臣一言。重壞紀綱者。此尤臣難贖之罪爲說。而又以爲目下病勢之外。不被不當被之律。以爲妄言者之戒。則夫夫也。皆曰波夫官高職親。有罪倖逃云爾。則其爲紀綱之乖損。反有甚於犯科守令之倖逃當律爲言。措語各別倔彊。如何如何。疏草出後。即示之也。]

By this point we should not be surprised to find that nearly all of this appears, often word-for-word, in Sim's memorial submitted on January 20, 1797.[68]

This puts a new spin on our understanding of events recorded in the *Veritable Records*. As it turns out, sometimes officials took positions contrary to the throne in open court at the express direction of the king. As an example, according to the *Veritable Records* account, Sim Hwan-ji staunchly opposed Chŏngjo's pardon of Princess Hwawan, at this time still legally a commoner known as Madam Chŏng. After Chŏngjo opened up the floor for discussion, Sim Hwan-ji immediately denounced Madame Chŏng and flatly refused any suggestion that she be forgiven.

> Councilor of the Right Sim Hwan-ji said, "Moral principles have their foundation and their implications, and rebels are composed of ringleaders and followers. The principles behind 1762 [Sado's death] became the righteous principles of 1775 [the execution of opponents of the regency], and the righteous principles of 1775 became the righteous principles of 1776. As for the traitors of 1762 and 1775, Madame Chŏng was the root cause of their treachery. People like Chŏng In-gyŏm, Hang Kan, Yun Yang-hu, and Hong Kye-nŭng, these traitors all secretly supported Madame Chŏng. If we were now to suddenly pardon and release her and news of this action spread to all corners of our country, and even to future generations, the *Record Illuminating Righteousness*[69] would become a useless book. The nation would no longer be a true nation and people would no longer be real people. The reason I rely on Your Majesty and serve is because of moral principles. I your servant may face death, but I do not dare to flatter you [by not opposing this]."
>
> The King said, "What Your Lordship has said is going too far."

> [右議政沈煥之曰義理有本末。亂賊有源委。自某年義理而爲乙未義理。自乙未義理而爲丙申義理。乙丙亂賊。鄭妻卽其根柢。而麟謙恒簡養厚啓能輩諸賊。皆以鄭妻爲奧援矣。今若遽爾宥釋。以此傳敎。頒之八方。垂諸後世。則明義錄將爲無用之書。而國不國人不人矣。臣所以藉手事君者。惟此義理而已。臣等有死而不敢奉承矣。上曰卿言過矣。]

After another official came to Sim's defense, the King cut him off and dismissed him. More opposition to Madame Chŏng followed, with Sim and his fellow Intransigent Yi Pyŏng-mo standing together until Chŏngjo angrily dismissed them both.

> Minister of Personnel Yi Si-su said, "When the terrible plot of Madame Chŏng was afoot, only the sagely Queen Mother saw clearly this evil treachery and with utmost sincerity protected [Your Majesty]. Now if

Your Majesty pardons Madame Chŏng, how could there be meritorious virtue in the Queen Mother's protection?"

Before Yi finished, the King said, "How can the Minister of Personnel try to blow this up all out of proportion? You are dismissed from your post. Get out." When Yi left, the King said, "You ministers of the State Council, if you have more difficulties to continually memorialize about, bring them before the Three Censorial Offices." Censor-General Song Chŏn and others also strongly complained that the *Record Illuminating Righteousness* explicated that traitorous ringleaders may not be forgiven, and so royal permission should not be granted.

Sim Hwan-ji said, "How can I maintain my dignity if I continue to occupy this position on the State Council? Since I have been immersed in the grace of the state [i.e., the King's favor], how could I dare to think of saving myself by asking to be dismissed? Yet I am truly shallow and unable to change Heaven [the King's mind]. It is appropriate that I resign and await punishment." He prostrated himself below the stairs and removed his official headgear.

The King said, "The Councilor of the Right's behavior is outrageous. Do not remove your headgear but instead approach the throne at once." Sim Hwan-ji did not obey the royal command.

[Councilor of the Left] Yi Pyŏng-mo said, "I your servant and the Councilor of the Right are no different in holding fast to righteousness today. Yet he cannot approach the throne before receiving the royal judgment. If you desire to relieve his distress, let him receive his punishment at once. This is my humble wish."

The King said, "In this matter, the Councilor of the Right is being totally ridiculous!" He commanded the Royal Secretaries to come in and take down a royal order. Sim Hwan-ji withdrew to await the order. The King said, "The Councilor of the Right in this matter has been exceedingly egregious." Thereupon he directed, "This is a serious affront to the dignity of the state. Not even a minute of thought was given to reverence or propriety. Moreover, today even after hearing my instructions, he [Sim] went ahead and continued to protest as though he had not heard me at all. This is not the sort of behavior I expect from a high official. The Councilor of the Right is dismissed from office."

Yi Pyŏng-mo said, "Speaking of my colleague on the State Council is the same as speaking of me, your servant. If he receives this rebuke, I your servant will also await such an order."

[吏曹判書李時秀奏曰鄭妻匈謀方劇之時。惟我慈聖。炳幾燭奸。至誠保護。今若有釋鄭妻。則其於慈聖保護之功德何如也。奏未畢。上曰吏判之奏。何可藉重爲說乎。吏判罷職。退出可也。時秀退出。上曰卿宰則有難一一盡奏。三司進前也。大司諫宋銓等。又力爭明義錄賊魁之不可有釋。不許。煥之曰臣以何顏。自處於具僚之上乎。厚被國恩。豈敢爲求退之念。而忱誠淺薄。不能回天。臣則當退而竢罪矣。伏階下免冠。上曰右相擧措。萬萬過矣。勿爲免冠。卽爲陞殿。煥之不膺命。秉模曰今日處義。臣與右相無異。而右相則未蒙兪音之前。必不陞殿。如欲慰釋。則卽爲還收處分。區區之望也。上曰右相事過矣。命承旨往傳下敎。煥之退而肯命。上曰右相事萬萬過矣。仍敎曰到今國體。事面爲重。敬禮有不暇顧。況聞今日之敎。而爲此擧。有非所知於此大臣者。右議政沈煥之罷職。秉模曰僚相之言。卽臣之言也。僚相既被譴。臣亦當待命矣。]

The King then turned on the Censorate, demanding that they censure Sim. They, in the face of Sim's "holding fast to righteousness," demurred, so Chŏngjo dismissed them as well.

> The King said, "All of you Censors are here. Why have you not prepared a charge for this offense?"
>
> Song Chŏn and others said, "As for the affair of Madam Chŏng, we are still in the early stages of dealing with it. First we need to recall the order for a pardon and then we can go on to the next step of preparing charges."
>
> The King said, "There is no need for you to stick up for each other. All the officials in the Three Censorial Offices are at once dismissed." Again he instructed, "When I requested a reaction to this proposal the other day, you said it would be difficult to pardon someone who had done wrong. And you said you could not be forced to implement this order. Censor-General Song Chŏn has to be replaced." The King went into his personal quarters and directed, "All the officials in the Three Censorial Offices are dismissed forthwith."[70]

[上曰臺臣既備員。何不傳啓乎。銓等曰鄭妻事。在於合辭之首。今宜先請還收全宥之命。然後始可以次第傳啓矣。上曰不必相持。三司諸臣。速爲退去。仍敎曰日前請對時。做錯有難寬恕。則不可强令察任。大司諫宋銓許遞。上仍還內敎曰三司諸臣。卽爲退去。]

Sim Hwan-ji certainly appeared to have openly defied the King and was dismissed from office as punishment for refusing to accede to royal desires regarding Madame Chŏng. The letter the King sent to Sim the previous evening, however, presents a different picture.

I omit the greeting. This time the situation is very difficult. Truly it has been a long time since Madame Chŏng has entered the capital. Whether the people at court realize it or not, this shows a serious lack of sincerity. I dealt with her just like the situation in the court of Hyojong, and old men say this issue should be forwarded to the Border Defense Command in the palace. At that time I did not hear of memorials regarding this. This being the case, would you not say that the ministers at court are not acting with sincerity toward me these days? I have heard enough about how to deal with this issue yesterday, but the relevant moral principles here are very strict. Now that Kim Chong-su has passed on, *you must not concede the leading seat.* This matter is related to the moral principles of the *Record Illuminating Righteousness*. How can we avoid bringing that record up when we discuss the matter? Tomorrow, I will solicit opinions from the ministers. When it is your turn, complain strongly. Then you will go down at once to the courtyard, remove your official hat, and request censure. Then I will look at the situation, remove you from office, and decide either to dismiss the State Councilors or to censure and remove them from office as well. I am even thinking of reappointing you, so give that some thought. I will make sure Sŏ Yong-bo understands my intentions, though it seems this letter will not reach his messenger in time. I will end here.[71]

[除煩。今番絲。極難處。而其實入置城內已多年所。朝廷之知若不知。太欠誠實。而昔在孝廟朝。亦有似處分。故老傳以謂上闕備邊司許接云。其時未聞以此上疏陳箚。然則今日廷臣。未必謂之不誠耶。至於日前處分。言足聽聞。而義理嚴。至於卿則夢閣去後。卿當不讓主人。事關於明義錄義理。寧過無不及爲可。明日當召見諸臣矣。出班力陳。仍卽下庭免冠諸譴。則當觀事勢。免相與譴罷間區處。其後復拜之道。自有料量者。似此連意。而當以此意。使徐俒以吾意傳之耳。此書想未及傳於徐使之前矣。姑此。]

Sim Hwan-ji's actions that day were in fact requested by Chŏngjo himself. The entire display of Sim's opposition to pardoning Princess Hwawan was a sham, probably staged to help Sim avoid the charge of being a royal puppet; whenever someone accused him of knuckling under to the King, he could point to this as a time he lost his office over principle, a badge of honor among the Intransigents. Chŏngjo, ever ready to be all things to all men, reassured Sim that he would remain a leader of the Intransigents and, in fact, might soon receive another appointment. It may also have been a way to get Yi Pyŏng-mo to remove himself from office as part of a public show of solidarity with his fellow Intransigent, an incentive for Sim, publicly his factional brother but privately his rival, to go along with the charade.

Chŏngjo routinely requested that Sim Hwan-ji intervene with his faction to deal with problems outside official channels,[72] and even consulted him for advice on how to protect Ch'ae Che-gong from accusations from within Ch'ae's own faction.[73] Despite Sim's public commitment to principle and precedent, Chŏngjo wooed him by offering to break with precedent—that is, to use the very royal discretion that fellow Intransigent Yi Pyŏng-mo criticized—in order to grant his request to leave the capital despite his recent appointment to central government office.[74] Chŏngjo was crafty enough to realize that men opposed to his expansion of royal discretion might be made more amenable were they to find that discretion exercised on their own behalf. Clearly, the King was able to placate to some extent even his avowed opponents, though those opponents would not hold back upon his untimely death.

Chŏngjo learned the game of politics through early mistakes. As we have seen, the King was initially uncertain of how to proceed, allowing his close friend and ally Hong Kuk-yŏng to dominate the first years of his reign and proving unable to protect royal relatives like his aunt Princess Hwawan and his half-brother Prince Ŭnjŏn from extreme banishment and death, respectively. Chŏngjo was a fast learner, however, and it was not long before he demonstrated what he had learned of the game of thrones. Hong Kuk-yŏng, seemingly at the height of his power, was cast down, all his might turned to vapor before the young king's wrath and aristocratic opposition to any attempt to supplant the king, their impartial arbiter. A plot against his second half-brother Prince Ŭnŏn was stymied, and Princess Hwawan was slowly but irresistibly restored to her old place in the palace.

When it came to the major political factions, Chŏngjo altered Yŏngjo's balance of power between two factions into a complex shifting of alliances designed to ensure that he himself was always in the supreme position. Like Louis XIV, who wrote to his grandson and heir, "never allow yourself to be ruled; be the master; have no favorites or prime minister; listen to, and consult your Council, but do decide yourself,"[75] Chŏngjo reserved the final decision to the throne and refused to be dominated or forced to act by others. He rewarded his staunch supporters like Ch'ae Che-gong but was not beholden to them, lest they entertain pretensions of becoming a second Hong Kuk-yŏng. Neither did the King wantonly punish his opponents, but sought ways both clear and shady to enlist their support. The consummate politician, Chŏngjo built relationships, portrayed himself as fair and impartial, and told his officials whatever it took to get them on his side. While the King was not the only skilled player of the game—men like Sim Hwan-ji were masters themselves who probably understood exactly what Chŏngjo was doing—they all, in the end, understood the system within which they had to work and knew they had to find some way to work together to avoid serious unrest and bloody purges, which no one by this point in the dynasty's history wanted to relive.

5

BUILDING A SYSTEM

KING CHŎNGJO WAS A MASTER OF BOTH THE IDEOLOGICAL TOOLS AVAILABLE
to him in Confucianism and the political realities of the eighteenth-century
Chosŏn state. He deployed his extensive education and the Confucian emphasis
on both kingship and scholarship to argue for increased royal discretion and
aristocratic subservience while cultivating relationships with both supporters
and opponents to accomplish his policy objectives. All of this relied, however,
on Chŏngjo himself. An energetic monarch with a keen mind, Chŏngjo was
able to weld together a core of support among at least the high officialdom for
his policies, but this would not be enough to perpetuate increased royal prestige
and power beyond his own effective ruling years. For that, institutional reform
was needed. This was a far more daunting task than managing factionalism and
convincing the independent-minded *yangban* to follow the throne's lead, but
the benefits would also be more long-lasting. Hence Chŏngjo sought to build
a system that would ensure the continued centrality of the king in decision
making. This chapter deals largely with reforms on the civil side in pursuit of
this goal, with the following chapter focusing on his military reforms.

The King sought to institutionalize both his own version of the role of
the king in government and his notion of expanded discretion. Thus, after an
early misstep with the position of selection secretary, he constructed the Royal
Library to serve as an institutional basis for a proroyal wing of the government and the royal selection system to educate officials in his own views on
Confucianism and to place himself in the position of teacher rather than student.
More than any previous ruler, he sought direct interaction with the people he
ruled and went to great lengths to keep himself informed of the administration of the country outside the capital, such as by making greater use of secret
inspectors 暗行御史 (*amhaeng ŏsa*) and reforming the inspector system.[1] Here
we will focus on how he expanded the king's freedom of action by recruiting
men into the government who had been traditionally excluded, by going on

frequent processions to interact directly with those he ruled, by dealing with problems directly through petitions rather than allowing officials to control his ability to take action through refusal to bring issues to his attention, and by planning the replacement of slavery with hired labor, thereby circumventing restrictions on the throne's employment of people for service.

The expansion of recruitment in particular represented Chŏngjo's most direct challenge to one of the pillars of *yangban* power, the virtual monopolization of office-holding by a small, self-selected group of *yangban* clans. The King attempted to bring men into the government who lacked a significant power base other than royal patronage, so as to ensure their support for his policies, just as Louis XIV attempted to do. These included men from the northern provinces (traditionally regarded as lesser *yangban* than those from the southern provinces whose capital branches dominated the central bureaucracy), secondary sons 庶孽 (*sŏŏl*, men born of a *yangban* father and a concubine), and men of the Southerner faction who had been effectively excluded from power since 1694. The last is particularly interesting, since the Southerners were ideologically in line with Chŏngjo, calling for a strengthened, activist throne as against the more aloof throne of the Patriarchs and Disciples. Yet, as Park Hyunmo points out, the King did not turn the government over to the Southerners, instead taking great pains to keep the throne above factionalism.[2] Chŏngjo kept a careful balance of bringing Southerners into the government as a source of support while not making them his sole pillar of power, lest they in turn gain power over him.

EARLY SETBACKS: THE STRUGGLE OVER SELECTION SECRETARIES

Yŏngjo and Chŏngjo both attempted to expand the pool of talent from which they could draw officials. A key to controlling access to the halls of power was the position of selection secretary 銓郎 (*chŏllang*). This was an office in the Ministry of Personnel of rank 5a, assisted by an official of rank 6a. A rank 5 office is not obviously important, but the selection secretaries had enormous influence over recruitment, such that the office could be considered a "gateway" to high office. The prestige of the position by late Chosŏn was such that, despite its middling rank, not only was an official expected to serve in the post before ascending to high office, but the sitting office-holders themselves, rather than the Minister of Personnel, had the power to recommend their own successors.[3] This power, coupled with the necessity of serving in the post in order to rise to higher office, meant that whichever faction controlled them could exert disproportionate influence on the highest levels of government, and the king was effectively eliminated from the process.

Indeed, the existing factional lines in the eighteenth century trace back to a dispute over appointments to this office in 1575, and eighteenth-century Chosŏn scholar Yi Chung-hwan blamed the office itself as the cause of factionalism. Even if the position of selection secretary did not cause factionalism, it was a key weapon of the factions. Through control of this gateway to higher positions, a faction could monopolize access to the highest official posts. Thus, much factional strife revolved around appointments to this office, since control of these appointments meant control of the highest offices of state.[4]

Yŏngjo recognized the divisive potential of selection secretary appointments and accordingly abolished their power to influence higher offices. Shortly after he took the throne, Chŏngjo restored this power. His reasons for doing this are not clear. Chŏngjo himself claimed he had no choice but to do so in the face of official clamor. Yi Han-u argues it was part of Hong Kuk-yŏng's bid for favor from the Patriarchs to secure his position early in Chŏngjo's reign, while Park Hyunmo notes that Royal Library officials could be recommended to the office,[5] suggesting the King may have initially intended to funnel his supporters into the position and so did not wish to weaken it. Whatever his reasons, the restoration led to problems, and the King would eventually abolish the power again. In 1782, he lamented that the selection secretaries were just as partisan as ever. "After the re-establishment of selection secretaries' recommendation [power], I occasionally held out hope that it would have some small effectiveness at changing things. Yet even now there has been not benefit, but harm [銓通復設之後。或冀一分有淬勵之成效。迄今無益而有害]." Thirteen years after restoring it, Chŏngjo abolished the power of the selection secretaries, never to reinstitute it. His old ally Ch'ae Che-gong presented his case, probably the King's own case. After the reestablishment of the power, said Ch'ae, contention at court only became more severe, due to the repeated abolition and establishment. Selection secretary was the most sought-after of all posts, such that even a state councilor or state tribunal was cowed by the selection secretaries. Ch'ae pointedly argued that it was no good to discuss whether the power should be kept or abolished based on precedent. Instead, it should be kept only if it was advantageous to do so. Several officials voiced their opposition to the power, and in response, Chŏngjo reiterated his earlier claim that he thought restoring the power was a bad idea.

> From the first moment it was re-established, I knew it was not beneficial, yet immediately after its re-establishment, my desire to end it was not possible to carry out and so it has been in place until now. According to what you have said, the words I hear from my ministers accord with

my own intention. How can I be restrained by any suspicion that it is not prudent? The regulations re-establishing the selection secretaries[' power] are abolished.[6]

[自初復設。決知其無益。而既設之後。欲罷不能。因循至今。適因言端。聞卿言。政合予意。銷刻何拘。吏郎復設之規。革罷。]

This fit in with the King's overall goal of increasing royal discretion, in this case flexibility in the selection of men for office. By eliminating selection secretaries' right to nominate their own successors, Chŏngjo removed a check on royal prerogative in the selection of officials to that office and, due to its importance, to all higher offices. Yet selection secretary remained a key office, and Chŏngjo developed another avenue for exerting royal control over it.

ROYAL LIBRARY AND ROYAL SELECTION SERVICE: EDUCATION AND TRAINING

King Chŏngjo understood that the amount of time he needed to implement serious reforms would have to be measured in months, if not years. Living in such a thoroughly agricultural society as Chosŏn, he would undoubtedly have understood the metaphor that one had to plant seeds that would only be harvested much later. Two of these seeds were the institutions of the Royal Library and the royal selection system. One began minor and slowly became major, while the other cultivated those who were minor in order to take advantage of them once they became major.

The Royal Library: A Place of Learning and Power

As part of his attempt to elevate the ruler and strengthen the throne against the aristocracy, Chŏngjo established the Kyujanggak, or Royal Library, an institution dedicated to the preservation of royal writings, using the precedent of China's Royal Library system, established during the Song dynasty (960–1276), to legitimize the construction. To its officials, Chŏngjo explained in moral terms his reason for setting up the library.

> I do not think establishing the Royal Library and creating rules and regulations for it are urgent matters, yet that is my intention. The morality of the scholar-officials these days has been swept from Earth. This means they are utterly without comportment and fail to act properly.

In their comings and goings and in their speech, they likewise have no habit of observing courtesy, to a regrettable extent, and even the officials close at hand imitate the officials who are far away. If they are made to go in and out of the Royal Library, they will show restraint and decorum and will not reach the point of behaving recklessly. If they are gentle, modest, and orderly, the effect will be that when they hear a baseless rumor, they will be strongly outraged. Would this not be sufficient to help bring order to the court and transform the officials?[7]

[設置內閣。刱立儀規。或當以爲不急之務。而予意別有在焉。近來士夫之名檢掃地。動作周旋之際。全沒收斂之意。進退相與之間。亦無揖讓之風。良足慨然。近臣者。遠臣之所效則者也。若使出入內閣之人。修飭威儀。不至放肆。酬接溫恭。秩秩有序。則風聲所曁。亦當有觀感之效。豈不足爲治化之一助乎。]

The Royal Library expanded, both in physical size and in scope and function, over the course of Chŏngjo's reign. In the beginning it served as a symbol of royal erudition and scholarship, but it would come to serve as a centerpiece of Chŏngjo's effort to bolster royal power through restructuring the central government. This vesting of importance in the Royal Library weakened the traditional aristocratic strongholds of power.[8] Kim Sung-Yun argues that the weakening of those government positions monopolized by powerful *yangban* meant that "a new power system [had] formed around [a] talent pool that received benefits and education directly from the king."[9] Coupled with the royal selection system, the Royal Library constituted a way to funnel proroyal officials into the bureaucracy; a majority of appointees to the Library came through the system. Young officials just beginning their careers were educated by the King in his own interpretation of Confucianism through the royal selection system, cultivating a relationship with him as he evaluated them. Then these men served in the Royal Library, and then as selection secretaries (weakened without their power to recommend their own successors but still important as a necessary step on the ladder of power), and finally reached the high ranks of officialdom, and by this point they were well known to the King through frequent meetings with him,[10] meetings that were held outside the regular royal audiences with high officials.

The Royal Library began as a repository for the writings of preceding Chosŏn monarchs. Chŏngjo ordered the construction of a "Pavilion for Receiving and Protecting the Writings of Previous Kings" 先朝御製奉安閣 in the rear garden 後園 of Ch'angdŏk Palace 昌德宮 immediately upon his accession to the throne, and the project was completed six months later. The familiar face of Ch'ae Che-gong was charged with the project, and key Chŏngjo support-ers like Hong Kuk-yŏng were immediately given high-ranking offices in it. Originally the lower floor of the building, the *ŏje chon'gak* 御製尊閣 or "Pavilion for Respecting Royal Writings," was to house the written work of the Chosŏn monarchs. However, a few months after establishing the Library, the King suddenly announced that his own material would be stored there and that a sepa-rate building, called the Hall for Receiving the Royal Plan 奉謨堂 (*pongmodang*), would be constructed for the writings of previous kings. Administratively, the Royal Library was headed by two superintendents of scholarship 提學 of minis-terial rank, specifically ranks 1b to 2b, and initially lacked a director 大提學. It also consisted of two auxiliary superintendents of scholarship 直提學 of ranks 2b to 3a, one auxiliary pavilion official 直閣 of ranks 3a to 6b, one assistant educator 待敎 of ranks 7a to 9a, and thirty-five lesser officials (including four examiners 檢書官), supplemented by seventy clerks. This last meant that the Royal Library had approximately 20 percent more functionaries than the Office of Special Advisers, marking it as administratively important.[11] Yi Tae-Jin compares the Royal Library to the Hall of Worthies 集賢殿 (*Chiphyŏnjŏn*),[12] the center of scholarship founded by King Sejong in 1420 that famously created the Korean alphabet, and contemporaries made the same comparison.[13]

In some ways the comparison of the Royal Library to the Hall of Worthies was apt. Both were centers of learning that stored royal writings, and the offi-cials of both bodies were personally chosen by the king and worked closely with him as advisers. Nor did either institution retain its importance after the reign of its founder. But the differences are as illuminating as the similar-ities. The Library had about forty officials while the Hall of Worthies typically numbered around twenty. While officials in the Hall of Worthies escaped the frequent transfers of office typical of government service in Chosŏn and might serve for years or even decades in their positions, a post in the Royal Library often signaled royal favor that led to further promotion in the bureaucracy.[14] The Royal Library was also the center of the royal selection system, which had no counterpart in Sejong's time, and it became involved in politics at a king's behest (discussed below) rather than in opposition to a king, as the Hall of Worthies did when King Sejo usurped the throne in 1455.[15]

At the time of its completion, the Royal Library finally received its perma-nent name, "Kyujanggak," a term that first appeared in Korea during the reign of Sejo, though it was not used. The Chinese equivalent, the "Kuizhangge" (rendered by Hucker as "Hall of Literature") originated in the Yuan dynasty in 1329, though the name was very quickly changed. It does not seem to have housed imperial writings but instead was a place to hold what Hucker calls

"Classics Colloquia," which resemble the Chosŏn royal lectures discussed below.[16] The Royal Library bolstered monarchical prestige because the institution itself drew on the precedent of Song China and gave central place to the writings of kings, and the name Kyujanggak reinforced Chŏngjo's portrayal of the king as being apart from, and above, everyone else in the state. "Kyujanggak" literally translated reads "Pavilion for the Writings of Kui," a Chinese literary deity whose name eventually came to refer to the Chinese emperor's writings, with corresponding connotations of divinity. By housing his writings in a building with such a name, Chŏngjo was not only implying equality with the Chinese emperor but comparing his scholarship to the divine. He did not state this directly, for obvious reasons, but he specifically cited the Song precedent, and only one of the *kyu* graph's two meanings was relevant to a library, so the implication was unlikely to be lost on the highly educated *yangban* elite.[17]

It was not long, however, before the Royal Library became more than a vehicle for boosting royal prestige and assumed a more direct role in politics. This new role was marked by Chŏngjo's suspension of the royal lectures, or "Lectures from the Mat" 經筵 (*kyŏng'yŏn*). These "lectures" were supposed to be readings of the classics and discussions of Confucianism between the king and senior officials, held three times daily. In reality, of course, the king's schedule did not allow for such frequency, and so even dedicated monarchs like Yŏngjo could hold but a fraction of what the ideal called for. JaHyun Kim Haboush notes that routinely having more than five of the regular royal lectures per month was unusual, and that having more than one on the same day was rarer still. In addition, they were freewheeling discussions that could stray far from the classic being examined and often ended up being about contemporary policy, which meant confrontation. Yŏngjo, through extreme dedication to learning over the length of his long reign, went from being lectured to by his officials to defeating them on "all critical challenges on matters of interpretation or policy."[18]

Chŏngjo, on the other hand, chafed under a system that placed him as the student to be instructed by his own ministers, as this hardly lined up with his assertion of authority on the basis of his status as teacher-monarch. Though Yŏngjo managed to turn the system against his officials, he was the exception rather than the rule, and he was only able to do so after decades of intensive effort, helped by the sheer length of his life and reign. Apart from Yŏngjo, the royal lecture system generally obstructed royal authority, and supporters of increased monarchical power like Yu Hyŏng-wŏn called for its elimination for this very reason. Further, Chŏngjo had been treated as heir to the throne throughout his childhood and youth, and he had therefore studied

Confucianism with the most able tutors Yŏngjo could find for two decades before he took the throne. He was already a master of Confucian rhetoric and probably saw nothing to be gained from taking up the position of diligent student once he was on the throne, as his grandfather, a man not expected to rule, had been forced to do. Up until 1781, the sixth year of his reign, Chŏngjo held the royal lecture at the Royal Library. However, on the eighteenth day of the third month of that year, he held his final royal lecture. From this point forward, *he* would be the teacher of young officials through his royal selection system.[19]

The catalyst for the expansion of Royal Library influence was the fall of Hong Kuk-yŏng. Hong had been in charge of its daily operations, and with his fall from power, Chŏngjo took over direct administration himself. Thus, in his fifth year, "Chŏngjo ordered all the civil servants at *Kyujanggak* to assume duties at such bureaus as the *Yemun'gwan* (Office of Royal Decrees), *Hongmun'gwan* (Office of Special Advisers), and *Sŭngjŏngwŏn* (Office of Royal Secretariat) in addition to their scholarly duties" in the Library.[20] Strikingly, the officials of the *Kyujanggak* had the power to censure officials in the existing government organs but were not subject to censure in turn by the *Sahŏnbu* (Office of the Inspector-General).[21] This gave the King a way to control overzealous censors short of punishing them directly and opening himself up to charges of closing the channel of speech言路 (*ŏllo*), that is, the right of censors and out-of-office country scholars to criticize the king's policies according to Confucian norms. Library officials could also be recommended directly to the office of selection secretary which, though weakened by Chŏngjo's abolition of its recommendation powers, was still a key office because it offered close contact with the King and crown prince and served as a stepping-stone to high office.[22] In keeping with Chŏngjo's emphasis on face-to-face interaction, officials in the Royal Library had frequent daily contact with him. Topics of discussion included order and chaos in both the past and the present, the troubles suffered by the common people, and political successes and failures of generations past.[23] This is vital, of course, because of the importance of "the face of the king." In an era lacking instantaneous communication, the king's authority diminishes away from his person.[24] Thus, service in the Royal Library was both a weapon against the established state organs and a method of getting Chŏngjo's own supporters into those organs. It became such an important body that even high-profile Intransigents like Sim Hwan-ji (in 1798) and Yi Pyŏng-mo (in 1790) served in it. Indeed, its highest offices were primarily filled by Patriarchs and Disciples rather than Southerners, again illustrating Chŏngjo's intention to institute a system that would produce loyalty to the monarch in all officials, not just in a single faction of them.

The Royal Selection System: Studying at the Foot of the Throne

So why were the royal librarians the King's "private officials"? Under the royal selection system 抄啓文臣 (*ch'ogye munsin*, "selecting and leading civil officials") system instituted by Chŏngjo, the King personally selected promising passers of the *munkwa* under age thirty-eight to be reeducated in his philosophy of government—sometimes receiving lessons from the King himself. If the candidate already held an official post, he was given an exemption from his official duties for the duration of his studies; if he did not hold a post, he received a military sinecure such as senior military protector 上護軍 (*sangho'gun*, rank 3a) or junior commander 司猛 (*sameng*, rank 8a). Chŏngjo instituted the system in his fifth year, not coincidentally the same year the Royal Library began to make its presence felt on the political scene. Due to his mastery of advanced Confucian texts, Chŏngjo was able to design the program he wanted these officials to learn, ignoring the demands of the older officials around him that he teach their preferred *sŏnghak* 聖學 (study of the sages).[25] Men reeducated under the royal selection system were the pool of talent from which Chŏngjo drew his support, and they were recruited without regard to faction. Even secondary sons like Pak Che-ga, Yi Tŭk-kong, and Yu Tong-mu were recruited, often by special appointment. Virtually all appointments to the Royal Library were graduates of the system, and they slowly began to take over other parts of the government as well. By the closing years of Chŏngjo's reign, half of all officials to serve in high office in the central government came through the royal selection system.[26]

In the course of the King's quarter century on the throne, selections of usually sixteen men were made for the system ten times, for a total of 138 graduates. They were examined on seven texts of the Confucian canon—the Four Books together with the *Rites of Zhou*, the *Book of Odes*, and the *Book of Documents*[27]—twice a month 試講 (*sigang*) and given problems to respond to once a month 試製 (*sije*). Also once a month, the King would personally administer an additional exam. All examinations were written by Chŏngjo himself. Outstanding responses—as determined by the King, of course—were published together 奎華名選 (*kyuhwa myŏngsŏn*), and students were rewarded based on their performance. An example of such a publication is the *Correct Written Responses* 正始文程 (*chŏngsi munchŏng*), a collection of responses from students at the National Academy—to whom the King also occasionally offered direct instruction[28]—and the royal selection system, published in 1795. Students were freed of nonessential duties in order to concentrate on their studies and were expected to graduate at age forty.[29]

In addition to training officials in the importance of the king, the lessons also imparted the tools Chŏngjo regarded as necessary to carry out reform. Students learned the Classics so that they would have the prestige of eminent scholarship to go head to head with other officials, and they discussed contemporary policy issues in order to understand the problems facing the government. They were frequently assigned policy questions, written questions from the King to officials about how to deal with a given problem or issue.[30] Chŏngjo was concerned with the proper arrangement of the Classics in ways that appear influenced by the School of Evidential Learning. An example of this is one of Chŏngjo's policy questions to the royal selection system students, calling on them to investigate the old text/new text problem that Evidential Learning scholars in China also revisited. After unifying China proper for the first time in the third century BC, the first emperor of China restricted access to unorthodox texts. His dynasty did not long survive his own death in 210 BC and many texts were destroyed in the chaos of its collapse, as the imperial archives housing them were sacked and burned. This left the succeeding Han dynasty to reconstitute the texts. According to tradition, the learned men in the Han reconstructed the texts from memory; these were the "New Texts." But then in the second half of the second century BC, the supposed original texts were discovered hidden, most of them in the walls of Confucius's old house in the city of Qufu. Despite being found after the earlier reconstructions, these were known as the "old texts" to reflect their alleged precedence. Each set of texts was popular in different periods of Chinese history, as scholars debated the authenticity of the one set over the other.[31]

Scholars in late Chosŏn Korea too took up this question, in this particular case in response to one of Chŏngjo's policy questions. He lamented that doubt and trust in the received text of the *Book of Documents* was "fifty-fifty [尙書其疑信相半]" and that the 3,000-year record of failure to determine the authenticity of the text was "surely a blot on the record of we Confucians [豈非儒家之一大欠典乎]." He demanded the scholars rectify this problem using, among other techniques, analysis of the writing styles of the Old and New Text versions.[32] He also requested responses on the problem of secondary sons, difficulties in recruiting from all over the country, land reclamation, and troop registers and military logistics.[33] Most of the texts discussed were the familiar classics: the Four Books, the *Zuo Commentary*, the *Changes*, the *Odes*, and the *Documents*. In 1795, the object of study was a little more practical. Instead of a Chinese philosophical text, memorials, tax codes, and law statutes were the texts under examination. The 1795 *Correct Written Responses* also served as a studied text.[34] Chŏngjo also put to his students the problem of the *Analects* and the compilation of the received text from the so-called Lu and Qi versions.[35]

Familiar names pop up as the official selector of men for the royal selection system. This official was of state councilor rank, and the list of men Chŏngjo appointed is conspicuously made up of his supporters. The by now familiar name of Ch'ae Che-gong appears twice, as do those of Sŏ Myŏng-sŏn, Hong Nak-sŏng, and Kim Ch'i-in, with Yi Pyŏng-mo holding the position shortly before Chŏngjo's death. With a Southerner (Ch'ae), two Disciples (Sŏ, along with Yi Sŏng-wŏn), two Intransigents (Kim and Yi), and one Expedient (Hong), the head position illustrates Chŏngjo's attempt to build a broad base of support. The system produced Tasan (1789) and his brother Chŏng Yak-jŏn (1790), Sŏ Yong-bo (1781), Yi Sŏ-gu (1784), as well as Kim Cho-sun (1786), who would institute rule by in-law families. It is telling that, as soon as Chŏngjo died, his opponents immediately attempted to exclude these men from power.[36]

The royal selection system and the Royal Library were Chŏngjo's efforts to develop and then employ officials amenable to his program of a strengthened crown. However, what incentive would powerful *yangban* clans have to accede to a resurgent throne whose increased authority would have to come at their expense? The King tried to persuade them that it was morally correct to do so. Yet he was astute enough to attack on another front as well, and so he turned to men who might be more open to changes in the existing power structure, that is, men who were disadvantaged by that structure.

EXPANDING RECRUITMENT: NORTHMEN AND BASTARDS

Of the people listed in the register of officials, there is but one from Kwandong [roughly modern Kangwŏn Province in central Korea]. How can we limit recruitment of men of talent according to their region in this way? Is this not especially narrow recruitment of people?[37]

[關東人在籍者。只有一人。人才。豈限地分而然乎。特取人不廣耳。]

—Chŏngjo, "Political Matters"

Chŏngjo believed that he alone, as king, was able to judge men appropriately and so had the power to select men without regard to faction, and he chafed under the prejudice of the elite capital families against men from the provinces and the resulting difficulty the King had in employing them. This marked a recurring theme in his writings.

In ancient times, Zhuge Liang[38] likewise said, "Those in the palace and those in the provinces are of one substance."[39]

[昔諸葛亮猶曰宮中府中。俱爲一體。]

Some people are not constrained by their lineage group, like many strange grasses and flowers that flourish in secluded alleys and filthy ditches.[40]

[人或不係世類。如奇花異草。多生於猥巷穢溝。]

Before the middle period of our dynasty, many distinguished officials and great ministers came from distant villages and local areas. After the middle period, I have not heard of any coming from outside the distinguished capital families. Those who were born and raised in the capital are not necessarily virtuous. Those born and raised in distant villages are not necessarily weak. So the ministers in charge of personnel must not misunderstand that the proper Way is to appoint worthy officials without regard to their lineage.[41]

[我朝中葉以前。名臣碩輔多出於遐鄉疎遠之地。中葉以後。簪纓世家之外。絕未聞焉。生長於簪纓者。未必皆賢。生長於遐鄉者。未必皆不肖。則甚非所以立賢無方之道。掌銓之臣。不可以不知此。]

There are certainly literate scholars living in the countryside and reading books. If we were to search wholeheartedly for them, we would not overlook important talent, right? What about searching again, more widely this time?

...

If I make up my mind to gather and employ literate men from the countryside, there would be names worth hearing. What need is there to be strict in choosing? What would be the [negative] result if I were to appoint them to the lowest rank?[42]

[此外必有卿居讀書之士。救之以誠。寧或遺珠。更須廣求如何。

...

卿外讀書之人。必以收用爲心。則當有得聞之名姓。何必峻選爲也。先自一名而試之。其效當如何耶。]

One of the greatest constraints on the authority of late Chosŏn kings was the monopolization of high office by a small number of *yangban* clans based in the capital. It was difficult for the king to impose his will on his officials when he could turn to no one else. Because the capital *yangban* were loath to implement any reforms that jeopardized their own sources of wealth and power—landed estates largely hidden from tax collectors, extensive private slaveholding, elite Confucian education, and illustrious family background—the government was hampered in its attempt to strengthen state power, and kings were likewise hindered in their struggle to expand their freedom of action. If an official obstructed a monarch's expansion of power, that official could be dismissed, but he would be replaced by a man from the same class, background, region, perhaps even family—in short, a man just as likely to obstruct the king's efforts as the man he replaced, at least when it came to expansion of state or royal power at the expense of the *yangban*. Thus, supporters of greater royal power like Yun Hyu (1617-1680) argued that the king should be able to choose ministers of any social class.[43] While Chŏngjo does not go that far—that would have been a truly revolutionary change, not the conservative innovation of the absolute monarch—he did recognize the problem of being limited to the capital *yangban*, elaborating on this at some length to officials of the Royal Library.

> What is the difference between a man of talent from the capital and one from a rural village? Now if I were to send only men from the capital out to all the outlying districts, I could not raise one man for every hundred I would need. Is this placing the worthy without restriction? A village of [merely] ten houses also has loyal and honest men. Why should worthy scholars in distant and isolated villages lament that they grow old without their talent ever being recognized? Moreover, Yŏngnam produces many excellent men of talent. Recently I have noticed and made use of them, and as with the men of Honam, I have selected men of talent. Some I will promote and others I will reward, and a thing of beauty will be constructed. Only those vested with screening men will not comprehend that this is my intention. I do not continuously appoint someone to office based on a single nomination. How could the court be even-handed and without discrimination if I treated men from the capital differently?[44]

[人才何間於京鄉。而近來銓注。皆出京華。至於遐方。則百不舉一。此豈立賢無方之道哉。十室之邑。亦有忠信。鄉曲遐外之士。亦豈無抱才虛老之歎乎。況嶺南。尤是人才之冀北也。

近來加意收用。竝與湖南而甄拔。或陞擢之。或獎詡之。庶有咸造之美。而但在銓衡者。莫
體此意。一番注擬之後。更無繼用之實。與京洛之人有異。此豈朝家一視之道哉。]⊠Part of
Chŏngjo's effort to combat this was to bring into the government men without
an existing power base in the capital, who would therefore owe their positions
to him alone. These men were also distinct from the capital elite in several ways.
The northern elite were not generally considered true *yangban* by the capital
elite and their branches in the southern provinces, nor were sons of *yangban*
fathers by consorts other than the legal wife ("secondary sons"). Thus, they
lacked the elite status granted to the capital *yangban* by birth. They were also
considered lacking in their Confucian education, northmen in particular due
to their involvement in commercial activity, something a good Confucian aristocrat avoided.[45] This emphasis on commercial activity as opposed to landed
estates was another point of divergence that, as it did in Europe, weakened the
perception of their status as nobility.[46]

The primary method to incorporate the northerners was the military
examinations. Neither Yŏngjo nor Chŏngjo could, at a stroke, flood the higher
offices with "barbaric" northmen. After all, Chŏngjo had enough trouble
overcoming factional resistance to getting a Southerner like Ch'ae Che-gong
into high office, despite Ch'ae's Confucian erudition and relatively illustrious ancestry. Resistance to employing men from the northern provinces in
high offices would have been far greater.[47] Therefore, these two kings, "in their
efforts to bolster royal power, tried to promote talented men from the north"
through the military examination system, which was of lesser prestige than
the civil system.[48]

> The regulations for administering the Northwestern Special exam have
> been this way for a long time. Moreover, I hear that now, because of
> official notices by the Ministry of War, there are many military men
> coming to the capital on the northern road. Now not only has the six-
> month evaluation already passed, but none has been recommended
> for office. So although I desire to appoint them to office, the situa-
> tion is such that I cannot. They all come with nothing, and they leave
> with nothing. Tomorrow I will hold a special military examination for
> Northwesterners. Receive my order.
>
> . . .
>
> Before, military men from distant regions could not obtain office,
> and I have repeatedly handed down instructions to change that. Now
> the action taken at this six-month evaluation has been so especially

disturbing to me that I should demand practical results. I have already found people in the three southern provinces, the two western provinces [P'yŏngan and Hwanghae], the northern frontier, and the Kaesŏng region, but will they be accordingly appointed to office? For this reason, I explicitly order the Ministry of War to do this.[49]

[西北別付料試射之規。自昔已然。況聞近因兵曹公文。北路武士。多有上京者云。今則都政不但已過。皆是無薦之類。雖欲收用。其勢末由。皆將空來空往。明日西北別付料軍官試射時。一體待令。

...

向以退方武士之不得沾官。屬勤飭敎。今番都政。須有別般聳動之擧。可責實效。三南兩西北關松都人。果已搜訪準擬乎。此意另飭西銓。]

According to Eugene Park, "the center's effort to accommodate northern residents through the military examination reached its limit by about 1800,"[50] that is, the year of Chŏngjo's death. This discrimination was, in turn, a direct cause of a serious rebellion in 1812.[51]

Less successful was Chŏngjo's attempt to get secondary sons into the government, partly because he also pushed for them to be included in the civil branch, which the powerful *yangban* clans more jealously guarded. While Yŏngjo began the process of appointing secondary sons, little had been accomplished even by 1772. Ch'ae Che-gong asked Yŏngjo to address secondary sons' failure to be listed to the list of candidates for government office despite their qualifications, but he refused to intervene on their behalf, citing the king's inability to draw up the list of official candidates himself (despite Yŏngjo's having flown into a rage at such lists when they contained the names of men from a single faction, in violation of his Policy of Impartiality).[52]

Chŏngjo argued against the discrimination facing secondary sons mostly by appealing to his prerogative as king to select whom he would, as noted above, but he did occasionally make a more general criticism of the distinction of secondary sons from "genuine" *yangban*. In 1791, the King ordered that the National Academy cease seating secondary sons apart from primary sons, remarking that, "when a sage instructs people, he only sees whether they are worthy or not and does not discuss whether their positions are noble or base [聖人敎人。只觀其人之賢否。不論地閥之貴賤]." He went on to say that secondary sons' not being permitted to "stand shoulder to shoulder [而不欲比肩]" with sons of the primary wife "has no basis in righteousness [義無所據]" and was "utterly unjust [萬萬無當]."[53] Though Chŏngjo pushed for secondary sons in the civil branch, he also worked to get them into the military, as resistance to their employment in military service was less severe. In 1777, the King directed that secondary sons be permitted to serve in military offices as part of his larger effort to revamp the military:

> The Palace Guards are none other than the military officers who are supposed to protect the king, but in recent years, they have not been shaping up. They are so ignorant that they cannot distinguish the word "fish" from the word "foolish,"[54] and they do not hone their military skills. That these rascals and untrained green troops fill the ranks, and that people say they think this constitutes a military unit, is truly pitiful. I want to determine a method to get men of talent as candidates for the Palace Guards. It is appropriate to hand down an order regarding this, but there is no one in the regular cavalry who is not base. When it comes to establishing a law to govern all their behavior, how can I strengthen the military? If I take the step of using *chung'in* or secondary sons to fill it out, the effect would be a great change.
>
> . . .
>
> My intentions are large-scale, and I mean to make great changes in the military system. Although we talk of the Grand Unity, we have to begin with small steps and slowly implement it.[55]
>
> [禁旅卽宿衛之士也。近年以來。漸不成樣。目不識魚魯。身不閑軍旅。無賴白徒。苟 充額數。言念軍制。良可寒心。予欲定宣薦內禁衛。取才入屬之法。當下敎而馬兵亦 無非下賤之類。全昧坐作之法。何以得力於戰陣乎。若以中庶塡充。爲遷轉之階。則 似有一變之效也。
>
> . . .
>
> 予意欲大其規模。一變軍制。雖以大同言之。先自一道始。次次行之]

The *yangban* swiftly condemned any attempt to allow secondary sons into the government on the grounds that this would blur the status distinction between primary and secondary sons and, therefore, threatened status distinctions in general. Officials of the Office of Special Advisors presented this argument:

> It has been the custom of our state to appoint men according to their family background. Now if we regard secondary sons of every family as if they are of the same group as primary sons with no way to distinguish them from each other, they will gradually come to realize this and

it will cause some awkward situations. If primary sons face obstacles because of the entry of secondary sons into service, so that secondary sons hold high office while primary sons are impoverished, then will there not be confusion and the vice of insulting primary sons? A law like this has never remained in place for long. We your servants say that looking at each primary son and placing him first is what the *Rites of Zhou* means when it discusses collateral lines' [of descent] being subordinate to the primary line, and so the law originally can be said to be free from any corruption. [56]

[我國之俗。既以族閥用人。今若以各族之庶。歸之一類。無復區別。則渠輩之稍有知識者。亦必恥之。而嫡之所枳。以庶而得通。庶則已顯。以嫡而反微者有之。則非但有混雜倒置之歎。亦必啓以孼凌嫡之弊。法如是而能久者。未之有也。臣謂當各視其嫡。而降一等。以附周禮小宗統於大宗之義。然後其法始可無弊矣。]

The *yangban* accordingly moved to block the appointment of secondary sons. In 1778, after Hwang Kyŏng-hyŏn and 3272 others from the three provinces of Kyŏngsang, Chŏlla, and Ch'ungch'ŏng sent in a memorial protesting the discrimination against them, Chŏngjo lamented that his instructions to remedy this were not being carried out, promising to "issue the instruction even more sternly [自當有申嚴之道矣。所請序齒等事]."[57]

Despite this, seven years later in 1785, he complained that secondary sons were still not appearing on lists of candidates for high civil offices.

The King instructed, "As for the matter of removing the misconception of secondary sons, the decree of the *chŏngyu* year [1777] has not yet been faithfully carried out. There has been a great loss of trust in the court. They are dejected at being tossed aside like this, as this is against their fundamental intention of not being treated as worthless. If they get a clause giving them permission for something important, it is only in name and not in actuality. I have heard of all of one or two appointments to the Ministry of Punishments, the Ministry of Taxation, or the Board of Public Works among the civil officials, and none among the top rank officials. In political affairs, from now on, act consistently according to the decree of the *chŏngyu* year. Now I have entrusted this business to you, so know for sure that it has not been effective. Although the offices of section chief of Taxation, Punishments, and Public Works are not presently vacant, I command that they be made so in order that secondary sons be recommended. Do not take into account the status within the family of the various candidates. Instead, list all the candidates together. Thereafter, we can say they are given permission to hold important posts. Make sure the Ministry of War and the Ministry of Personnel know this."[58]

[教曰庶類疏通事。丁酉節目。尙不遵行。朝家之失信大矣。渠輩落莫。姑捨是。殊乖疏鬱之本意。又若許要一款。有名而無實。文臣之經三曹郎者。僅止一二人。而蔭官之判官。絕未聞差擬。始自今日政。一遵丁酉節目。着意修明。近來凡事任之。決知無其效。三曹郎官該司判官。雖無見闕。其令作窠。以庶類備擬。排望之際。毋或較量。通同排擬若是。然後始可言許要。銓曹知悉。]

The son or grandson of a high official was entitled to automatic appointment to a low-level office without passing the examinations, known as a "protected appointment" 蔭 (ŭm). Appointments to even low-level positions in the Six Ministries were respected, those to district magistrate less so. The King is pointing out that inexperienced recent graduates gain immediate access to higher offices while experienced secondary sons are passed over for even the lowliest posts.

While his efforts to get secondary sons into the regular civilian bureaucracy were stymied, the King had much more control over the officials of the Royal Library, and by this means he was able to get some secondary sons into the government. In April or May of 1779, Chŏngjo appointed Pak Che-ga 朴齊家, Yi Tŏk-mu 李德懋, Yu Tŭk-gong 柳得恭, and Sŏ Yi-su 徐理修—all secondary sons—to the position of editor 檢書官 (kŏmsŏ'gwan) in the Royal Library. Pak, Yi, and Sŏ were all members of the Northern Learning School 北學派 (pukhakp'a), again revealing Chŏngjo's willingness to employ men who took advantage of Qing knowledge even as he disparaged the Qing to staunch traditionalists like Sim Hwan-ji. Each editor also concurrently held a military post of rank 5 or lower; through this entrance into the military bureaucracy, Pak Che-ga would eventually receive an appointment carrying the substantial rank of 3a. Though the military was the less prestigious branch, senior third rank was part of the tangsanggwan 堂上官 ("officials permitted to go up to the palace"), the elite of the high officials. As Eugene Park notes,

The vast majority of officeholders never attained the sixth rank, the lowest level at which officials were eligible to attend court meetings held in royal audience, and achieving this rank was considered to be a break-through in one's career. The next milestone, which only a small minority of officials ever passed, was to achieve the senior third rank, divided into upper and lower sublevels. Receiving the upper-senior third rank signaled admission into the top stratum of officialdom.[59]

Thus, military office or not, Pak Che-ga achieved a singularly high rank as a secondary son, due at least as much to Chŏngjo's shepherding of his career as to his own brilliance.

Chŏngjo attempted, with limited success, to take advantage of men from untapped *yangban* branches in order to expand his freedom of action and create a coterie of men without their own power bases who would therefore be dependent on him alone for their positions. The military, being less favored by the most prestigious *yangban* clans, was more open to this sort of maneuvering. Yet Chŏngjo fought on many fronts, and even as his efforts to build a coalition of previously-excluded officials that would support him were stymied, he sought to restrict the necessity of that he use officials at all.

PERSONAL RULE: CIRCUMVENTING MINISTERS

Though Chŏngjo was adept at overcoming ministerial resistance to his policies, he also sought ways to avoid having to go through ministers altogether. Like a good absolute monarch, he wanted to do everything, or at least as much as humanly possible for one person to do. James Palais has argued that the ideas of Chosŏn reformer Yu Hyŏng-wŏn, who argued for direct royal action over issuing instructions to intermediaries, did not have much impact before the rule of the Taewŏn'gun. It is possible, though, that Chŏngjo was influenced by Yu's proposals for reform. Yŏngjo in 1770 ordered the compilation of an institutional encyclopedia along the lines of Ma Duanlin's *Comprehensive Examination of Documents* 文獻通考 (*Wenxian tongkao*), itself completed in 1307 in Jiangxi and published by the emperor in 1322.[60] This encyclopedia neglected Yu's work, among that of others, and so Chŏngjo ordered the production of a second edition that included writings both by Yu himself and by others familiar with his ideas. By this time, Palais tells us, "Yu's work had to have been known to the most prestigious scholar-officials at court,"[61] and it is not unreasonable to assume it was known to the King as well, given the inclusion of Yu in the second edition. As will be discussed later, Chŏngjo's writing on slavery shares some commonalities with that of Yu Hyŏng-wŏn, and Yu was also the first to suggest that military defenses be built in Suwŏn, which Chŏngjo ordered in 1796. In any case, Yu believed that it was vital for the king to meet with ministers face to face rather than issuing orders to them through intermediaries and that ministers should in turn present themselves in person rather than passing messages up the chain of command. Whether or not Chŏngjo read Yu's work, he must have agreed with Yu on these points, since he attempted to circumvent layers of officialdom to obtain information and issue orders directly and insured personal meetings between himself and Royal Library officials. He sought to expand his power of recruitment outside of the standard recommendation system. To take one example, he asked the assembled officials what they would have thought if he had appointed a candidate for the office of Superintendent of the Capital Police who had not served in the required prerequisite offices. After another official responded that there was no need for the candidate to have that record of service, we find Ch'ae Che-going saying, "If we are to make use of people, then although there is a set of recommendations, there is truly no harm in considering others [人苟可用。雖將望不害直通以亞將]," to which the King responded that it should be carried out "as was done in the old days [復舊施行]."[62] Here Ch'ae Che-gong has rather deftly changed the subject from appointing men who are recommended even though they have not served in the prerequisite office to "considering others" *apart* from recommendations. That is, the king should be able to consider not only men who have not served in the prerequisite offices but men who were not even recommended, cutting the Ministry of Personnel out entirely. Chŏngjo's phrasing of his agreement with this, "to do as it was done in the old days," is another example of his claims of restoring ancient practice that had fallen to corruption in his own day when, in fact, he was instituting a new policy.

Chŏngjo's officials, naturally, did not wish to be bypassed by the King, and so his efforts were resisted. Nevertheless, Chŏngjo persisted, as we shall see in the first example below. Two ways that the King attempted to gain more direct influence over the running of the state were through the expansion of direct petitions to the throne and through the limitation and eventual abolition of hereditary slavery.

Petitions and Processions

The absolute monarch is the source of all power and the ultimate recourse for those over whom he ruled, including those who exercised power in his name.[63] Chŏngjo instituted measures that allowed people to come directly to the throne with problems rather than following the traditional bureaucratic channels. Yi Tae-Jin points to Chŏngjo's frequent trips outside the palace and the resulting contact with his subjects as evidence of Chŏngjo intervening directly with the people, bypassing his ministers.[64] Ko Donghwan agrees that, because of this frequent direct contact with his subjects—from whom he learned about their exploitation at the hands of local officials—the King intended to eliminate the influence of midlevel officials and deal with grievances directly.[65] Petitions allowed the King to act without waiting for, prodding, or cajoling an official into bringing a matter to his attention. By ordering investigations and redress of grievances based on petitions even from commoners and slaves, Chŏngjo expanded his freedom of action, for ministers generally did not wish to be seen as blocking such redress. Processions outside the capital "advanced royal goals and diminished ministerial interference" in the administration of the realm, since the flurry of activity required to support the royal movement centered attention on the monarch.[66]

Since Chŏngjo was making it possible to receive petitions during his processions, he found excuses to make processions—a lot of them—especially visits to royal tombs and the tomb of his father. Yi Tae-Jin offers a striking contrast in the number of such visits: Yŏngjo made only two confirmed processions to royal tombs outside of Seoul in his fifty-two-year reign, while Chŏngjo undertook between sixty-three and seventy such processions in twenty-four years, each typically lasting between three and five days. His first visit took place before he even took the throne. As part of the rehabilitation of his father, it was Sado's tomb he went to.[67] This was undoubtedly because, once he became king, his first procession was ritually required to be to the tomb of his adopted father Hyojang, which he duly carried out early in 1777, soon after his accession. Indeed, Chŏngjo undertook travel outside the palace for any reason an average of 2.7 times per year, a 50 percent greater rate than Yŏngjo, whose own annual rate was already nearly double that of any of the five previous kings. Chŏngjo's son and successor posted a paltry procession rate of one every two years (sixteen processions in thirty-four years).[68] Chŏngjo's rate is nearly 50 percent higher even than that of Elizabeth I, well known for her frequent trips outside of London, though the queen's trips lasted much longer since staying in the homes of prominent local figures was an integral part of her processions, along with avoiding outbreaks of disease and adverse weather. Like Elizabeth, Chŏngjo tended not to stray too far from the capital, preferring to stay in wealthy, politically central areas that were safe for royal authority; these were not tours of the distant frontier regions with military significance, as were those of the Qianlong Emperor.[69] The total number of petitions that Chŏngjo addressed is not known, but to take the year 1785, he dealt with between thirty and eighty petitions a month.[70]

The initial petition system, the *sinmun'go* 申聞鼓, was implemented during King T'aejong's reign early in the fifteenth century. It involved striking a large drum located at the palace. It was highly restricted, being limited to threats to the throne and appeals of death sentences, and it soon fell into disuse and was replaced by striking a gong. While the *sinmun'go* petitions could only be made while the king was in the palace where the drum was located, gong petitions could be made during royal processions, since they could be made even with small gongs (*kkwaenggari*). The sight of petty *yangban*, commoners, and even slaves petitioning the King on the road would have been shocking to Elizabeth's court in England, where the poor and other riff-raff were forbidden even to approach the procession, which, ostensibly due to the very real threat of political assassination, was restricted to licensed visitors.[71] The petition could then be made in writing 上言 (*sang'ŏn*) or orally 擊錚 (*kyŏkchaeng*). The volume of petitions under this new system quickly led to its being restricted, such that petitions were only accepted in four cases: protesting punishment of oneself, resolving disputes between a father and son, resolving disputes between a wife and a concubine, and resolving disputes between commoners and base people 賤民 (*ch'ŏnmin*). These four cases were collectively known as the "four matters" 四件事 (*sa kŏnsa*). During the reigns of Sukchong and Yŏngjo, the system was expanded with the "new four matters" 新四件事 (*sin sa kŏnsa*), which allowed petitioning on behalf of another: a descendant for his ancestor, a wife for her husband, a younger brother for his elder brother, and a slave for his master. Yŏngjo also reinstituted the *sinmun'go* as a replacement for petitions initiated by striking the gong.[72]

Chŏngjo not only kept the gong petition system, he expanded it still further. He noted that, though Yŏngjo had reinstituted the *sinmun'go* to make it easier to petition, the elimination of gong petitions actually made petitioning more difficult.

> [The King] explicated the law examining oral petitions outside the palace. He instructed, "When [the ruler] is in the palace, oral petitions are made at the front and rear gates. When [the ruler] leaves the palace on a procession, oral petitions are made outside the palace. This is an ancient system. The Late King re-established the drum petition [*sinmun'go*] and ordered a ban on the system of oral petitions. His Sagely intention was merely that people petition by means of a drum rather than a gong. Now that this is linked to petitions made elsewhere as well, it effectively bans all petitions whenever I travel outside the palace. Therefore there is no way for me to hand down orders to the appropriate bureau. Memorials of officials with rods only give me a vague idea of officials' behavior, and so now the drum is there for oral petitioners when I am in the palace. Oral petitions are not something that have

been discussed, and I will hand it over to the Ministry of Punishments to examine the matter of [petitions] outside the palace so that I might hear of it."[73]

[申明衛外擊錚推問之法。教曰御闕則擊錚於差備。動駕則繫錚於衛外。古制也。先朝申聞皷復設後。命禁擊錚之制。聖意祇在勿以錚而以皷也。今則幷與動駕時而亦禁擊錚。故初無下該曹之擧。以金吾長之奏。可知其有司之昧於擧行。從今以後擊錚者。闕內則既有皷矣。錚非可論。而衛外則依古例移付刑曹。推問以聞。]

A few months later, the Minister of Punishments argued that Yŏngjo had abolished petitioning during processions. Chŏngjo refused to accept this unless the situation fell outside of the four matters.

> Minister of Punishments Chang Chi-hang said to the King, "After the Late King established the *sinmun'go*, there was an instruction that those who make oral petitions in the road be flogged and banished. After that, it goes without saying that whether a situation is one of the four matters or not, it is to be punished with flogging and banishment to a distant place. While Your Majesty was out on a procession yesterday, a woman of Koryŏng made an oral petition in the street. I request that she be treated according to this precedent." The King responded, "The palace gates are stout and there is no road leading into the palace, so the sentiments of the common people cannot reach my ears. See if the petition regards one of the four matters. If it is not one of the four matters, strike her about the shins so that she will not do this again."[74]

[刑曹判書張志恒啓言。先朝設申聞皷後。街路擊錚者。有杖配之教。伊後無論四件事與否。竝決杖遠配。日前動駕時。高靈女人街路擊錚。請依舊例擧行。批曰門禁嚴則無入闕擊皷之路。然則下情不可上達。此後四件事例刑捧供。非四件事。則刑推後勿施。]

By doing this, Chŏngjo greatly expanded the petition system, since people no longer needed to travel to the palace itself to reach him, and the palace guards' ability to choke off petitions by denying access to the drum was circumvented. Allowing petitions to be presented wherever the king was rather than at a fixed point also meant that the king ruled no matter where he was, focusing power on him personally at the expense of the central government apparatus. Four years later, Chŏngjo allowed petitions from outside the four matters as well, perhaps his most truly revolutionary act. For this reason, it is worth quoting his explanation of this decision at length.

The King personally administered the examination for the royal selection system. Thereupon he held an audience. Chief State Councilor Sŏ Myŏng-sŏn said, "... Royal processions within the city originally lacked incidents of an oral petition [kyŏkchaeng]. These days, the ignorant common people do not know the meaning of the law such that as many as six petitioners try to present their petitions, and this matter is greatly alarming. In the opinion of I your servant, anyone petitioning about something that is not one of the four matters should be specially punished." The King said, "As for this matter, I have wished to issue an instruction regarding it, but I have not yet done so. If a matter falls outside of the four matters, what law would it fall under?" Minister of Punishments Kim No-jin said, "We should apply the law that requires military service in a distant location." The King instructed, "Once someone is sent off to serve in the military in such a fashion, they cannot be pardoned, even if they committed only one offense. What kind of a compassionate king would I be then? In ancient days, the gatekeepers were not severe, and so those making an oral petition struck the drum as they liked outside the Yŏnyŏng [Spreading Flower] Gate. Then the Central Palace Guards accepted the petition and brought out the relevant official. The drum at Chinsŏn Gate [for the sinmun'go] has been in place since the last reign, but oral petition was abolished. Now the gatekeepers have become severe and do not permit anyone to enter and strike the drum. Therefore, I will not forbid oral petitions during processions outside the palace so that there will truly be a Way for me to learn of the condition of the people."[75]

[親試抄啓文臣課講。仍行次對。領議政徐命善啓言...城內擧動。本無擊錚之事矣。近來愚民不知法意。至於衛外擊錚者。多至六人。事甚驚駭。臣意則四件外擊錚人。亟施別般勘律宜矣。上曰此事業欲下敎而未果。係是四件事外。則其律當照何律乎。刑曹判書金魯鎭言用充軍律矣。敎曰充軍之法。一次充軍。則終不入於赦典。是豈欽恤之道乎。昔則閣禁不嚴。擊錚者任自擊錚於延英門外。則中禁奪其錚。而出付其人於該曹矣。始自先朝。置鼓於進善門。而擊錚之法遂廢矣。近因閣禁之稍嚴。不得入來擊鼓。故不禁衛外擊錚者。實爲通下情之道。]

Chŏngjo's lifting of the restriction to the four matters "meant that the government permitted the common people to petition on non-sakŏnsa, namely, social and economic sufferings. It was an epoch-making measure in the development of the petition system."[76] Permitting petitions during royal processions, together with Chŏngjo's frequent travel and the expansion of petition subjects beyond the four matters, led to an explosion in petitions. In 1783, the Inspector-General sent a memorial requesting a ban on petitioning the King when he was outside the palace, on the grounds that there were too many of them. Chŏngjo refused, citing the need to keep the path of communication open.[77]

The only European monarchy I came across in my research that had a petition system anything like that of Chŏngjo's Korea was that of his contemporary, Holy Roman Emperor Joseph II (r. 1765–790). Eighteenth-century Britain lacked any sort of direct petitioning to the monarch at all, while in France only certain constituted bodies had such a prerogative, not individuals.[78] Historian Derek Beales has written extensively about Joseph and lamented the neglect of petitions to the monarch among historians of Europe, noting that their content and the decisions the king made regarding them remain an untapped treasure trove for researchers.[79] Perhaps a brief comparison of petitioning under Joseph as analyzed by Beales with that of Chŏngjo might be fruitful for dialogue between historians of Asia and Europe.

Beales notes the same tension between the absolute monarch's desire for direct interaction between ruler and ruled, minimizing ministerial impediment of the royal will, and ministers' attempts to interpose themselves between the ruler and the common people. Ministers sought to do this "partly no doubt so that they could interpret and apply [royal edicts] as they pleased."[80] This helps to explain Chŏngjo's greater issuance of edicts with accompanying Korean vernacular (han'gŭl), much more than either of his predecessors, to ensure his actual intentions reached even commoners in villages.[81] He also accepted petitions from women written in han'gŭl with little fuss, which had been hotly debated in earlier periods, another indication of early modernity.[82] Accepting direct petitions from commoners provided a means to avoid this ministerial interference in central Europe as well as Korea, and Joseph, along with Frederick William and Frederick the Great of Prussia, also received petitions as they toured the realm, though among them Joseph alone actively solicited petitions.[83] Joseph told his mother Maria Theresa that his travels outside the capital were necessary in order to check up on his officials, lest he be entirely reliant on only the information flowing into the capital. He also wrote that touring and hearing petitions were not "an eccentricity" but "necessary instruments of government," and he declared that "I give the whole universe freedom to bring me their complaints," which he would then investigate so as to punish the officials responsible.[84]

Like Chŏngjo, Joseph's personal attention to so many matters, viewing decisions he made as his personal responsibility that he would make with ministerial advice but not beholden to it, attracted both praise and criticism.

Catherine the Great thought he "ruined his health with his eternal audiences," while one of his officials argued that

> From my standpoint, the only good system is one that enables the prince to see in every single village whether his orders are carried out, and whose fault it is if they are not. Your Imperial Majesty, who every year undertakes arduous travels through his far-flung states, is the only reliable and non-partisan judge of whether this dual aim is achieved under the present arrangement.[85]

The reform of the petition system presents another textbook example of Chŏngjo's ruling style: slow, painful, subtle alterations, carried out over the course of years, until he finally achieved his aim. From allowing oral petitions, to allowing them as long as they regarded the four matters, to allowing them as they pertained to any matter, the King step-by-step instituted change that, by the end of his reign, gave him discretionary power that even Yŏngjo had not achieved during his fifty years on the throne. This pattern would be repeated in Chŏngjo's handling of slavery, though his premature death prevented him from reaching what appears to have been his final goal.

Slavery

Hereditary slavery in Korea, not abolished in Chosŏn until 1888 (and all slavery not until 1894), had a long history, existing from the start of Koryŏ and probably during the Three Kingdoms as well.[86] Chosŏn defenders of slavery stretched back its history still further, claiming it existed from the founding of Korea as one of the Lord of Ji's eight laws, though the slavery of the Lord of Ji's law as recorded in the *Book of Former Han* is clearly not hereditary.[87] This connection with the Lord of Ji made it difficult for reformers to argue against it, and when Yu Hyŏng-wŏn did so in the seventeenth century, he declined to address its relationship to the Lord of Ji's laws altogether.[88]

Hereditary slavery was a contentious issue at various points throughout the latter half of the dynasty, because private slaves were exempt from both military service and corvée labor and taxes and, thus, were essentially outside the control of the state. It was not until the Imjin War that successive kings succeeded in getting some state control over slaves. On the throne during those invasions, King Sŏnjo directed that slaves be conscripted into mixed units with commoner soldiers, beginning a slow breakdown between slave and commoner that would lead to calls for the outright abolition of hereditary slavery in the eighteenth century. Further, this precedent of slave military service meant that slaves could be assessed the military cloth tax when that tax was assessed in the eighteenth century, though they paid less than commoners.[89]

Another method the government used to combat the expansion of slavery and increase the state's access to the country's human resources was the matrilineal inheritance law, that is, the limitation of the inheritance of slave status to the mother's line rather than from either parent, but this law's effect on reducing the number of slaves is mixed at best, and other causes for the marked decline of slavery in the eighteenth century have been cited. Among these are the early modern commercialization of Korea, which meant that the effort expended to recapture runaway slaves was worth less than their labor as against the ready availability of hired labor.[90] Chŏngjo did take some steps during his reign to reduce the slave population, with the aim of eventually eliminating hereditary slavery altogether. Like Joseph II, who accepted that aristocratic resistance prevented radical changes to the serf system,[91] Chŏngjo knew better than to even attempt to abolish hereditary slavery right away. Instead, he proceeded as he always did, as he had to when taking on the interests of the powerful *yangban* class who provided the very people expected to execute his policies: in fits and starts, spread out over a long period, protesting all the while that this was what he was forced to do. In his capacity as a judicial legislator—the king being regarded as the source of law in Chosŏn—Chŏngjo usually sided with the weak against the powerful, which included former slaves who were legally commoners but were still expected to treat their former masters with special deference. As an example, in one case the King was lenient to a master who killed his former slave, but he explicitly rejected the governor's request for leniency on the grounds of that former relationship and proceeded to offer different reasoning for clemency. A manumitted slave, Chŏngjo insisted, was legally a commoner, and so the former master could not be forgiven for continuing to treat his former slave as servile. This was not because Chŏngjo was rigid when it came to law, as in another case where he disciplined a governor for (correctly) recommending a death sentence according to the letter of the law. Chŏngjo argued that the governor should have recognized the letter of the law did not apply in this case and commuted the sentence to banishment, even though the law did not actually allow this.[92] Thus, in the case of the former slave, it was not a matter of Chŏngjo's rigidity in insisting that the *legality* of commoner status had to be protected at all costs but the protection of former slaves from slipping back into bondage. He also protected contract laborers from slipping into effective slavery, substantially raising the status of long-term contract workers and declaring short-term contract workers to be "ordinary persons" 凡人 (*pŏm'in*), that is, legal commoners. William Shaw notes that this "new policy . . . undoubtedly ran against the grain of much traditional sentiment," since contract laborers, especially those under a long-term contract, were held in almost as low regard as slaves.[93]

In 1791, after refusing to abolish hereditary slavery outright on the grounds that it would disrupt the Chosŏn status system 名分 (myŏngbun), the King did offer a number of ways to allow slaves to escape from their lowly station, again using the military as a way to expand state control over the people without challenging that which the yangban held dear. It began with Chŏngjo's complaint that Yŏngjo's reforms had not eliminated corruption associated with slavery—such as commoners committing themselves to slavery to avoid taxation (a loss for the state that represented a gain for the private slave owner, which goes some way toward accounting for why the yangban officials were not zealous in eliminating the practice) and slaveholders' flagrant defiance of the matrilineal inheritance law by enslaving the children of any mixed marriage involving a slave—or alleviated the plight of slaves.

> The King summoned high official of the Border Defense Command Cho Chŏng-jin. He instructed, "In every province the slave labor system is corrupt, as we all well know, yet last year after the secret inspector returned from Hamyang, I began to hear more frequently that this corruption must be rectified. If there is no remedy, is this not lamentable? The Late King's directive of 1755 was a special dispensation, and it allowed more than 10,000 people to offer payment in lieu of labor service to the Ministry of Finance, but the National Academy and the Bureau of Royal Attire continue to hold out and still collect this labor tax. I do not even know if [those people] have any onerous obligations beyond that. Nevertheless, the corruption in the slave system in the various provinces is truly pitiful. Immediately after scrutinizing the slave register of the Palace Offices and the various Ministries, I will go to a discussion among the high officials, and come up with special ways to deal with this situation. I will inform the relevant offices in every province to take measures to ensure that not a single man or a single woman suffers unnecessarily. The year I ascended the throne, I made a special decision to abolish the directorate of slave registration, yet I have not been able to reform the slave labor tax system. I have not been firm enough about this matter. After examining each case one by one so that escaped or deceased [slaves] are recorded accurately, make a report to the relevant department. After assessing these things, if there is [any corruption] to expose, mete out severe punishment according

to the relevant laws, and if there is something to report, inform the examiner."[94]

[召見備局堂上趙鼎鎮。教曰諸道奴貢之弊。曾所稔知。而昨年咸陽御史之還。益聞
此弊。不可不矯,尙無擧行。寧不駭痛。先朝乙亥節目。實爲莫大之特恩曠典。萬有
餘口。自戶曹使之給代。而獨成均館尙衣院。尙今收貢。未知別有委折。而諸道奴弊。
誠甚切矜。就考本曹及內司奴婢案後。往議大臣。各別措辭。行關諸道。俾無一夫一
婦之冤也。予於初元。特罷刷官。而若干貢弊。尙未夬革。是所憧憧焉者。一一查櫛
後。逃故據實後錄。使之報本司。此後摘奸時。若有綻露。該倅依法典重勘。如有可
以稟處者。道伯狀聞。]

In the ensuing discussion two days later, the King suggested that slaves with skill in the military be permitted to take the military examinations and be placed in special units of approximately commoner rank, leaving behind the stigma of the label "slave." They could also buy their freedom outright, though the price was probably beyond what most slaves could hope to amass. Ch'ae Che-gong lamely offered up that there was no plan to accomplish the King's aims, while another Chŏngjo supporter, Yu Sŏ-rin, voiced tentative support.[95] In 1797, with the support of Yi Pyŏng-mo, Chŏng Min-si, and Kim Hwa-jin, Chŏngjo eliminated the distinction between slave troops and commoner troops in the Military Training Agency 訓鍊都監 (hullyŏn togam), which Hiraki Minoru calls an "epochal" moment in the history of Chosŏn slavery.[96]

In 1801, a decree was issued in the name of King Sunjo that abolished official slavery. Private slaves, by far more numerous than public slaves, were of course excluded. However, even among public slaves, only 66,067 were freed by this decree: "those of the Royal Treasury, palace estates of royal relatives (kungbang), and the capital bureaus of the regular bureaucracy,"[97] in short, only those of the king and central government.[98] Thus, the power of the yangban class was not threatened, and their vast slaveholdings withered away through social forces other than government abolition. According to Palais, the decree's explanation for abolishing official slavery was distinct from Chŏngjo's view, and he quotes the decree in support of this.

Slavery [in Korea] in recent times is more reflective of an age of decline because officials impose great burdens on slaves, and ordinary people treat them as extremely base. Their lineages and communities are kept separate [from the rest of the population], they have to live in separate villages or areas, and for their whole lives neither sex is capable of legitimate marriage. How could the Lord of Ji ever have been called a sage if he [devised] a system like this?[99]

However, if we look at Chŏngjo's explanation of his plans for slavery in his introduction to a collection of Hong Pong-han's memorials 翼靖公奏藁 (*Ikjŏnggong chugo*), compiled in 1800 shortly before the King's death, it does not seem that distinct after all.

> Slavery originates in the male and female servant system of the *Rites of Zhou*, the service it requires stops at a single body and is placed in the same category as hired labor. When the Lord of Ji came east, he established the teachings of the eight items, and [one of these was that] thieves are to be made slaves, and this law has been handed down from the period of the Three Hans. Those [who serve] the officials were called "public base people," and those [who serve] in the home were called "private base people." Their responsibilities were clearly defined, and their taxes were determined and levied. When our dynasty was first set up, an order was issued that the child of a common father and a slave mother would be a commoner. At the same time, a directorate to distinguish slaves and determine slave status was established. T'aejong established the Great Limiting Law, three years later completed it with a ledger of slaves, and twenty years later completed it with a rectified ledger [for slaves] that was kept in both the capital and in the provincial government offices.

> [周官臣妾爲奴婢之始。而其役止於一身與賃傭等耳。箕聖東來。設八條之教。相盜者沒入爲奴婢。自三韓。行世傳之法。屬於官者。謂之公賤。屬於家者。謂之私賤。設職而理之。定貢而收之。我國朝定鼎之初。立勒令。爲賤者從良之法。又立辨定都監。辨別之。獻陵朝立大限法。三年成續案。二十年成正案。藏于京外官。]

Chŏngjo introduces the Chosŏn distinction between public and private slaves, but this distinction is immediately dropped. After claiming a patrilineal slave law at the start of the dynasty, he proceeds to argue that the Lord of Ji did not intend that slavery be hereditary, while also detailing the discrimination suffered by slaves.

> I have thought that, of the injustices in the realm, there is none more urgent than slavery. The Lord of Ji's tenets were simply intended as temporary punishment of evil, yet it has continued without change from generation to generation. Those who endure it are lowly and regarded with disdain. They are bought and sold in the same way as beasts, with

their price determined by the size of their families and their ages. They are distributed to sons and grandsons as inheritance, no different from the way land is treated. Certainly deriving their status primarily from the mother and taking a slave surname instead of their father's surname is a custom that puts us closer to the barbarians. Slaves are not permitted to marry, and they are treated differently from those who live near them. They contort themselves beneath the high and bend themselves to the wealthy, as if they have no place to go. How can it be that people to whom Heaven gave birth are caused to be like this? Although I rely on the royal ancestors and their cultivation of benevolence to protect my virtue and act in accordance with the respect due the throne on which I sit, I have the utmost concern and sympathy [for them].

[予嘗以爲天下之冤。莫切於奴婢。箕聖敎條。不過出於一時懲惡之意。而歷代沿襲。莫之變更。生生世世。受人賤蔑。計口計齒而賣買。則便同畜產。傳子傳孫而分析。則無異土地。必先母而與胡相近。不從父而以奴爲姓。婚姻不通。隣比不與。跼高蹐厚。若窮無歸。天之生人。豈宜使然哉。雖因列聖朝煦濡漸磨之仁。保其身奠厥居。而哀矜惻怛則極矣。]

Given his concern and sympathy for slaves, what did Chŏngjo plan to do about their plight? In the next selection, he makes clear his intention to replace slaves with hired laborers.

When I rest from the myriad affairs of state, I worry that there is no easy method to deal with these two things. First, the regulations regarding slavery should be swept away and a law establishing hired labor be set up. Slavery should be limited to individuals and will not be inherited by later generations. Specific measures should be enacted that will provide compensation [for freed slaves] according to a fixed amount. In consultation with a few like-minded officials, I will propagate such an order. Next I will consider that our state esteems moral obligations according to social status. If the common people mix with base people and the *yangban* families are not clearly distinguished, then criminals will come together and arise, mothers will [be required to] carry out corvée labor [instead of raising their children], sons will resist their rulers, small fortresses and post stations will have no underlings, and impoverished scholars and poor wives will have no way to stoke their stoves. Truly there is concern that driving off one vice gives rise to another vice, and because of this there is hesitation [to abolish slavery]. But is this a reason not to offer relief to [slaves]? Do not say that the abolition of the slave registrars [carried out by Yŏngjo] indeed sufficiently fulfilled the royal command. This particular section is problematic. If [slaves] can be made to occupy the humble position of commoner while still protecting the social distinctions without contradiction, then [abolition] must be carried out resolutely. Due to public memorials, I have outlined my intentions this way.[100]

[予於清燕萬幾之暇。思得均齊兩便之策。一掃奴婢之規。辦行傭雇之法。限以己身。不許世傳。措處指劃。先定方略。給代出處。皆有定數。一二臣同。行將發令。第念我國專尚名分。若使良賤相混。班閥不明。則凌犯者必接迹而起。母方執役。子反抗主。殘驛小堡。廝圉乏人。窮士貧婦。樵爨無路。實有袪一弊。生一弊之慮。此所以遲徊趑趄者也。然則其將因此而不之拯救耶。莫曰推刷官革罷。亦足以迓續景命。此特節目間事耳。苟可使之廁平民守常分。竝行不悖。則斷當決然行之。因公奏藁。略示予意如此云。]

Again we see a connection between Chŏngjo and Yu Hyŏng-wŏn, as the King refers to the replacement of slavery with hired labor. Also like Yu, he calls for abolition of slavery quickly, though not immediately. Unlike Yu, however, he also makes the argument of reformers like Yu Su-wŏn regarding the Lord of Ji, pointing out that the slavery of the Lord of Ji carries no implication that this status is to be inherited, as it is a punishment for criminal activity[101] that Chŏngjo probably accepted. The 1801 decree cites, as Chŏngjo does, the suffering of slaves and their mistreatment even by commoners, along with their segregation and lack of legal marriage. Unlike the decree, however, Chŏngjo's preface gives no indication that he refers only to public slaves. He simply notes that there are two categories of slaves but does not refer to the distinction again, including, crucially, in the section declaring his intention to abolish hereditary slavery. This is the key difference between Chŏngjo's intention and the actual measure that was implemented after his death; with Sunjo a minor and Queen Chŏngsun's influence restrained by attitudes toward gender and literary prejudice, the Patriarchs in charge of the government had no intention of freeing their own private slaves. *Ikjŏnggong chugo*, with its extensive introductory material penned by the King himself, was not completed until shortly before Chŏngjo's death in 1800, and the abolition of hereditary slavery would wait another eighty years.

As with the Hong Kuk-yŏng affair, Chŏngjo erred early in his reign when he restored the recommendation power of selection secretaries that his grandfather had abolished. Realizing his mistake, the King eventually abolished the power again while also looking for other ways to control an office that remained important even without that power. Through the creation of the Royal Library, he both exalted his own position and gave his personally selected ministers a way to restrain official criticism of his policies. The royal selection system put his scholar-king rhetoric into action, with Chŏngjo instructing young officials rather than being beholden to the wisdom of aged aristocrats. The library also served as a vehicle for another of his policy objectives, namely, the inclusion in the state apparatus of men who had long been excluded from power: members of the Southerner faction, men from the northern provinces, and sons of *yangban* fathers by concubines. This dilution of political power among a wider group of *yangban* was fiercely resisted, though less so on the military side. Finally, Chŏngjo greatly expanded the direct petition system so that he would be less reliant on his officials when it came to addressing administrative problems. He also took advantage of changing economic and social conditions to progressively restrict slaveholding and seems to have intended to abolish the inheritance of slave status entirely, though his sudden death ensured that this intention would be ignored.

6

MILITARY MATTERS

THE MILITARY OF CHOSŎN KOREA IN THE EIGHTEENTH CENTURY WAS hardly an intimidating force. Long gone were the days of ancient Koguryŏ, the Korean kingdom that menaced China's borders in the fifth century, and Silla, the tiny state that first unified the southern two-thirds of the Korean peninsula and fought China to a standstill in the seventh century. After two centuries free of major invasion, the military of late Chosŏn was primarily a force to put down domestic rebellion,[1] a role it performed adequately until confrontations with the modern world unleashed social forces that led in 1894 to a rebellion of a kind never before seen in Chosŏn. Chŏngjo made no serious effort to build a military capable of waging war, even defensively, against Chosŏn's neighbors. Protected by the Qing Empire to the north and west and facing a Japan uninterested in further continental adventures, there was no pressing need to do so; the window of opportunity to overhaul the military sufficient to enable it to repel either the Qing or the Japanese had passed two hundred years earlier, when the Imjin War (1592–1598) revealed a Chosŏn army disastrously unready to fend off a major invasion.[2] Nor did Chŏngjo experience the humiliation of living as a hostage in the Qing Empire as his ancestor Hyojong had, and so there was no question of his revenging himself on the Manchus. By the time of his reign, the notion of a Northern Expedition was effectively dead, and Chŏngjo was more interested in what benefits he could gain from Great Qing than in fighting it. Unlike Europe, where alliance-making and breaking, military campaigns, and strategic international marriages were part and parcel of the absolute monarch, early modern Korea, especially after the fifteenth century, was largely at peace. Its diplomacy was almost entirely confined to placating China and diverting Japanese piracy into regulated trade relations, particularly after the Jurchens in the northeast had been subdued through a combination of low-intensity war and tributary relations modeled on those of

China; the Ryūkyū Kingdom was another key relationship.[3] Chosŏn's was not a "war-driven expansion of the state."[4]

What Chŏngjo did do, though, was strengthen the military's ability to serve his own purpose, namely, giving him a freer hand to rule than even his grandfather had. He primarily did this in two interconnected ways. First, he ordered the construction of a large, modern (by Chosŏn standards) fortress to guard the tomb of his father, the Illustrious Fortress 華城 (Hwasŏng) in the city of Suwŏn. Taking nearly three years to build, the Illustrious Fortress stands today as a testament to Chŏngjo's filial piety, but the Fortress was more than a symbol. It was strategically placed to provide the King a refuge that would be well-protected from the greatest threat to his throne—his own officials in command of ostensibly royal armies. Second, Chŏngjo established a new military unit to be stationed in the Fortress, the Robust and Brave Regiment 壯勇營 (chang'yong'yŏng). Beginning as a tiny company to protect Sado's tomb, the Regiment was continuously expanded at the expense of existing army units. It stood outside the regular military hierarchy, since its command was held as a concurrence with the governorship of Suwŏn. By appointing a supporter to this office, Chŏngjo brought a significant military force under his control, without which he could not exercise independent royal action.[5] The Illustrious Fortress garrisoned with the Robust and Brave Regiment under Chŏngjo's control represented a formidable military challenge to officials' control over the military.

THE ILLUSTRIOUS FORTRESS: A MONUMENT TO SADO?

In February of 1794, construction began on the Illustrious Fortress in what is now Suwŏn, thirty kilometers south of the capital. Yu Hyŏng-wŏn first suggested that defenses be constructed in Suwŏn, and Chŏngjo cited this as suggested in Yu's Collected Works 磻溪隨錄 (Pan'gye surok) when discussing the construction of the Fortress.[6] Its ostensible purpose was the protection of the tomb of Prince Sado, which Chŏngjo had moved to Suwŏn in 1789. Initially, scholars accepted this explanation at face value, but as Roh Young-koo puts it, "[t]he naïve understanding that the construction of Hwasŏng Fortress was an embodiment of Chŏngjo's filial devotion to his father has been completely overturned." Roh also notes later that the construction of an elaborate tomb for Sado effectively recognized him as royalty rather than criminal, thus strengthening Chŏngjo's own legitimacy.[7] Despite his legal adoption, Chŏngjo continued to regard Sado as his true father, and the dead prince's shadow hung over his entire reign. While it is true that the fortress was part of the King's desire to rehabilitate his father, it was also intended to be a center of royal power. Like his displays of

public displays of grief as recorded in the *Veritable Records*, the Fortress represented both Chŏngjo's genuine commitment to his father's memory and his
willingness to use the sympathy generated by it to accomplish realist political
ends. In the words of Kim Sung-Yun, Chŏngjo's "intention was to set this area
as the background for full-scale reform by creating a pro-monarch region."[8]
To this end, the King stationed royal guards at the fortress and designated it as
an administrative center. He also took measures to develop commerce in the
area that was not tied to Seoul by lending money to merchants to open shops in
Suwŏn and relaxing restrictions on merchants in the area, leading to increased
commerce and, accordingly, an increased population.[9]

Preparations for Construction

In his familiar pattern, Chŏngjo moved slowly, step by step, laying the groundwork for the Fortress's construction years before he ever broached the subject.
As noted, in 1789, he ordered that his father's tomb be relocated there. Four
months later, in March of 1790, the King and his officials discussed improv-
ing the Suwŏn area.[10] That same year, a midlevel military official, one Kang Yu,
proposed the construction of military defenses in Suwŏn. As this area was both
important to national defense and the "precious ground" where Prince Sado
was buried, wrote Kang, the new military garrison being set up there needed
fortifications and, because it was not a mountainous area, a defensive moat.
A fortress in Suwŏn would support Toksŏng Mountain Fortress—an ancient
fortification in Kyŏnggi Province dating from the Three Kingdoms period—to
discourage raids. Kang noted that using expensive stone to build the fortress
might incite resistance to construction of this necessary defense and so earthen
walls should be built instead. (Kang dubiously claimed that earthen walls, if
well-planned and built, were just as strong as stone walls.) He also argued for
bringing duty soldiers and directing them to construct dwellings for themselves to replace the scholars-in-training 儒生 (*yuhak*) living there, which he
claimed were upward of half the population of the area. He suggested that the
King divert farmland set aside to cover shortfalls from tax exemptions given
to meritorious subjects for support of these troops. They would need to work
the land themselves instead of remaining "idle."[11] (Kang apparently did not
consider intensive military training to be honest work.) The same year, one Sin
Ki-gyŏng also suggested strengthening Suwŏn's defenses.[12] Kang's suggestions
were largely accepted, though Chŏngjo must not have been convinced of the
equality of a well-constructed earthen wall with a stone wall, as he ordered the
Illustrious Fortress to be constructed of expensive stone.

The following year, while Ch'ae Che-gong was serving as the sole state councilor, the King pushed through the Commercial Equalization Law 辛亥通共 (sinhae t'onggong). This loosened restrictions on commercial activity in Suwŏn by permitting it to take place outside the confines of the Six Licensed Shops 六廛 (yukchŏn). This law was part of Chŏngjo's more liberal economic policy compared to Yŏngjo's more tightfisted, fiscally conservative policy, as evidenced by his effort to encourage greater import of precious metals and frequent minting of currency, ordering the latter five times between 1785 and 1798. While these efforts did not initiate a commercial revolution and commerce still lagged behind China's and Japan's, greater circulation of money did result and continued through the nineteenth century.[13] The Commercial Equalization Law also "meshed with the political intent of diluting the vested commercial rights of Seoul licensed merchants in order to attract and recruit merchants and thus nurturing the Hwasŏng commerce."[14] Also in furtherance of this aim was Chŏngjo's policy to move prosperous commoner families to the area around the Fortress, discussed in the following section. In the winter of 1792, the King instructed Tasan to review existing fortress designs and develop plans for a new fortress system to be used for the Illustrious Fortress. While a number of other officials also drew up plans, the Fortress was largely based on Tasan's design.[15]

In 1793, Chŏngjo changed the name of Suwŏn district to the name of the fortress itself and raised the status of the official in charge from the more common and generic *magistrate* 府使 (*pusa*) to *prefect* 留守 (*yusu*), a term reserved for the official running an important city apart from the capital, and also personally wrote a tablet 懸板 (*hyŏnp'an*) to be hung from the front gate of the governor's office. The presence of the "guard" character 守 (*su*) is significant, giving the title a more military character in keeping with the city's importance to Chŏngjo's military reforms. The governor of the Fortress District was concurrently made minister of the Robust and Brave Outer Garrison 壯勇外使 (*chang'yong oesa*), a position commanding Chŏngjo's new military unit whose importance will shortly become clear. Unsurprisingly, the first man to hold this elevated-status office was none other than Ch'ae Che-gong. He was appointed, again by special appointment bypassing the normal recommendation process with the Ministry of Personnel, the very same day the position was created.[16]

Building the Fortress

At the end of 1793, final plans for construction of the Illustrious Fortress were drawn up, and construction began in the first lunar month of 1794. Chŏngjo personally inspected the construction three times, once in each year of the project, including a large celebration for his mother's sixtieth birthday and his twentieth year on the throne. Due to the advanced techniques involved, the relatively rapid completion, and Chŏngjo's insistence that the Fortress be constructed of stone rather than wood, the cost was substantial, coming out to 873,517 *yang*, nearly three and a half times the original estimated cost of 250,000 *yang*.[17] Roh Young-koo notes that the King broke with Chosŏn precedent by paying wages to the workers building the Illustrious Fortress rather than using the corvée system, including different pay scales for different jobs, and that this likely contributed to its quick construction.[18] It is also an example of the King's preference for hired labor over coerced labor, since the former was not subject to the latter's restrictions on the number of working days permitted. If Chŏngjo did intend to eliminate hereditary slavery, this would have vastly increased the available pool for both hired and corvée labor.

This construction period included a six-month halt ordered by the King shortly after construction began, due to a drought.[19] Key Chŏngjo supporters like Ch'ae Che-gong, Cho Sim-t'ae, and Yi Pyŏng-mo opposed the delay, arguing that stopping and restarting construction would be very difficult, but the King rejected this reasoning. The discussion was rather lengthy and carried out over an extended period, but the *Veritable Records* entry for November 11, 1794 is typical.[20] The King broached the subject of the Fortress in an audience at the Pavilion of Purification 齋室. Given the unprecedented famine and the dire state of the common people, he had inquired at an earlier audience about issuing an order to reduce the royal tribute and received official praise. But when he mentioned stopping the construction of the Fortress in order to concentrate on relieving the bad harvest, the officials objected that construction was not a burden on the people because it paid wages. If it were stopped, they argued, the men working on the project would be worse off. The King rejected this reasoning, positioning himself as the champion of protecting the people from excessive hardship, even when that hardship was in the service of his father's memory. He goes on to discuss the problems with his officials' reasoning in the face of the people's suffering. While it was true that funds for the construction were not part of the regular budget, those funds nevertheless had a major impact on state finances. Work would need to cease—at the appropriate time, of course, and not immediately—so that a surplus could be accumulated. Only then could work resume. Thus Chŏngjo, who usually positioned himself as arbiter between bickering sides whose bickering was getting in the way of taking any action, thought it no trouble to restart work on the fortress. His ministers were not convinced, with Ch'ae Che-gong objecting that interrupting such a major project was difficult. Since artisans and conscripted laborers had been assembled from all over the country, if they were released and allowed to leave, Ch'ae claimed, it would be difficult to get them back to Suwŏn again to resume the work. Plus, those paid workers committed to the project were dependent on those wages, and so a shutdown of the work would harm their livelihood. Too, hauling the stone materials to the Fortress's location was expensive, and that cost was sure to rise in the future. For Ch'ae, the work of building the fortress was itself a way to alleviate the famine. The King reiterated that the funds were lacking and that the project, though important and necessary, had been planned to take ten years and so need not be regarded as especially urgent now. He also rejected the notion that it would be difficult to get the laborers and artisans back to Suwŏn.

With Ch'ae failing to persuade the King that restarting the work would be difficult and costly for the government, the State Council took the tack that it would be difficult and costly for the people. Councilor of the Left Kim Yi-so and Councilor of the Right Yi Pyŏng-mo complained that the work was vitally important to the state, such that the availability of funds was rendered a nonissue, but the King was not convinced by this, either, and the work was stopped. The work stoppage is an example of Chŏngjo's mastery of the political process. It may seem strange at first glance that Yi Pyŏng-mo, an outspoken opponent of the Fortress, would counsel that its construction not be stopped on account of drought. Nor was Yi known for working with Ch'ae Che-gong, as Kim Chong-su and, on occasion, even Sim Hwan-ji were willing to do. It is possible that Yi wanted to stir up resentment against the Fortress by portraying the King as unwilling to ease the burden on the common people through ordering a halt on its construction. Chŏngjo, though, again took a long-term view. Six months was not a serious delay, as it gave him time to further expand the Robust and Brave Regiment. Instead of appearing uncaring or even oppressive by forcing its completion, Chŏngjo was able to win political points by portraying himself as a benevolent monarch who put aside even his own widely known and sympathetic concern for his father's memory for the sake of alleviating the common people's suffering. Chŏngjo also proved to be correct that construction, once halted, did not prove particularly troublesome to restart. He emerged from the months-long controversy as the champion of mercy and charity against the officials, even his own key supporters, who had urged him to remain steadfast. Despite the six-month delay, two years and nine months after construction began, the Illustrious Fortress was complete.

A Center of Royal Power

So King Chŏngjo constructed a new fortress. This was nothing new for Chosŏn monarchs. Nor, in an age when grave robbing could be a lucrative business, was there anything particularly special about constructing a fortress to guard royal tombs specifically. Why then does the Illustrious Fortress figure so prominently in scholarship on Chŏngjo?

There are a number of reasons the Illustrious Fortress was more than just another building project. The first and most obvious reason is that it served as another step in Chŏngjo's long, slow, meticulously careful rehabilitation of his father, which would culminate in Sado's being posthumously made king by Kojong in 1899, on the grounds that it was Chŏngjo's unspoken wish.[21] Having such a large and impressive structure built to protect Sado's tomb boosted not only his prestige but that of his son and of the dynasty as a whole. Also, as noted above, the King could cloak his other intentions for the Fortress in the mantle of filial piety and the rehabilitation of Sado, which even the Intransigents found hard to oppose in principle.

But Chŏngjo had more concrete reasons for constructing such a large and expensive building than mere prestige, and this is revealed in part by the details of its construction. One obvious detail is his insistence that it be constructed from stone. Unless grave robbers routinely pack trebuchets and ballistae, it is difficult to see why a tomb would need to be guarded by a colossal fortress of stone and not wood or earth, as Kang Yu suggested. At the time of its completion, the Illustrious Fortress was the most technologically advanced military structure of Chosŏn Korea. When its architect, Tasan, submitted initial plans that were too conservative and traditional, the King instructed him to use works from the Qing Empire that incorporated Western techniques in order to make use of all the latest advances from the Qing Empire in its design.[22]

The Fortress's location was also significant. Being in Suwŏn, it anchored the capital's southern flank, and together with Kaesŏng to the north and Kangwha Island to the west, constituted a key component of the capital's defense.[23] However, crucially, the Fortress was not intended to defend against foreign enemies, but domestic ones. According to Kim Sung-Yun, the Fortress was part of a comprehensive plan to defend the King from "an attack from Seoul rather than from outside enemies."[24] This plan included the rebuilding of Kwangju South Fortress and of Toksŏng Mountain Fortress near Suwŏn, the latter's commander receiving a division of soldiers from Kyŏnggi Province. Combining the military commands of Sihŭng, Kwach'ŏn and Kwangju—three areas that controlled access from the capital to the rich agricultural areas in the south, providing a supply line in case of a lengthy conflict—"formed a defense line that surrounded the lower part of Seoul," a defense line anchored by the Illustrious Fortress.[25] That is, in keeping with the purpose of the late Chosŏn military, the King reinforced its ability to protect the dynasty from rebellion rather than invasion. In furtherance of this, he stationed the Robust and Brave Regiment there. This military unit was directly under his own command because it was controlled by the governor of Suwŏn, a position to which Chŏngjo consistently appointed key allies, rather than falling under the existing hierarchy in the Ministry of War. Two Chosŏn monarchs, Yŏnsan and Kwanghae, had been overthrown by officials in command of ostensibly royal troops, and Chŏngjo's own grandfather faced a rebellion of extremist Disciples in key military positions; had the conspirators not been betrayed almost before their rebellion began, they would have been well-positioned to seize the king and capital before they could have been effectively countered.[26]

There exists the possibility that Chŏngjo intended to abdicate and retire to the Illustrious Fortress, perhaps in 1806. While none of his writings or public speeches directly state such an intention, there is circumstantial evidence. The auxiliary palace 行宮 (haenggung) he constructed as his residence there when visiting was the largest in Chosŏn, so large that it was not completed until the Fortress itself was. This may suggest that Chŏngjo considered it more than just another auxiliary palace. Further, the King based his new military unit in the Fortress. The *Regulations for Royal Processions* 園幸定例 (wŏnhaeng chŏngnye) records that, during Chŏngjo's annual progressions to his father's tomb there, the royal carriage was accompanied by 6,200 guards and that Chŏngjo himself wore military dress. Upon his arrival at the Fortress in the year of his mother's sixtieth birthday (1795), the King held a massive celebration, including a personal review of the troops. When the Fortress was completed, he again conducted a review of troops, including personal inspection of the cannon there, and he demonstrated his own personal archery skill in front of his officials at every opportunity. While the *Veritable Records* continue their tradition of exaggerating the king's skill at archery when describing these displays, their frequency implies that Chŏngjo did have some skill; if he lacked skill with the bow, his cause would not have been served by constantly revealing his ineptitude in public. These steps, in addition to emphasizing the oft-neglected martial role of the king, may also have been meant to intimidate the *yangban* with a display of the military power at his disposal when combined with the Fortress's power. Indeed, Yi Pyŏng-mo once opposed the King's calling up of troops for the mere purpose of "displaying the army's capabilities [觀保障軍容]" since such a military display was frightening to officials.[27]

Why would Chŏngjo have wished to abdicate? Assuming the King's penchant for cloaking his real intentions behind the obvious held in this case, abdication may have been another ploy in his drive to strengthen his position. 1806 would have been his thirtieth year on the throne, and his son Sunjo would have been sixteen, old enough to reign but not quite old enough to rule as long as his father lived. If he had successfully abdicated, he could have ruled on the model of King T'aejong, who had abdicated to his son Sejong in 1418, but continued as the effective power until his death four years later. In this scenario, Chŏngjo, free of the ritual and moral burdens of a reigning king, could have ruled behind the scenes. (Of course, it is unclear if Chŏngjo's abdication in favor of his adult son would have been acceptable in late Chosŏn.) As Peter H. Wilson noted, the pomp and ceremony of royalty "consumed much of [rulers'] time, fixing their daily routine and often placing a considerable physical burden upon them."[28] Far enough away from the capital to escape prying eyes yet close enough to influence events there, protected by loyal troops located in a place where they posed a significant threat to the capital, and no longer weighed down by onerous ritual obligations, Chŏngjo could have had significant freedom from the restraints on the Chosŏn monarchy, perhaps even greater than the Taewŏn'gun had when he ruled through his young son in the 1860s. And unlike the Taewŏn'gun, Chŏngjo had been king himself and so could have resisted attempts by his son to rule in his own right, which in any case Sunjo would have been unlikely to attempt for at least the better part of a decade.

Two of Chŏngjo's contemporaries wrote of his intention to retire to the Illustrious Fortress. Tasan wrote in his "Tomb Inscription for Yi Ka-hwan" 貞軒墓誌銘 (Chŏnghŏn myojimyŏng) that the King said, "After ten years, I will be an old man myself, and I will make the Illustrious Fortress my place of residence to grow old [後十年。予將老焉。 故華城有老來之堂]." His mother Lady Hyegyŏng directly states that the King intended to abdicate and retire to the Fortress in 1804, and that this would coincide with the exoneration of Sado and of her brother Hong In-han, along with everyone else unfairly punished as a result of the Sado affair, such as Princess Hwawan.[29] This vindication of Sado by Chŏngjo's son rather than by Chŏngjo himself would be in line with Yŏngjo's intention to have Sado vindicate Yŏngjo himself from the specter of his alleged involvement in Kyŏngjong's death; since a king could not directly overturn his predecessor's decisions, he was left to intimate to his successor that this be done, in such a way as to maintain what modern politicians call "plausible deniability" in the eyes of both their officials and the historical record.[30] Of course, Yŏngjo probably did not have his brother poisoned, whereas Sado probably was guilty of a capital offense, but Chŏngjo may not have accepted his father's guilt, given that he was only ten years old when Sado died and Yŏngjo immediately banned any discussion of the whole affair.

The King also attempted to develop the Suwŏn area economically. As noted earlier, the Commercial Equalization Law was implemented to encourage commercial development. He offered government loans to wealthy families that agreed to relocate to the area. He also encouraged craftspeople to move there and promoted their cooperation with merchants. His efforts seem to have been largely successful, at least relative to the rest of central Korea, as Suwŏn did experience a comparatively rapid population growth.[31]

One scheme that did not succeed, however, was the King's plan to relocate twenty of the wealthiest merchant families in the capital to Suwŏn. Kim Sung-Yun notes that the King worked to stimulate commerce in area, issuing a decree in 1797 giving the families both relocation funds and exclusive control over the sale of government-style headgear and ginseng, the latter being a mode of payment in the China trade. Permission to engage in that trade was contingent on successful management of the headgear trade in an attempt to force prosperity in the Suwŏn area through government enforcement of both domestic and foreign trade there.[32] In a rare political blunder for this period of his reign, the decree would have offered government posts to families who accepted this offer.[33] While the sale of offices was already becoming common, there had been controversy from the start over funding the Fortress's construction, including a rumor that the King had sold offices to raise funds for it.[34] It is also difficult to see how the families would have been encouraged by receiving a government monopoly, since the King had already effectively legalized merchant trade outside the Six Licensed Shops system. Further, Chŏngjo's go-to weapon for suppressing opposition to the Fortress, his filial piety, could not really save him here. How would moving merchant families—merchants not exactly being the most righteous men in the Confucian worldview, since they produced nothing themselves while profiting off the labors of honest folk—to the area around his father's tomb be a filial act? This gave the Intransigents—who despite being willing to work with Chŏngjo on other issues were never comfortable with the Fortress or its garrison—an opening to block the implementation of the decree. Chŏngjo wrote to Sim Hwan-ji to gain his support for the relocation, to no avail.[35]

THE ROBUST AND BRAVE REGIMENT: WHOM DO THEY SERVE?

With the Illustrious Fortress, Chŏngjo had a base of royal power to strengthen his hand against opponents among the official class and the landed *yangban* elite. But a fortress is nothing without soldiers to garrison it, and just as he sought a power base outside the vice-grip of the aristocracy, so the King needed a new military unit apart from the existing military apparatus. Rather than a military unit led by a civil official from a prestigious lineage who had performed not a day's worth of military duty or training and made up of old men, dead men, and slaves who had long since run away, Chŏngjo wanted an actual effective unit. After all, two Chosŏn kings had been forced off the throne by officials in command of government troops, and the gravest threat to Yŏngjo's throne had been Disciple opponents in key military positions.[36] Like T'aejong, a former soldier who preferred direct royal control over military units, Chŏngjo knew he could not effectively rule without control over military assets and their attendant economic resources, and like his father, he was determined to pose a credible military threat to a *yangban* class that was not shy about manipulating the succession in the face of a direct challenge to their power. The King's increasing control over the military alarmed the Patriarchs, and even close associates of Chŏngjo among their number opposed it.[37]

The creation of the Robust and Brave Regiment followed the by-now-familiar pattern of Chŏngjo's ruling style. It began in 1777 with the creation of the "temporary" Office of the Palace Guard 宿衛所 (*suk'wiso*) to provide a high official post for Hong Kuk-yŏng, commander of the Palace Guard 宿衛大將 (*suk'wi taejang*). This office was abolished after Hong's fall in 1779, but the precedent was set for creation of a new military unit. In 1782, Chŏngjo created the *muye ch'ulsin* 武藝出身 and in 1785 changed its name to the Robust and Brave Guard 壯勇衛 (*chang'yong'wi*). Its purpose was to guard the king—despite the criticism that military units for this purpose already existed. Chŏngjo brushed aside the concerns of men like O Ik-hwan, who complained in 1788 that "[f]or guarding Your Majesty inside [the palace], there are the Palace Guards and the Office of Military Arts. For outside, there are the generals and men of the Five Military Divisions. There are no gaps in the defense of the perimeter of the palace, yet you for some reason pursue this path of excessive expense [殿下內則 有禁軍武藝。外則有五營將卒。環衛不缺。綢繆甚固。乃爲此冗長之物。以廣糜費之路歟]."[38] This incarnation of the Guard consisted of three companies 哨 (*ch'o*) of about ninety men each. Thus, despite its designation as a guard 衛 (*wi*), at this time it was only the size of a battalion 司 (*sa*) of 270 men. In 1787 it was enlarged and renamed the Robust and Brave Office 壯勇廳 (*chang'yongch'ŏng*). The following year it was made a regiment 營 (*yŏng*), giving it its final name of the Robust and Brave Regiment, though as yet it remained well under regimental strength.[39]

It was not until Chŏngjo's seventeenth year on the throne (1793) that the unit expanded to become a real force to contend with. Not coincidentally, this occurred alongside the construction of the Illustrious Fortress, and this would only be the beginning of their intertwined relationship. The Fortress was designated as the "southern fortress" 南城 (Namsŏng) for the defense of the capital, which meant that the Robust and Brave Regiment, being headquartered there, was on equal footing with the Five Military Divisions 五軍營 (*o'gun'yŏng*), effectively making it permanent. In February of 1793, the Regiment was expanded to coincide with its division into an Inner Regiment 內營 (*naeyŏng*) and an Outer Regiment 外營 (*oeyŏng*). The Inner Regiment was to guard the royal shrine at Ch'angdŏk Palace in the capital, while the Outer Regiment was stationed at the Illustrious Fortress to protect Sado's tomb, the capital, and the king when he was in residence at the Fortress. Chŏngjo justified the maintenance of a military unit in Suwŏn by noting the importance of having military officials in charge of such a strategic area: "The southern fortress [i.e., the Illustrious Fortress] is only for protection, yet those high ministers appointed to administer [Suwŏn] have been exclusively civilians. For the sake of defense, rather, military officials are to be nominated for the southern fortress. Is not this land, this district, a place of importance [南城只管保障。而大臣爲使。居留專差文宰。而爲保障。則武臣通擬於南城。況是地是府之所重乎。]?"[40]

While military officials did figure prominently in leading the Regiment, the principle of civilian control over the military was maintained. The King did indeed place a civilian official in charge, but in a startling break with his strategy on other fronts, he consistently selected Expedients alone, including his prominent allies Sŏ Yu-rin, Sŏ Yong-bo, Chŏng Min-si, Yi Si-su, and Cho Sim-t'ae. This is probably a result of both his desire to keep the Regiment (along with the Illustrious Fortress) exclusively under his supporters' control and of the Intransigents' unflagging opposition to it. Kim Chong-su consistently opposed the King's military reforms, and Yi Pyŏng-mo switched from Expedient to Intransigent over the building of the Illustrious Fortress.[41] While Chŏngjo's successful use of the rhetoric that the Fortress was an expression of filial piety made it impossible to oppose its construction outright, Kim circulated a letter critical of the Fortress while Yi attempted to obstruct troop transfers there and to cancel the military training carried out there.[42] Sim Hwan-ji may have half-heartedly supported it, but this can only be inferred from Chŏngjo's letter to him regarding the relocation of wealthy families to Suwŏn, which Yi Pyŏng-mo also opposed. In this letter, the King asks Sim not to reveal his knowledge of the planned relocation and to highly praise it.[43] It appears, however, that Sim did not praise it, as the official record is silent as to his stand on the relocation question, despite a second letter from the King that seems to play on Sim's dislike of Yi Pyŏng-mo to gain his support.[44] Perhaps Intransigent opposition was so great that none among their number could express open support for the development of the area around the King's new fortress.

Of the two parts of the Regiment, the Outer is our primary concern here, since it was assigned to the Illustrious Fortress. At the same time the commander of the Inner Regiment was raised from commissioner 壯勇使 (chang'yongsa) to grand military commander 壯勇兵大將 (chang'yong pyŏngdaejang), the governor of the Illustrious Fortress District 華城部 (Hwasŏngbu) was assigned the concurrent appointment of commissioner of the Outer Regiment 壯勇外使 (changyong oeyŏng), inextricably linking the unit to the defense of the Fortress. The Outer Regiment was also further expanded, becoming a respectable standing regiment of over 3,000 men, and was tasked with protecting the detached palace at the Fortress. In his decree ordering these changes, Chŏngjo noted that he had been conserving funds for some time in order to pay for the Regiment's needs. Not surprisingly, he justified these reforms as expressions of filial piety to his father, whose tomb should not be in the charge of an official of merely third rank. He also inflated Suwŏn's importance in laudatory terms, drawing on both geomancy and (Chinese) history to make the area appear of central importance to the dynasty.

Since I ascended the throne, I have regarded conserving resources as important. Fortunately, with the mysterious help of my royal ancestors in unfathomable Heaven, here on the site of the coiled dragon and crouching tiger,[45] we will be blessed with great fortune for countless years to come. This land we cherish truly has prospered like the Feng lands of the Zhou and the Pei lands of the Han.[46] Only by striving to defend this area even more effectively will our prestige be exalted and our state institutions be revered. This is why I feel it is important for me to express my feelings. It is like the rite of the royal shrine in which the first beautiful part is the high officials arrayed before it. If there is any example connected to what is important, this is it. Since the Manifestly Abundant Garden was prepared, this land in Suwŏn District has been more important because it guards the flanks. How beautiful it is! I honor [Sado's] cap and gown each month. In preparing to establish the detached palace, my first thoughts were of trust and respect. I hung up his portrait, and I served my mother faithfully, but the child's longing to connect with his father knows no restraint. For the three hundred days of every year, not a day goes by that I do not count and wait with anticipation [to pay homage to Sado in Suwŏn]. I pass the time in the performance of these rites [for Sado] on one day a year, but as soon as I complete the rites and start the return trip to the palace, when I stop on the hilltop at the boundary of Suwŏn, I turn my face to the sky and hesitate to leave, and I cannot rouse myself from this hesitation to continue on. When I summon the magistrate of my father's tomb before me, I continually insist that he should guard it with reverence and due respect. But if you look at his position, it is that of a township head. When you ask his rank, his is the third rank.[47]

[御極以後。峙藏儲用。爲所重也。幸荷皇天祖宗之默佑。而龍盤虎踞之宅兆。永奠千億萬年無疆大曆數。是地之所重。實與周之豐漢之沛。竝盛而齊隆。惟其拱護之方。愈勤而愈密。使體貌尊嚴。制度肅虔。卽予小子情文之所當然。譬若宗廟之禮。先言百官之美。其有關於所重者如是矣。是地水原府。自卜園寢。關防增重。美哉。天作之襟帶。長奉月出之衣冠。預建行宮。先寓瞻依之思。摸揭圖像。用替定省之誠。而孺慕結轖。迷不知節。每歲三百日。無日不屈指而企者也。亶在於禮行一日。而旣展省將還駕。駕住府界峴上。瞻望躊躇。不自覺其吾行之遲遲。輒召至[致]守臣於前。申之以恪謹拱護之義。顧其職則一邑倅也。問其品則三品窠也。]

In the middle of 1793, the 300-strong cavalry unit of the Regiment was reorganized as the Brave Detached Company 壯別隊 (changbyŏldae), and two months later it was designated the King's Personal Military Guard 親軍衛 (ch'in'gunwi). In 1795, twelve more battalions were transferred from regular army units to the Robust and Brave Outer Regiment, three months after their associated villages of Yong'in, Chinwi, and Ansan were put under the administration of the Illustrious Fortress District. Three months after that, the regular army was further weakened when two of the Five Armies, the Defensive Resistance Command 守禦廳 (Suŏch'ŏng) and the Chief Military Command 摠戎廳 (Ch'ongyungch'ŏng), were gutted, effectively putting the Robust and Brave Regiment on the level of the remaining three armies. Here, Chŏngjo's cultivation of Sim Hwan-ji paid off; Sim, serving as minister of war, gave his assent to the decision.[48] The next year, Yi Chu-guk, a proponent of Chŏngjo who served as minister of war despite having only passed the military examination,[49] proposed the abolition of all provincial armies. Though this was not carried out, the proposal attracted royal praise, and the Regiment eventually came to number approximately 20,000 troops. It is unclear whether the

Regiment could actually have fielded this number of duty soldiers, since it was never tested. Chosŏn Korea's military forces on paper were consistently much larger than the armies that were ever mustered, since old men and dead men remained listed as active and the registers were always several steps behind men's movements from one area to another.[50] Like most early modern states, Chosŏn struggled to raise needed duty soldiers and often had to make do with "the mere scumme [sic] of our provinces" as the upper-class and even well-to-do commoners escaped service.[51] But as we have seen, absolute monarchy was at least as much about image as reality. If the Regiment could never have actually fielded a full 20,000 troops, any rival force would be no more likely to field its full complement of troops on paper. The *perception* of the King in control of such a force, or something even close to it, was enough.[52]

The Robust and Brave Regiment, then, represented a serious royal challenge to aristocratic control over the regular army as represented by the Border Defense Command 備邊司 (*pibyŏnsa*), as it weakened the central army at the expense of a proroyal unit. From its place in the mighty Illustrious Fortress, commanded by a King's man, the Regiment represented a strong deterrent to any aristocratic challenge to Chŏngjo's hold on the throne. Absolute monarchs tended to have a stronger position in the areas of military policy and war, as we have seen here as well as in Chŏngjo's relative success in expanding recruitment of military officials to include previously excluded groups as compared to civil officials.[53]

The Illustrious Fortress stands today as a visible reminder of Chŏngjo's devotion to his father's memory. It was not just a symbol but a functional military installation that the King garrisoned with a new military unit centered on it. This military unit began as a token tomb guard that Chŏngjo quietly built into a formidable force. He entrusted command of this unit and its fortress to his close allies, and he may have intended to retire to the safety of its stone walls. Some members of the aristocracy opposed these developments, understanding the danger posed by a powerful military unit stationed near the capital that effectively operated under the King's direct control and outside the regular military command. They were outmaneuvered, however, by Chŏngjo's skillful manipulation of filial piety. He turned the weakness of Sado's shadow into strength, playing on the sympathy of Sado's tragic end to justify the grand fortress constructed in his name and the elite guard to defend it. The fortress survives, but the guard was not so lucky.

7

CHŎNGJO IN AN EARLY MODERN WORLD

DESPITE THE LONG-STANDING CULTURAL INTERACTION BETWEEN THE peoples on the Korean peninsula and the peoples in the Chinese heartland—interaction that continued to flourish despite upper-class Koreans' disdain for the Manchu barbarians—absolute monarchy in the late Chosŏn more resembled that of seventeenth-century France than contemporary China. Counterintuitive as it may seem, vastly different cultural contexts were shaped by geographical, political, and social factors such that "Confucian" rulers in Korea ruled in a manner closer to Catholic France than to similarly "Confucian" China, an example of what Daniel Lord Smail compares to convergent evolution: "It is similarity of ecology, not relatedness, that often determines convergent evolution—similarity of behavior."[1] Jisoo Kim, though without using the term, recently found another example of this kind of convergent evolution. Her research into the status of women as legal persons in Chosŏn and the Islamic world revealed that "[d]espite the geographic proximity of China and Korea, women of the Chosŏn shared more similarities with those in the Middle East in terms of their recognition as legal subjects."[2] This chapter examines Chŏngjo's absolutism by contrasting it with his immediate processor, Yŏngjo, and with a prominent Ming absolute ruler, the Yongle Emperor. It then looks closely at Chŏngjo's absolutism in relation to two other important rulers: the Qianlong Emperor of the Qing Empire and the Sun King Louis XIV of France. All three monarchs—Qianlong, Louis, and Chŏngjo—deployed similar methods to flex their autocratic muscle, though these methods were shaped by their respective contexts of seventeenth-century France and eighteenth-century China and Korea, and some channels that were closed in one context were open in another. As we will see, though, Qianlong's position at the top of a vast multiethnic, multilingual empire marked his version of absolutism off from the more constrained absolutism of Louis and Chŏngjo in their much smaller, culturally and linguistically more unified kingdoms, in terms that could be considered analogous to Fukuyama's "strong" and "weak" absolutism. Despite the enormous cultural distance between the opposite ends of Eurasia, political and social conditions were such that absolutism in early modern Korea more closely resembled that of early modern France's "weak absolutism," as opposed to "Chinese-style absolutism," to use Fukuyama's terms.[3] While there were a number of similarities between Qianlong's and Chŏngjo's absolutism due to the cultural context in which each man operated, there was a vast gulf between the lands they ruled. The Qing Empire was a sprawling multiethnic composite state with a population of 300 million, while the Chosŏn kingdom, tucked away in the eastern corner of Eurasia, boasted a population smaller than that of the larger Chinese provinces. This meant that Chŏngjo ruled in a way more recognizable to a kingdom of more comparable geographic size with a dominant hereditary aristocracy—seventeenth-century France.[4]

Before getting to the Chinese and French rulers, it may be useful to examine the contrasting ruling styles of Chŏngjo and a strong king from the former period, Sejong the Great (r. 1418-1450) and his own predecessor and grandfather, Yŏngjo. Sejong preferred to listen and keep quiet during audiences, in contrast to the verbose Chŏngjo, who seemed to delight in confusing and tripping up his ministers and whose forceful personality dominated court audiences. Indeed, whereas Sejong's audiences were concerned with winnowing down to converge on good ideas though discussion, Chŏngjo's audiences were about the King instructing ministers on the need for reform and insistence on obedience.[5] In the late eighteenth century, Chŏngjo sought to overawe his ministers with the majesty of four hundred years of the Yi dynasty, the centrality of his place in the political world and the cosmos, and his own personal brilliance and moral mastery. Sejong, the son of a usurper, taking the throne within three decades after the dynasty's founding and only twenty years after the Strife of the Princes,[6] ruled in a consultative, consensus-building fashion. He preferred to lead from the rear, encouraging his officials to "take him to task."[7] To take a well-known example, his proclamation of the Korean alphabet in 1444, Sejong went to some length to keep the project secret, among a few trusted officials, before suddenly springing it on the court.[8] The predecessor to Chŏngjo's Royal Library, the Hall of Worthies, was not so firmly under Sejong's control. Despite many of its members being involved in the creation of the alphabet, none other than one of its own deputy chiefs, Ch'oe Mal-li, was perhaps the most eloquent opponent of the alphabet, remarking,

> The land and customs of the nine ancient provinces [of China] differ, yet there was never a separate writing system for regional languages.

Only the five ethnic groups of Jurchens, Japanese, Mongols, Tibetans, and Tanguts have their own scripts. These are all barbarian affairs and not worth carrying out. It has come down to us: "Use the ways of the Xia [China] to reform the barbarians." I have never heard of the civilized becoming barbarian. For generations China has considered us the heirs to the teachings of the Lord of Ji. Our writing, implements, ritual, and music all follow those of the center of civilization. Now we create this vernacular writing, pushing aside China and making ourselves no different from the barbarians. This is what is called rejecting the fragrance of civilization and embracing the dung of beetles and grasshoppers. Is this not a great disgrace to civilization?[9]

[自古九州之內。風土雖異。未有因方言而別爲文字者。唯蒙古西夏女眞日本西蕃之
類。各有其字。是皆夷狄事耳。無足道者。傳曰用夏變夷。未聞變於夷者也。歷代中
國皆以我國有箕子遺風。文物禮樂。比擬中華。今別作諺文。捨中國而自同於夷狄。
是所謂棄蘇合之香。而取蜣蜋之丸也。豈非文明之大累哉。]

In contrast with the institution's successor, the Royal Library, whose officials usually served as preparation for higher office in key ministries like War and Personnel, men in the Hall of Worthies could hold office there for decades and served as more of a "think tank" for discussing issues of the day than a stepping-stone to later office. Thus, it was accepted that they had the freedom to pursue their own interests.[10] Clearly Ch'oe Mal-li did not consider the Korean alphabet to be one of his interests.

One of Sejong's officials, one Sin Kae (1374–1446), noted that it was acceptable to employ discretion (*kwŏn*) when establishing a new dynasty, but since Sejong was (according to Sin) in the "consolidation" phase of dynastic building, the king should not employ discretion but follow the Rectified Path 正道, which meant canvassing the officials for their thoughts on state matters and then acting according to their recommendations.[11] Park Young-do characterizes Sejong's monarchy as "co-governing of ruler and vassals [臣]."[12] Sejong's "leading from the rear" meant that he sought consensus-building rather than pretentions to absolutism. Even after canvassing the officials and receiving support from the majority of his officials, he did not move forward with a fixed land tax because the minority opposed to it contained a number of high officials, whom he was determined to bring into the consensus. It took seventeen years (from 1427 to 1444) to finally implement the system, and even then it only applied to a single province and scattered villages by Sejong's death in 1450. Kyŏnggi Province was not included for another twelve years (1462), and the system was not implemented throughout the entire country until 1489. Park Hyunmo points out that Sejong only succeeded by adopting "public sentiment [公論]," introducing amendments, and applying the law in only a small part of the country.[13]

Sejong was very concerned with law and ordered the compilation of a new law code, the *Great Code for Managing the State* 經國大典 (*Kyŏngguk taejŏn*), that served as the basis of Korean law until the twentieth century. He personally approved each section of the code, generally intervening only to lighten the punishment for certain crimes.[14] Chŏngjo ordered the compilation of the *Complete Compilation of the Great Code* 大典通編 (*Taejŏn t'ong p'yŏn*) in 1785. This was a supplement to both the Great Code and Yŏngjo's *Supplement to the Great Code*, and all three were printed together. An analysis of the changes and additions the King made to the two existing codes remains to be written, but the *Complete Compilation* does include strengthened military tests (focusing more on actual skill over theoretical knowledge), in line with Chŏngjo's stress on actual results and directly connected to his frequent processions, which often included grand displays of military training exercises.[15] He also standardized the format of inquest reports to resolve confusion in criminal investigations and ordered the compilation of the *Record of Royal Reviews* 審理錄 (*Simnirok*), a record of past decisions to serve as a kind of "case law" for later generations in the king's capacity to administer justice, and a collection of decisions on cases in the Ministry of Punishment that was maintained until 1893, though all decisions originally collected before 1822 are now lost.[16] Yi Tae-Jin has even argued that Chŏngjo (and Yŏngjo) used their decisions in lawsuits to send a message to the *yangban* that, despite their status, they were not guaranteed to prevail in disputes with commoners.[17] In the context of Europe, Ziad Elmarsafy views absolutism as an instrument of liberation from aristocratic dominance for those at the bottom of society, since it "brought with it a space where rule of law was viable" that put nobles "on a par with the peasantry."[18]

In stark contrast to Chŏngjo, Yŏngjo had a weak claim to the throne and only became king due to "a series of accidents." His father Sukchong, despite having ten wives and consorts, had only three sons who survived into adulthood. Once his sickly brother died at age thirty-five after only four years on the throne, only Yŏngjo, the son of Sukchong by a lowly consort, was left as a viable candidate. He responded with a combination of a sharp eye for attacks on either his parentage or on the early death of his brother (the latter continuing to hound him with accusations of poisoning for years) and an attempt to prove himself the moral superior to his officials, since "[o]ne of the few tenets the bureaucracy could not challenge was ideal of the sage-king upon which the

Yi monarchy was premised." This meant both ruling and living according to a strict definition of what constituted the Confucian sage.[19] Like Chŏngjo, he obsessed over the status of his mother and gradually raised her posthumous status, though also like Chŏngjo he was never able to make his mother a queen.[20]

In contrast to Chŏngjo, Yŏngjo did little for secondary sons, despite his extraordinarily long reign by Chosŏn standards. In 1772 he took an action to address the discrimination, appointing three secondary sons as censors, but he made no move to follow up or support this action, and it did not become a regular practice.[21] He also cut somewhat of a less impressive figure than his grandson, though this was partly by design. Whereas Chŏngjo demanded his ministers recognize his centrality and defer to his leadership, overawing them with his mastery of Confucian rhetoric and classical writing style, Yŏngjo adopted the modesty of his vision of the sage-king who points out his own faults and does not raise himself above others, crying out at the ancestral altar that his own lack of virtue brought disgrace on the royal line.[22] Whereas Chŏngjo intimidated his officials by dressing in military uniform and personally inspecting military drills, Yŏngjo, when his officials failed to listen to (his) reason, engaged in "tantrums" and refused to eat.[23] Yŏngjo was concerned that he not be viewed as arbitrary but as morally perfect in the eyes of his officials, though his increasing restriction of the channel of speech severely tarnished that image, while Chŏngjo presided over a vast expansion of the channel of speech that blunted criticism of the actual increase in his power.[24] The two kings' contrasting characters are revealed in their approaches to the royal lecture. Yŏngjo struggled for decades to assert his position within the royal lecture system. He sought to master it, to show his officials he could beat them at their game, and this weakened his Policy of Impartiality.[25] Chŏngjo eventually refused to hold the lecture and replaced it with a system of his own devising that placed him in the superior position. He felt no need to prove anything to his officials. Yŏngjo would often refuse to come to audiences or to meet with any officials when he judged that his policies were being obstructed, bringing the business of government to a halt as the ministers begged him to return and assume his rightful position.[26] His ultimate weapon was to make his withdrawal permanent, that is, the threat of abdication.[27] By late Chosŏn, the whole theory of government was predicated on all authority being concentrated in the reigning king, and Yŏngjo's officials balked at the notion of abdication even when he had an heir old enough to rule. Just as there could not be two Suns in the sky, there could not be two kings in Chosŏn. Yŏngjo's nuclear option was even weaker in the wake of Prince Sado's death. Yŏngjo, whose overriding goal was to protect the dynasty, the legacy of his ancestors, could never have seriously considered abdicating to a child, as it would have threatened to throw the state into chaos. Yŏngjo's ultimate way to hold onto power was to threaten to give up that power, a threat everyone knew was empty but had to pretend to take seriously because of the gravity of it. Yŏngjo of course never expected to be king and probably never wanted to be. Chŏngjo by contrast was groomed to rule from birth and probably would have agreed with Henry II in *The Lion in Winter*: "Oh God, but I do love being king!"

THE CENTER HOLDS: CHŎNGJO AND QIANLONG

When talking about the history of Korea, especially before 1910, comparisons with contemporary China often leap to mind. The extensive diplomatic contacts, the shared use of the written Literary Sinitic language, the similarity in the political and legal systems (at least on paper) and the official sanction of Cheng-Zhu Neo-Confucianism all point to important similarities. By the eighteenth century, both China and Korea were thoroughly dominated by Confucian ideology, at least at the government and elite level. Unlike the Catholicism of early modern France, there was no church of Confucianism or single leader of the religion in East Asia. In all three polities, the sacred and the secular were fused, but only in East Asia was it true that there was "no 'Confucian' clergy or pope, no alternative establishment (before the nineteenth century) around which dissidents could rally or whose ancient authority they could invoke," meaning that dissenters in both China and Korea were outshone by the court's ideological resources.[28] Whereas in France absolutism was defined in part by independence of Rome, and Louis XIV knew little of the finer points of Catholic theology and doctrine, both Qianlong and Chŏngjo strove to out-Confucian their officials. On the other hand, there is little question that Louis, if theologically unsophisticated, was a true lay Catholic believer, while Qianlong regarded Confucianism as more a tool to manipulate his Han Chinese subjects than a belief system to which he himself was committed. To the other ethnicities of his Eurasian empire, the emperor made no Confucian pretensions. He was *cakravartin* to the Tibetans and Great Khan to the Mongols and Manchus, and the lack of such a position as supreme authority among his Muslim subjects meant Qing control over them, at least in an ideological sense, was always tenuous.[29] Chŏngjo combined both impulses. A true believer in Confucianism, the King was not hesitant to use the religion to further his political goals.

Chŏngjo's absolutism was quite different from that of Ming. The pattern of absolute rule in that dynasty was laid down not by its founder Hongwu but by his usurper son, the Yongle Emperor (r. 1402–1424). A violent man "filled with great contradictions," Yongle was "part villain and part visionary" as he expanded administrative service by eunuchs, the "minions of the throne" who served as the linchpin of Ming absolutism.[30] Yongle also had a much freer hand than Chŏngjo in selecting officials. The civil wars in the wake of his father's death and the purges at the beginning of his own reign took a severe toll on the bureaucracy, such that the government had a pressing need for new talent. A military man, Yongle preferred a frugal soldier's life and had no qualms about working with lower-ranking scholars.[31] He was happy to use Confucian moral teachings right alongside "the terror and violence bequeathed by his father" to get his way, and he was willing to use the Chinese literati for their talents in the former despite his personal distaste for them and their ways.[32] Chŏngjo, with four centuries of Confucian hegemony in the political sphere behind him, sought to portray himself as the ultimate Confucian leader. Yongle, a military man in a time of strife and bloodshed, had little patience for the niceties of Confucian discourse. An example is their respective approaches to history. Chŏngjo only once challenged the sanctity of the composition of the dynastic annals, which was insulated from royal interference, when he prevailed on Yŏngjo to expunge from the record what were presumably incidents of his father's madness. Yongle, on the other hand, ordered his "spin doctor" Dao Yan to revise his father's entire *Veritable Records* three times, such that it was not completed until two decades after Hongwu's death.[33]

Both rulers, however, sought to control doctrine. Yongle produced his own versions of the Five Classics and Four Books, omitting many texts that he did not approve of, since he regarded as the main purpose of literary projects the legitimization of his own reign.[34] He also tried to build a clique of supporters in the official bureaucracy, though for Yongle his eunuchs were at least as important to his power base. Nevertheless, he built the Grand Secretariat as a secret council of his own supporters whose meetings were closed to nonmembers, and the secretaries' power stemmed from their connection to the emperor rather than from their official ranks.[35] He also attempted to move families, though his motives were due to loyalty rather than commercial development, and his efforts were on a much grander scale, shifting 3,000 families from the south to rural areas around the capital, though many of them later fled.[36]

Qianlong also regarded control of Confucian discourse as vital, as did Chŏngjo, since it was a Confucian framework in which both rulers had to justify their rule. (Qianlong deployed multiple discourses for different parts of the empire, but for the largest, most populous, and wealthiest part of that empire, China, Confucianism was dominant in politics.) Thus, both men questioned the lack of focus on the ruler in the commentaries of Zhu Xi and looked back to older, ruler-centered commentaries, exemplified by Chŏngjo's preference for such commentaries and for the Five Classics over Zhu Xi's Four Books, due to their greater concern with the art of governance. In the same vein, Qianlong ordered the restoration of Zheng Xuan's tablet in the Scholar's Temple 文廟 (munmyo), leading Pamela Crossley to remark that "Zheng Xuan's place was reestablished under the Qing."[37] Zheng (127–200) was regarded as one of the most important commentators on the Classics, and his interpretation of Confucianism as authoritative, until Cheng-Zhu learning became prominent under the Mongols in the thirteenth century, when he was eclipsed by Zhu Xi.[38] The Scholar's Temple was a shrine reflecting the legacies of those whom the state regarded as orthodox thinkers. Thus, Qianlong's restoration of Zheng's tablet meant that his more ruler-focused thought was as acceptable in the emperor's eyes as that of Zhu Xi, and indeed Qianlong's writings became increasingly critical of Zhu over the course of his reign. Also like Chŏngjo, Qianlong favored scholars of Evidential or "Han" Learning, in part due to Han arguments limiting sagehood exclusively to rulers such as himself, and he exercised personal control over the publication of his own editions of the Classics and which commentaries would accompany them.[39] As we have seen, Chŏngjo sought to replace the royal lectures with a system in which he did the lecturing as part of his attempt to portray himself as the source of learning and controller of Confucian interpretation. Similarly, David Nivison notes that "[w]e find the Qianlong Emperor lecturing his censors instead of being lectured by them, as he would have been in an age in which men of learning restrained the throne."[40] Qianlong lectured scholars; he was not beholden to them.

In the seventeenth century both Chosŏn and the Qing Empire faced serious population increases without concomitant increases in the number of offices. This meant that, by the eighteenth century, both polities had too many examination passers and not enough offices to go around, and in both cases government officials in office were forced to govern more people with the same administrative resources. (France, on the other hand, faced the opposite problem; Louis's creation of new offices meant too many officials without enough work to do.) There were, however, key differences as well. Even before the Qing conquest, China was a vast empire of more than 100 million people even at its lowest point during the five hundred years of Chosŏn Korea, while the latter's population probably never exceeded 14 million. During the eighteenth century, China proper boasted nearly half a billion people, a staggering number for a society not exploiting the power of fossil fuels on a large scale, leaving aside Qianlong's other realms of Manchuria, Mongolia, and Tibet. The sheer size of the Chinese bureaucracy alone meant it functioned quite differently than that of Chosŏn, despite the Korean elite's conscious attempt to implement a Chinese-style bureaucracy. The Chinese aristocracy's stranglehold on central government offices had been eliminated centuries ago, while Korea's aristocratic class was only beginning to see the erosion of the privileged place it had occupied for at least half a millennium. Still, despite the vastly different circumstances facing the two rulers, Qianlong and Chŏngjo responded in similar ways, not necessarily through conscious imitation. Instead, they deployed the weapons of early modern monarchs against the background of their respective cultural contexts, which naturally led to marked differences as well.

In the eighteenth century, China was the largest, wealthiest, and most important part of the Manchu Qing Empire. And for most of that century, the Empire was ruled by Hongli, better known as the Qianlong Emperor. Qianlong ruled for sixty-three years, though he officially abdicated after a sixty-year reign to avoid eclipsing the achievement of his similarly long-living grandfather, the Kangxi Emperor (r. 1661–1722). He was the fourth son of the Yongzheng Emperor (r. 1722–1735) by his father's concubine, Lady Niuhuru. Reportedly he was favored by Kangxi, a boon for his future accession despite Kangxi's death thirteen years before Qianlong's succession became an issue. The early Qing emperors, in a departure from Han Chinese practice in the later Ming dynasty, did not practice primogeniture in the imperial succession. The Kangxi Emperor attempted to institute Chinese-style primogeniture by naming his eldest son the heir, but this attempt ended in disaster among a Manchu-Mongol elite still accustomed to northern acclamation-style succession (see below). Instead, the reigning emperor, in secret, chose a successor from among his sons and wrote that son's name on a scroll kept hidden and not revealed until his death. Still, Kangxi's open favoritism of young Qianlong meant few were surprised with Yongzheng's choice of successor.

Both Chŏngjo and Qianlong ascended the throne at age twenty-four as grandsons of long-reigning rulers (Yŏngjo fifty-two years, Kangxi sixty-one years), and neither had any serious challenge to their legitimacy, unlike their predecessors. Yŏngjo was the son of a concubine and was forever haunted by the probably baseless rumor that he had murdered his older brother in order to seize the throne, while Yongzheng had to contend with having never been Kangxi's designated heir. Indeed, Kangxi deposed and arrested his heir, Prince Yinreng, only to reappoint him heir again some years later and then depose and arrest him a second time. After this second deposal, Kangxi refused to appoint an heir at all, but princely rivalry did not abate. The leading contenders were Yinzhi, who had the support of two other brothers whose own prospects for succession were dim, and Yinti, then serving as general-in-chief for the Pacification of Distant Lands 撫遠大將軍 (*muwŏn taejanggun*); the future Yongzheng Emperor was a distant third. But when Kangxi died, it was Yongzheng who outmaneuvered his brothers and secured the throne in the best Manchu style. After his accession, opponents of Yongzheng spread rumors that he had manipulated his father into choosing him over Yinti, or had even poisoned his father. Yongzheng was unaware—or pretended to be unaware—of these rumors until 1728, whereupon he ordered their instigators punished and, the following year, published a defense against these charges, among others; five hundred miles away in Seoul, Yŏngjo, facing probably false accusations of poisoning his predecessor, would have understood.[41]

Early modern China, lacking Korea's overweening concern with hereditary status, did not begrudge Qianlong his position due to his mother's lowly court rank as early modern Korea did Yŏngjo's. As beloved heirs (declared almost immediately in the case of Chŏngjo, known as an open secret in the case of Qianlong, though he was not officially educated as heir), both men received the best education available in eighteenth-century East Asia, though their language education was quite different. Chŏngjo's linguistic education focused entirely on learning Literary Sinic, the *scripta franca* of East Asia, Sheldon Pollack's cosmopolitan written language of civilization that transcended national boundaries and culturally bound the region together.[42] He also learned "vulgar writing" 諺文 (*ŏnmun*), as the Korean alphabet was derisively referred to by Korea's elite men, but this would not have been considered part of his formal education. While it is impossible to know, he might have learned it informally from the palace ladies who attended him daily, as the Korean alphabet was widely used by women, including princesses and queens. For Qianlong, Literary Sinic was just one language among several. He also had to learn his own ethnic script, Manchu, along with one of the interethnic languages of Central Asia, Mongolian. The multilingual Qing Emperor reflected the multiethnic Qing Empire, while the notion of Korea as the domain of a single people was already entrenched by late Chosŏn.

Still, absolute monarchy did not function entirely differently in China and Korea in the early modern period. For instance, both Chŏngjo and Qianlong were limited by precedent. As monarchs, they were legitimized by their dynastic heritage, but that very heritage also acted as a constraint on innovation. Qing emperors sought in many ways to portray themselves to the Chinese as Confucian rulers, and so their imperial propaganda emphasized the morality and good governance of their ancestors. As in Korea, this made it hazardous to alter the policies of these worthies—it opened the ruler to the charge of unfiliality—leaving reform to be characterized by Mark Elliott as tentative, unofficial, and indirect.[43] Indeed, when the Kangxi Emperor froze the land tax in 1721, the cash-strapped government turned to other forms of revenue rather than reversing the freeze, despite the turmoil the Empire experienced in its struggles with the modern West in the nineteenth century. Like Chŏngjo, the Qianlong Emperor made subtle criticisms of his two predecessors to create space for him to deviate from their policies, but it was a fine line to walk, and he was vigilant against charges of violating precedent. An unfortunate official, one Wang Shijun, met with execution when he leveled that very charge against the emperor.[44] Both rulers also sought ways to circumvent the influence of ministers at different layers of bureaucracy and intervene more directly, such as Chŏngjo's "secret letters," analogous to the secret memorial system of early Qing. This permitted a high official to submit to the emperor an "eyes-only" memorial whose contents were seen by no one else, what Silas H. L. Wu calls "a direct and secret communication device."[45]

Perhaps the most striking of these methods is frequent procession. The importance of processions to governing the Qing Empire cannot be overstated. Michael Chang titled his monograph on Qing processions *A Court on Horseback*, reflecting the early emperors' reluctance to remain sequestered in the Forbidden City, and called imperial tours "centerpieces of High Qing political culture" that "played a pivotal role in the formation of Qing rule during... the 'long eighteenth century.'"[46] Their Korean contemporaries were not unaware of the imperial penchant for frequent travel. In 1753, when returning envoy to the Qing capital Yu Han-so reported to his king and Yŏngjo asked, "What goes on over there in China [彼中事何如]?," Yu replied, "The [Qianlong] Emperor is not willing to remain in the capital even one day. He comes and goes constantly. The rumor over there in China is his is a court on horseback [皇帝不肯一日留京。出入無常。彼中有馬上朝廷之謠矣]."[47] Both Qianlong and Chŏngjo increased the touring rate over their predecessors, whose rates were already higher than earlier monarchs,' and Qianlong specifically cited Kangxi's frequent touring to justify his violation of Ming precedent; Ming emperors were notorious for remaining sequestered in their palaces.[48] (While Yongzheng was actually his immediate predecessor, Qianlong astutely tended to refer to Kangxi's more illustrious and acclaimed reign when he needed to claim he was following his predecessors.) Qianlong averaged two to three tours per year, a rate comparable to Chŏngjo's nearly-three-per-year average. Qianlong also received direct petitions from those who were not government officials on these tours, including from commoners, as he did on April 4, 1762.[49] Both rulers used processions as occasions for display of their positions as military commanders. Qianlong inspected troops personally in Jiangnan on his Southern Tours, and tour life purposefully modeled the experience of a military march; they also served as examples of the Manchu Emperor "roughing it" the way his Jurchen ancestors had. Still, these military maneuvers were probably more symbolic than anything else; like Chŏngjo, Qianlong demonstrated his skill in archery rather than musketry despite the latter's centrality to eighteenth-century warfare. Yet, in keeping with the vast Qing Empire's military endeavors, Qianlong did seem during his military inspections more concerned with the troops' actual effectiveness than Chŏngjo, who was more interested in demonstrating his control over the military vis-à-vis his officials.[50] After the deaths of both monarchs, touring their respective realms precipitously declined, since government officials consistently opposed touring as wasteful and useless.[51] In the Qing Empire after Qianlong's death, the bureaucracy even went so far as to put these words into Qianlong's mouth, claiming that in his old age he regretted the expense of his youthful tours. This was a significant hindrance that hampered his successor's ability to undertake tours.[52]

It is also important to note that Qianlong's travels were much more extensive, meaning he was out and about longer and wider; even when Chŏngjo made a trip outside of the capital, it was usually to Kyŏnggi Province, which surrounded it. Equivalents of Qianlong's Southern Tours must have been infrequent, and Chŏngjo probably never traveled to the northern frontier since, in the absence of any serious threat of invasion from that quarter, the northern *yangban* were expected to hold the border against raiders and other small-scale conflicts without bothering the central government about it. Qianlong's claim that he needed to inspect the distant frontiers and to conduct diplomacy with the various peoples on the Empire's vast borders carried no weight in the Eastern Kingdom. Chŏngjo, like Elizabeth I, used processions to display and reinforce his power rather than to seriously investigate the realm. Similarly, Qianlong held special recruitment examinations during his tours that targeted men from families who lacked a degree holder or officeholder, and there were a number of laws in place restricting these examinations to such men.[53] Of course, such an examination was out of the question in Chosŏn Korea, especially in the long peace of the eighteenth century, when there was no pressing military emergency to permit the rare exception allowing talented commoners to obtain military degrees.

NO SUCH THING AS PASSIVE LIFE: CHŎNGJO AND LOUIS XIV

L'État, c'est moi.

—Louis XIV, apocryphal

The periods of Bourbon France and Chosŏn Korea share an important historiographic characteristic: Each has, for most of the twentieth century, been studied for what came after it rather than for its own sake. For France, it is the ancien régime that *caused* the Revolution, leading to entire libraries being written with the express purpose of studying the seventeenth and eighteenth centuries by determining the conditions leading to 1789. Another unfortunate effect was to take the succeeding generation's analysis of its predecessor with rather less criticism than might be warranted. The revolutionaries, eager to cast their actions in the noblest possible light, were quick to lambast the Bourbons as maniacal tyrants, the eighteenth century as one of decadence and war, the French state one of oppression and exploitation. It was only toward the end of the twentieth century that scholars began to look with a more critical eye on these claims, finding more continuity after 1789 than the revolutionaries would admit and wondering if our knowledge of earlier centuries might be better served by viewing those centuries on their own terms rather than parsing them for the answer to the question of why the Revolution happened.

For Korea, the Ultimate Question is why Korea failed to defend itself from Japan. Just as in France, the eighteenth and nineteenth centuries have been combed for decades in search of the source of Korea's failure, the sad orchestral overture before the 1905 aria, when Korea became a Japanese protectorate and for all intents and purposes lost what little political autonomy it had maintained over the previous thirty years. Further, the combers remained, unknowingly, in the thrall of the views of those who wrote history after the opening of Korea in 1876. For them, the late Chosŏn state was hopelessly corrupt, riven by constant and intransigent factionalism, and dominated by lazy and out-of-touch dandies, who executed each other in disputes over clothing styles and periods of mourning. The dominant view of nineteenth-century Chosŏn was that it was backward, stagnant, and in decline. Even after independence in 1945, many scholars—even, or perhaps especially, those in Korea itself—challenged none of these assumptions, taking them as given and trying to figure out how the *minjok*民族, the Korean race, had fallen from its heights in the glorious sixth and seventh centuries, when the kingdom of Koguryŏ sat astride

Manchuria and northern Korea, fending off continuous invasions from the mighty empires of Sui and Tang, until Tang finally got help from the treacherous Silla. That by premodern standards Chosŏn was not especially corrupt, that factionalism did not cause the government to be permanently ineffective, that Confucian disputes were no less important than Christian disputes in Europe to men of that time and place, that the late Chosŏn state was surviving and even thriving—these factors were not taken seriously by most scholars until the end of the twentieth century. Instead, the late Chosŏn period was parsed for signs of impending modernity, with this or that trend or personage classified as "conservative" and "progressive" (read: modern) or "future-oriented" and "past-oriented."[54]

If we look at the eighteenth-century state on its own terms, we find that early modern absolutism saw the increasing importance of institutions, though power remained primarily invested in individuals.[55] In seventeenth-century France, for example, officials' functions were defined more by their place in relationship to the king than the supposed duties of the offices they held.[56] The king sat at the top of government organizations, and "there were no institutions capable of stopping a determined monarch from overriding any resistance."[57] There were, of course, ways to pressure him, but the absolute monarch had no institutional check on his authority that could reverse or block his decisions, whether *parlement* or Censorate. Neither institution had the authority to actually *stop* the king from passing laws. Instead, they sanctioned laws, or not, by granting or withholding their consent. This meant that both institutions remained strongholds of the defense of aristocratic privilege, while also to some extent acting as a channel for grievances,[58] and allowing them to remonstrate and even to obstruct legislation was vital to the king, since it was political suicide to be viewed as behaving despotically by squashing dissent in a heavy-handed manner.[59]

Thus, while there may have been little dispute that the king's authority was unchecked by institutions or other actors in theory, no absolute monarchy actually functioned with unchecked authority. Instead, absolutism was continuously negotiated and contested by the monarch and his ministers, in which "skillful management of ruling elites rather than armed force" characterized the political landscape.[60] Effective absolutism required cooptation of the elite into the monarch's program and "preferred to exert its theological authority through carefully managed cooperation rather than confrontation and coercion."[61]

Most absolute monarchs not only lacked unfettered power but did not even seek to obtain it, and few of the aristocracy in early modern Eurasia sought to challenge the king's right to rule both de jure and de facto; those who did found little support, either ideological or practical. So even as Louis smarted at the remonstrance of the *parlements* and struggled to eliminate this thorn in his side, he protected the *parlements* from encroachments—and the *parlementaires'* own social positions—in other ways.[62] The tangible rewards the absolute monarch could offer aristocrats for obedience to his will in early modern France and Korea were limited indeed, but royal praise and expressions of gratitude, along with practically dubious but symbolically important gifts, like examples of royal calligraphy, could serve in place of fabulous wealth, and both Louis and Chŏngjo excelled at this form of cooptation.

Absolute monarchy, then, meant the king's word was final, but it did not mean the ministers were silent, ignored, or powerless. Julian Swann notes that in France "the king was expected to seek counsel before making decisions" and, as discussed earlier, "was restrained by the fundamental laws of the kingdom."[63] Another form of restriction was public opinion, though with quite a different meaning in early modern Eurasia than in the twenty-first-century global community. "[I]n a vast majority of cases [royal policies'] effectiveness depended on the support of public opinion."[64] Of course, here Lossky means by "public" opinion the opinions of those in the public sphere, namely, government officials, nobles, and other political movers and shakers, aptly encapsulated by the Chosŏn equivalent *kongnon*公論, also translated as "public opinion," but perhaps better understood in this context as elite reaction to a given policy. Without favorable public opinion—that is, support from the elite—absolute monarchy could not function.

Still, one may ask, why compare two such vastly different states as seventeenth-century France and eighteenth-century Korea? Perhaps surprisingly—though it really should not be—there are a number of similarities between the two polities. Both countries saw over the course of the sixteenth and seventeenth centuries a drastic change in public views of the relationship between ruler and subject, that is, from the king as a leader among the nobles to the king as both separate from and placed above the nobles. Likewise, by the times of Louis in France and Chŏngjo in Korea, the monarchs "had managed to secure a general recognition that all political authority in their kingdom emanated directly or indirectly from them."[65] Late Chosŏn Korea was uncomfortable with regencies, abdications, and uppity ministers—anything that implied devolvement of power away from the king. The same was true in early modern France, where, William Doyle tells us, "the French liked their kings to rule as well as reign."[66] The French in the seventeenth century considered monarchy superior to republican government, because the king could be above contesting factions and cliques in a way a republic never could. While Yŏngjo may have been the first king to give a name, the Policy of Impartiality, to the balancing of factions—even if he was not always consistent in applying it—he certainly was not the first to carry out such a policy. Though the French king did not have to deal with the hereditary factionalism of late Chosŏn Korea, what was well recognized was "the need for the king of France to be a good juggler." Louis XIV knew that "balanced distribution of his favor was the key to harmony," and "[a]n equilibrium of factions was always the aim," so that no single actor or group of actors monopolized the king's attention—and indeed it may well have been Louis XVI's downfall that he "was unable to preserve an image of impartiality" when mediating between factions, one of the most vital kingly roles.[67]

Similarly, as in Chosŏn, royal favor was the prime requisite for ministerial success. Officials reached the apex of political power when they had the favor of the king and tumbled into death or exile when they lost it. Likewise, "[t]enure of power in the Bourbon monarchy depended to a large extent on the favor of the monarch, and the ability of the holder of power to resist attempts to dislodge that favor."[68] Political conflict in early modern France and Korea was characterized by "tensions within a consensus of shared beliefs rather than between rival value systems."[69] By the seventeenth century, the military prowess and power of individual nobles had been replaced by the paramount importance of influence at court, and the king's conduct was scrutinized for any hint of who was the beneficiary of royal favor and who was on the outs. Thus, while the French king may not have had Chosŏn historians observing and recording his every move, he still had to communicate through subtle innuendoes and hidden meanings to keep the nobles guessing as to whom he favored the most at any given time.[70]

Absolutism, as well, had a similar meaning. Absolute monarchy was not an impudent king riding roughshod over the aristocracy. Instead, "absolute power really rested on a compromise with the families and groups who controlled the key institutions of central and provincial France. In return for the latter's political conformity, the monarchy sustained their material interests through a system of patronage from which both parties benefited."[71] Substituting Korea for France in this quotation makes it apply to early modern Chosŏn as well. In both countries in the centuries under discussion, "many of the royal powers . . . were potential rather than real; everything depended on the skill with which the king played his several appointed roles."[72] Even when ministers made decisions, they did so in the king's name, because "it was royal authority which was invoked and could not be legitimately resisted. In that sense the king's power was absolute."[73] Institutionally, then, there was no legitimate appeal above the king, no higher court or body to which to turn. But like ministers in Chosŏn, French officials could impede the king's will through "patchy enforcement," selective reading, and bogus interpretation, along with delaying implementation of a new policy, as devices to persuade the king to change it.[74]

As early modern societies with increasingly centralized governments, France and Korea were seeing the fruits of the corrosive effects of absolutism and selling of office on hereditary privilege, at least in the long term. Still, in both countries, despite increasing commercialization, there remained a lack of security in merchant enterprises, since the law and the ruling class continued to view land as the basis of wealth and so only provided guarantees of wealth based therein. Thus, "[m]erchants who wished to acquire social status, political influence or simply consolidated their assets invested in office and land."[75] This meant that, in the short term, these solvents did not undermine aristocratic privilege. Like the true *yangban* in Chosŏn, France's "traditional warrior elite soon became committed . . . to active collaboration in upholding royal authority," and those who bought office were, in effect, buying a share of the king's prestige, meaning they had no interest in undermining it.[76] For the true *yangban*, who largely succeeded in excluding from the main halls of power those who purchased *yangban* status, government service remained a cornerstone of this exclusivity, separating them from new men. So the aristocracy never supported a weakening of the monarch to the extent that service at his court lost its prestige. Yet these aristocratic attempts to monopolize the king's attention led both Louis and Chŏngjo to chafe at this restriction and move to expand government service, including attempts to reach outside the high nobility, in order to create a group of supporters who "owed their exalted positions entirely to royal favor."[77] Louis's men were nobles but often *homines novi*, new men from families that had not been nobles a century earlier. As Louis himself tells us, he avoided men of high birth because they usually demanded a share of his authority.[78] In this Louis was more successful than Chŏngjo, who struggled to get even illegitimate sons of the nobles into office. So despite their nature as "absolute" monarchs, both Louis and Chŏngjo had to create space for action within the confines of continued aristocratic privilege. They each recognized the highest nobles as partners in government and so could not take the "tyrannical" step of launching an all-out attack on them and their status. Indeed, for Louis, it was "inconceivable that the social status of the nobility should be diminished,"[79] and in fact his "fastidious emphasis on hierarchy and distinction" only benefited the elite.[80] Likewise, the kings of France and of Chosŏn owned all the land in the realm, and the throne itself was their exclusive provenance, which could not be legitimately contested. However, we must not anachronistically apply twenty-first-century conceptions of ownership onto the early modern period. By "own," it was understood that the king had the duty of preserving the realm and the throne in order pass it on to future generations rather than the modern notion of ownership of property equating to complete control over it. So any new tax or significant raising of an existing tax was always a thorny, perhaps even dangerous, endeavor, since it struck a major source of aristocratic status; and the French state "tried but ultimately failed to get its hands on the wealth of the oligarchic elite," due to the elite's skill at avoiding taxation through underreporting and underassessment of value, devices of wealthy tax evasion familiar to any historian of Chosŏn Korea.[81]

There were important differences in the two polities, of course. The late Chosŏn monarch faced a thoroughly Confucianized court, which meant not only a continuation of the Korean tradition of rule by consultation but a very clear and unbending understanding of who was to be consulted. Thus, ministers of the highest ranks had not only the right to meet the king but the power to *demand* an audience. Strictly speaking this was not a "power," but no king could afford the tremendous loss of face that would ensue by refusing to meet officials of such eminence. Conversely, ministers of the lowest court ranks could not expect to see the king at all, to say nothing of men who did not hold any rank. This led to the retention of numerous sinecures in the state apparatus whose sole purpose was to permit elderly men of prominence to retain a consultative role in decision-making without the bother of actually having to do any work. This contrasts sharply with Louis's France, where ministers had no right to see the king and "the principle had become established that the king of France consulted over his policy with whomsoever he pleased."[82] Score one for French absolutism, but Chŏngjo did have other advantages. The Chosŏn monarch retained undisputed power to appoint and dismiss officials. Following the Chinese example, ministers had no recourse when they were dismissed. The government owed them no severance package, and there was no *official* requirement that they ever be reinstated, to the same office or any other, though prominent men had such social and political clout that it could be difficult to keep them out of office for long without ample justification. The French king, by contrast, had to reimburse an official dismissed from office.[83] Since the funds earned from the sale of offices was a primary motivation for giving men office in the first place, giving them the money back in order to get rid of them was counterproductive.

The *yangban* were remarkable, though, for their ability to maintain a stranglehold on power and influence, both in and outside the state apparatus.

The musical chairs of the Chosŏn government, in which officials rarely held high office for more than a few months, contrasts sharply with France, where Louis could rely on key ministers holding power for decades, in some cases. In addition, the distinction between robe and sword nobles, and even that between established families and those of new men who purchased office (where the stigma of purchase tended to fade away after three generations of nobility),[84] was less rigid than in Korea. There, despite prevalent upward social mobility between slave and commoner and commoner and *yangban* in the eighteenth and nineteenth centuries, the line between the twenty or so top *yangban* lineages and everyone else—commoners, government functionaries, *chung'in*, secondary sons, even lesser *yangban* (including the military officials and their clans)—remained an impassable barrier. Nor did Chosŏn Korea have anything like France's Commerce Council, a governing body on which merchants served that could advise the king. Despite their growing economic importance, Korean merchants saw no appreciable rise in their status in the eighteenth century, and the mere idea of such people serving in government or advising the king was unthinkable.

Another striking difference concerns war. Louis remains well known for his diplomacy, wars, and expansion of his realm, and the French army became much larger in early modern France than it had been before. Chŏngjo fought no wars and led no armies into battle. He did reform and restructure the military in the course of creating and expanding the Robust and Brave Garrison; he did not enlarge it to any significant degree. Indeed, the early modern Korean military was probably smaller than it had been in earlier centuries, dwarfed in comparison to its height during the fifteenth-century campaigns to incorporate the northeastern part of the peninsula into the Korean realm. The diplomacy of Chosŏn consisted not of alliance making and breaking but of placating the two major powers in the region, the Qing Empire and Tokugawa Japan, neither of whom was much interested in Korea in the eighteenth century. Scholars are divided on the relationship between absolutism and the maintenance of great armies: Is absolute monarchy only possible on the back of a large military, or is it the absolute monarch who builds up a large military? The Korean case implies the latter, or at least does not support the former, since Chosŏn did not recover its pre-1600 military strength even as absolute monarchy developed. The Korean case thus supports Hillay Zmora's argument that the "prevailing thesis that early modern war acted as a catalyst of growth of state power" needs to be seriously questioned.[85] As Peter H. Wilson points out, "[w]ar did not automatically favor the growth of absolutism and could also undermine it."[86]

These important differences should not blind us, though, to the remarkable similarities of kingship for Louis XIV and Chŏngjo. Earlier I discussed similarities in early modern kingship in France and Korea, but there are also striking parallels specific to the Sun King and the Lord of the Shining Moon.[87] In France, Pelletier wrote, in reference to nobles falling under royal jurisdiction: "The stars are luminous but this light derives from the Sun which bestows it."[88] Nearly a century later, half a world away, Chŏngjo in the preface introducing his new pen name, wrote: "In myriad streams, there are myriad Moons. Yet there is only one Moon in the sky [川之有萬。月亦如之。若其在天之月。則固一而已矣]."[89] Both men sought to expand their discretion. Though Louis did not use the term specifically, he "was committed to a dynamic concept of monarchy through which he sought to manipulate and extend the conventions within which he ruled."[90] In his instructions to his son and heir, Louis wrote that "[t]rue maxims of state are not immutable, however, for they may change with new circumstances."[91] When we recall Lady Hyegyŏng's quotation of Chŏngjo, "[t]he right way is not unalterably fixed; rather, it changes with circumstances and time," we can see the influence of discretionary thought on the two monarchs.

David Sturdy noted in 1998 that historians of early modern France had neglected the importance of ritual to royal power, and Ronald G. Asch noted in 2014 that understanding ritual is vital for understanding early modern politics and kingship.[92] This is somewhat ironic since this importance had been, to Louis XIV, self-evident. He tells us, "People who think that [courtly rituals] are merely ceremonial affairs are seriously mistaken.... The people over whom we reign are unable to penetrate to the core of things and base their judgements on what they see on the surface...."[93] After all, "elaborate ceremonial was also important across Europe in declaring the legitimacy of monarchy,"[94] and in Louis's France, proper titles and the arrangements of chairs and seating were important enough to spark endless disputes over them in ways that would not be unfamiliar to someone who has read accounts of Confucian experts arguing over proper decorum as described in the *Record of Rites* 禮記 (*Liji*).[95] The centrality of ritual in governance in Confucian polities like Chosŏn hardly needs to be noted. To Confucians, proper observance of ritual is vital to maintaining social order, a sentiment that would not have been alien to Louis, even if he would not have expressed it in quite those terms. Indeed, both Louis and Chŏngjo sought to uphold traditional religious ritual and piety in the face of challenges from foreign religion: Louis to defend Roman Catholicism against Protestantism, Chŏngjo to defend Confucianism against that same Catholicism. Both kings banned the upstart religion in their realms, though Louis's revocation of the

Edict of Nantes was a much more disruptive affair than Chŏngjo's hope-it-will-go-away policy, both because tolerance had allowed the Huguenot community to grow substantially and because Louis himself vigorously pursued the ban. Korean Catholicism in 1800 was nowhere near the numbers it would attain in the second half of the nineteenth century, and Chŏngjo was consequently quite lax in enforcing the ban in spite of Catholic converts' refusal to observe Confucian rituals, not least because Catholics were concentrated in the very Southerner faction that he was laboring to rehabilitate.

Similarities began even in early the two reigns. Neither king had a serious contender to their succession. Chŏngjo was the twenty-second ruler of a dynasty that had ruled continuously (though not without contention) for more than three hundred years, and "[t]he Bourbon monarchy was a sturdy institution in the seventeenth century."[96] They both had good reason to emulate their illustrious grandfathers over their more divisive and morally compromised fathers in their kingship. Each man, perhaps understandably, relied a little too heavily on favorites—Chŏngjo on Hong Kuk-yŏng, Louis XIV on Jean-Baptiste Colbert—leading Louis to instruct his grandson to have no favorites.[97]

Both young kings also had legitimacy issues that haunted them throughout their reigns, and in both cases these issues stemmed from events that struck them as young boys. Chŏngjo, of course, was hounded by the death of his father in the rice chest when he was ten. Louis was thrown into the midst of rebellion from age five until he turned ten, a period known as the Fronde (1658–1653). Each of them learned from their experiences that, as ruler, they could trust no one too far and that the throne must be dominated by no one in order to facilitate the smooth functioning of the state.[98] Both sought to be independent of any other political actor in their domains and strove to achieve that independence, however unrealistic the achievement of that goal was. There were factions in each man's kingdom that believed in royal supremacy and a strengthened kingship. Lossky notes that many in seventeenth-century France believed that "the only way to protect society from depredations by individuals and pressure groups [was] to establish royal absolutism, to make the king independent of any human institution or group."[99] While Southerners like Tasan would not have used a Literary Sinitic equivalent of "royal absolutism"—lacking, as they did, the French explicit conceptual distinction between absolute rule and arbitrary rule, between enlightened despotism and tyranny—similar sentiments can be found in their writings, such as Tasan's praise of the centrality of the king through the Imperial Pivot metaphor, where blocking the king's will is equated to the cosmos itself misbehaving. Both kings worked tirelessly on issues great and small (being an absolute monarch is hard work) to limit opportunities for ministers to control the flow of information, and both learned to avoid favorites, as Louis reminded his grandson in the *Memoirs*.

In both France in the seventeenth century and Korea in the eighteenth, one of the most important duties of the king was the selection of men for office. With increasing centralization and fiscal extraction of wealth for the state—coupled with the weakening of hereditary privilege as a guarantor of high office—the question of staffing the government with the right kind of men was likewise becoming increasingly vital, to the ruler and the aristocracy alike. Both Louis and Chŏngjo, keen observers of their times who were attuned to the political realities they had to grapple with, seized on this point as a site of royal strength. They each portrayed themselves, as king, as the only ones who could be entrusted with this power, because only they could see the true character of people. Louis, who believed his power came directly from God, told his heir that "the art of knowing men" was very important, and he enjoyed figuring out what his ministers were attempting to hide from him, their hidden intentions concealed behind their surface rhetoric.[100] Chŏngjo echoed this sentiment in his *Preface to the Lord of the Myriad Streams and the Shining Moon* 滿川明月主人翁自書 (*Manch'ŏn myŏngwŏl chuinong chasŏ*), when he writes of his ability to discern people's characters.

> I have a lot of experience with men. In the morning they come in [to court] and in the evening go back out, jostling as they come and go. Their looks and complexions differ, as do their eyes and hearts. There are those who have insight and those who are dense, the strong and the mild, the ignorant and the foolish, the narrow-minded and the shallow, the brave and the craven, the clear and the shrewd, the wild and the rash, the square and the round, those who are far from their destinations yet believe they have reached them, those who take the simple as important, the hesitant to speak and the clever in speaking, the stubbornly proud and the alienated, and those who love [their] reputation and those who take their work seriously. There are all these types, and a hundred or a thousand others. From the beginning I have pushed forward with my heart, knowing who to trust.

> [予之所閱人者多矣。朝而入。暮而出。羣羣逐逐。若去若來。形與色異。目與心殊。通者塞者。強者柔者。癡者愚者。狹者淺者。勇者怯者。明者黠者。狂者狷者。方者圓者。疏以達者。簡以重者。訒於言者。巧於給者。峭而亢者。遠而外者。好名者。務實者。區分類別。千百其種。始予推之以吾心。信之以吾意。]

As noted earlier, William Beik has applied the term "conservative innovation" to Louis XIV's reforms, and the term is apt for Chŏngjo as well. Both men thought, or at least claimed, that they were restoring a glorious past, not boldly blazing a new path. Sturdy notes that the social change Louis wanted "was in the direction of restoring an idealized past rather than working towards some unprecedented future," and Chŏngjo tells us, "As for governing, those who do not regard the Three Dynasties [of ancient China] as the heart has taken leave of their senses. Moreover, it is the ruler's shame not to equal [exemplary ancient Chinese rulers] Tang and Yu and to have his ministers constantly divided [爲治不以三代爲心者。蓋自棄也。況恥君不及唐虞。卽亦人臣常分]."[101] Chŏngjo's absolutism was about less seizing new powers than exploiting his existing powers to their utmost, stretching and extending them outward, and the same could be said for Louis as well. (And in fact, Nicholas Henshall has.)[102]

There are limits, after all, to the social changes that can be imposed from the top down,[103] and Louis XVI may have lost his throne in part because of his more radical tendencies, upsetting the Sun King's careful balance that was effective at "absorbing and harmonizing conflict" but not at radical change, particularly in the teeth of entrenched interests.[104] Both also faced a rollback, "an aristocratic reaction that Louis foresaw after his death."[105] Louis had kept the *parlements* apart from Versailles, and their remonstration could only take place *after* a law had been registered. After 1715, these barriers broke down, permitting the *parlements* to block registration of laws and even bringing down ministers who proposed odious laws.[106] In Chŏngjo's case, the Catholic purge of 1801 proved a convenient excuse to eliminate many of his proroyal men, thwarting the late King's attempt to build an independent coalition of officials dependent solely on him for influence. This illustrates once again the conflicting efforts in which Chŏngjo engaged. A coterie of officials dependent on him was left helpless without him and thus was unable to assist his successor.

Early modern rulers in Eurasia were absolute in theory but in practice governed in consultation with other centers of power, who themselves were on board with theoretical absolutism because they shared in the monarch's government and legitimacy. Even in England, where the Whiggish tradition contrasts English limited monarchy with French and German absolutism, at least one scholar has argued that tyranny was not avoided by institutional checks on monarchical power but by moral education of the heir and moral counsel of the reigning king by important councilors. Jacqueline Rose notes that, in early modern England, "counsel . . . was a crucial part of absolutist discourse" for kings who "were *self*-limiting" due to their absolutist core; tyranny could not be legitimately resisted, and a king who violated the law could not have restrictions forced on him.[107]

Like Chǒngjo and his ministers, the Stuart monarchs and their nobles sought (and found) justifications for their respective positions in their Scriptures, for both the Christian Bible and the Confucian canon—being ancient compilations subject to endless interpretation and reinterpretation over nearly two millennia—included strands that supported obedience and resistance, tyranny and wise rule. The English king was also expected to sit through sermons intended to change his behavior, not unlike the Chosǒn royal lectures that Chǒngjo suspended, and ministers insisted that the "channel of speech" was not for their own sake but for the ruler's. Without frank counsel, the king could not avoid being locked into an echo chamber of flattery. Nor could one person know everything there was to know or be free from error, so even the greatest king must have the "collective wisdom" offered by ministerial advice. (Recall O Chae-sun's complaint that Chǒngjo relied too much on his own brilliance.) Free speech was then a duty to an absolute monarch, not a weapon to be used against him, at least in theory. The kings of Chosǒn had to aspire to the highest (dare we say unattainable?) virtue, with the assistance and counsel of his loyal ministers, and so did those of England. Indeed, Charles I's troubles lay not so much in his refusal to implement his ministers' counsel but in his refusal to even pretend to consider it, in his rejection of the very notion of counsel. It was this that crossed the line from "kingship" to "tyranny."[108] Thus, when Andrew Lossky says of the French king that his power and prestige arise from "a skillful combination" of roles "requiring the talents of a juggler, and played with vigor," he could have been talking about Chǒngjo.[109]

CONCLUSION

I take no joy in being a ruler.

[無樂乎為君。]

—King Chŏngjo to his officials, March 14, 1787[1]

THIS EPIGRAM IS A PARAPHRASE OF *ANALECTS* 13.15.[2] INTERESTINGLY, Chŏngjo, like other Chosŏn monarchs who reference this passage, left out the second half of the sentence. The full quotation reads, "I take no joy in being a ruler, except that no one dares to oppose what I say [予無樂乎為君。唯其言而莫予違也]." Since all Chosŏn officials memorized the *Analects* in its entirety as part of their basic education, even if the King did not speak the words of the second clause, they nevertheless hung ominously in the air. Thus absolute monarchy in Chosŏn was established. Chŏngjo constantly walked the line between absolute rule and arbitrary rule, enlightened despotism and tyranny.

The man born Yi San 李祘 ascended the throne of Chosŏn Korea in 1776, under the long shadow of his father's execution on the orders of his grandfather. His mother's family was a rival of his close associate Hong Kuk-yŏng; the court was riven by a faction supporting the execution of his father and a faction vehemently demanding justice for the fallen crown prince, and groups such as secondary sons and northern *yangban* were agitating for their share of influence in the government. The king of Chosŏn was not alone in wielding influence. He had to contend with wealthy aristocrats from illustrious lineages that had been respected and politically dominant since before anyone knew of the royal Yi clan. The same Confucian ideology that he used to demand loyalty and obedience from his ministers could also be used by those ministers to constrain and obstruct his autonomy. But ultimate authority rested in the king, and no institutional checks bound his power. He could not be removed except by coup d'état and rebellion. The Censorate could remonstrate, but it could not compel compliance. The limits to the royal authority were constantly negotiated and contested, reworked and reimagined, according to the shared understanding of the distinction between enlightened rule—with due attention to wise counsel—and arbitrary rule, which was felt to exclude a significant number of legitimate key political actors from the decision-making process. By the eighteenth century, the long peace under Qing suzerainty, the increasing penetration of the central government into the localities, the widespread dissemination of Confucianism among the different social classes, and the notion of Chosŏn as the last bastion of civilization combined to allow a Korean ruler of sufficient skill, drive, and motivation to maximize monarchical power within the Chosŏn polity.

The *yangban* were divided across several factional lines, but using one faction against another could be a bloody business, as Chŏngjo's great-grandfather Sukchong had discovered, and in any case those divisions were rendered irrelevant when it came to any perceived direct threat to the perpetual power of the *yangban* as a whole. The effective absolute ruler understood the political system in which he operated. He sought to actualize his powers, to co-opt rather than crush his ministers, and to enlist their recognition of his rule as absolute rather than arbitrary. Forbidden by tradition from meeting officials privately, Chŏngjo communicated his intentions to bolster his own power to officials who might be sympathetic, while cloaking those intentions from those who would not. Lacking those weapons of his Ming and Qing counterparts—namely, permanent dismissal from office or execution as punishment for mere refusal to carry out the king's orders—Chŏngjo instead made and broke alliances, took advantage of supporters without being beholden to them, and pushed his agenda using the methods available to him: his mastery of the Confucian canon, his shrewd judge of character, and the tragedy of his father's death.

Believing Yŏngjo had been misled into ordering Sado's execution, Chŏngjo was determined to be master of his own fate, and he did not shy away from making this clear in ways that were acceptable in the political world of late Chosŏn. That world was one that had come to terms with Manchu domination of China. In the seventeenth century, Chosŏn largely rejected all things Qing and maintained fierce loyalty to the fallen Ming. A century later, the Qing barbarians were viewed much as the Western barbarians soon would be: culturally inferior but practical and useful. So Chŏngjo was able, in early modern Korea, to portray himself ideologically as the ruler of the last bastion of civilization and the world's ideological center—the Celestial Kingdom relocated east—while also taking advantage of Qing military, technological, and intellectual advancements. He argued that the king was properly the teacher of his officials, placing himself in the superior position. He worked with scholars who took advantage of textual criticism techniques employed in the School of

Evidential Learning to "reconstruct" the classics along the lines of earlier, ruler-centered interpretations, even as he ostensibly condemned that very School. Chŏngjo drew on the long tradition of the ruler's discretion to justify his reliance on his own judgment, to the point that some ministers complained that he was excessively cutting them out of decision making, but he never crossed the line to arbitrariness and tyranny, or at least the most important political actors were never sufficiently convinced that he had.

Chŏngjo was not always successful in persuading his ministers that he knew what was best, especially early on. As a new king whose legitimacy was under scrutiny, he initially relied excessively on a close associate, Hong Kukyŏng, and proved unable to save his half-brother from death. He learned quickly, however, and perceived that his old friend Hong was making an unwise bid for power. Hong was disgraced and politically destroyed, and the King would never put so much trust and power in any one man again. Nor, several years after his half-brother's death, would he permit his other half-brother to face a similar fate. Instead, he "punished" his brother with a minor exile—one that he himself continued to violate, to the consternation of his ministers. As the institutional changes he put in place began to bear fruit—with graduates of the royal selection system and close confidantes from the Royal Library entering high office—the King found it easier to accomplish his goals. Only then could he take more overt steps against aristocratic power by constructing a royal stronghold within striking distance of the capital, protected by a separate army unit, and breaking down the barriers between commoner and slave.

The inheritor of his grandfather's Policy of Impartiality, Chŏngjo altered it in subtle ways to further his own ends. Rather than attempt to balance the two dominant factions of Patriarchs and Disciples, as Yŏngjo had, Chŏngjo expanded the policy to include the politically eclipsed Southerners. It was no longer a matter of balance but of the King's discretion to select whom he would. He did not seek to balance enemy factions but to reconcile them to the view that he himself was their primary concern. This is revealed by his canny manipulation of three key leaders of the Intransigents faction, the group of men most visibly opposed to his royal project. Even a staunch opponent like Sim Hwan-ji could be manipulated by the King. While Sim—no green lad himself when it came to politics—undoubtedly manipulated Chŏngjo as well, it was a small price to pay to have a powerful, if inconsistently reliable, friend in the "enemy" Intransigent faction. Chŏngjo's clandestine correspondence with Sim complicates our understanding of Chosŏn factional politics. Factional identity was more fluid and less straightforward than it was portrayed even at the time, and declared factional affiliation was not always reflected in people's actual behavior. In those cases where Sim could not be counted on, Chŏngjo had other men he could manipulate, not the least of which included other important Intransigents, as he played on that faction's own leadership intrigues. Even Ch'ae Che-gong, perhaps the King's closest, staunchest, and most consistent supporter, could not presume that he was above criticism. Chŏngjo was determined not to allow another Hong Kuk-yŏng, who thought his position so secure that he could become a threat to the King. Both Chŏngjo and Louis XIV were masters at one of the keystones of absolute power, being "extremely successful at baron-management, putting an end to the French aristocratic tradition of open opposition and rebellion," and bringing their respective polities "stability and tranquility [they] had lacked before."[3]

Chŏngjo ran into another problem with the selection secretaries. New to power, he perhaps did not realize why Yŏngjo had abolished their privileged power to recommend their own successors. It did not take long before he realized his error, though it did take some time to correct it. Nevertheless, the Royal Library was set up quickly, though initially it was not obvious what its real purpose was. Over time, as was his general practice, the King slowly built up its influence, by small increments that were not individually objectionable, but that combined over the years to create a formidable institution for the imposition of the royal will. Following on with his rhetoric of the king as teacher, Chŏngjo replaced the royal lectures, in which he was his ministers' student, with the royal selection system, in which he was their teacher. He also labored to expand the pool of talent from which he could recruit men. The Southerner faction was one example, but he reached even wider, to groups that had been neglected not just for a century but for most of the dynasty: sons of concubines and *yangban* from the northern provinces. His efforts to get these men into the civil branch of the government were largely (though not entirely) frustrated, but he did have some success in the military branch, particularly for northmen. These efforts did not continue beyond his reign, perhaps fostering resentment that erupted in the Hong Kyŏng-nae Rebellion.

Chŏngjo also expanded the petition system so that he could take a more direct role in administering justice. Again by increments, he permitted the expansion of situations in which a petition could be submitted, and he made it easier for petitions to reach him by allowing them to be presented to him during processions and having numerous processions in order to provide such opportunities. In addition, he appeared to have been in the process of working to abolish hereditary slavery, to be replaced by the more efficient and more humane system of hired labor. This would have adjusted the law to the realities of the late Chosŏn economy and also improved the military situation by adding thousand of men to the commoner rolls for military duty.

The military was the site of perhaps his most successful reform efforts of those under examination here. As he so often did, Chŏngjo professed filial piety for his father that, while entirely genuine, also provided a pretext to construct a fortress and a new military unit he could use to offset aristocratic military power stemming from its official command of dynastic armies. The Illustrious Fortress was the most advanced in Chosŏn at the time of its construction, reflecting the King's willingness to take advantage of the techniques of the barbarian Qing. Likewise reflecting his general distaste for forced labor, Chŏngjo ordered that hired labor be used to construct the fortress. Aware that building the fortress was a suspicious (and expensive) project, he also took opportunities to win propaganda victories with it, as when he refused his officials' recommendation that he force workers to continue laboring on the project during a famine, instead painting himself as putting aside his personal filial piety on behalf of relieving the people's suffering.

To garrison the Fortress, the King formed a new military unit, the Robust and Brave Regiment. This he placed under the direct command of the magistrate of the Fortress district, removing it from the standard military hierarchy. The importance of this unit is revealed by his first appointment to its command— none other than his closest associate, Ch'ae Che-gong. As in other areas, the King gradually built up the size and strength of the Regiment, at the expense of the five central armies in the capital that were strongholds of aristocratic power. Whether or not Chŏngjo planned to abdicate and move his residence to Suwŏn, the presence of a large army under the control of a royalist magistrate only a day's march from the capital was certainly a powerful new arrow in the King's quiver.

Park Hyunmo has written that Chŏngjo was not a great politician, since he was unable to accomplish the impossible. But perhaps "accomplishing the impossible" is not a reasonable standard to which to hold a political leader, at least an early modern monarch. Perhaps Nicholas Henshall's standard for greatness in reference to the Bourbons is a more apt standard to measure Chŏngjo against: ". . . [S]uccessful exploitation of prerogatives distinguished able monarchs from incapable ones—and the ability to push out the boundaries while minimizing opposition signified a great one."[4] By that definition, Chŏngjo's reign at least was great. The French kings after Louis acting despotically rather than absolutely because they were ineffective at obtaining aristocratic acceptance of the legitimacy of their use of absolute power. Louis XV damaged his legitimacy when he dissolved the *parlements* in 1771. The king had long had this power in theory, but Louis XIV had been astute enough not to actualize it. His successor was not so adept, and Louis XV was forced to reinstate the *parlements* amid a firestorm of protest and united resistance.[5] Likewise, Korea's Kojong (r. 1863–1907), who tolerated official criticism of his father's de facto regency, responded harshly to criticism of his own leadership, provoking a confrontation that resulted in his own loss of face.[6] Absolute monarchy, then, was never about unfettered royal power totally divorced from the cultural and political context of norms, written and unwritten; for all his ministers' kvetching and complaining, no rebellion against Chŏngjo erupted, no coup d'état was launched.

In the comparison between China, Korea, and France in early modernity, it is at first blush perhaps rather surprising that France and Korea shared more in common politically than either did with China, considering the enormous cultural importance of the Middle Kingdom to East Asia. But despite the conscious attempt by the Korean ruling class to adopt Chinese political institutions and to actively participate in the culture of the sinographic cosmopolis,[7] these could not ride roughshod over existing political, social, and cultural forms. Rather, they morphed and adapted to their new context, shaping that context even as they were shaped by it. Korea in the late Chosŏn was not a vast multiethnic, multilingual empire with multiple frontiers, ever expanding and contracting, but a modest peninsular kingdom dominated by one language and one ethnic group with a single salient, but stable, border. A Chinese aristocracy that choked off access to high central government office was a distant memory by Qing times, while Korean and French kings still grappled with theirs. So Confucian absolutism did not, indeed could not, operate identically in both Chosŏn and Qing. On the other hand, France was a large and powerful state by European standards, but the Qing Empire was unimaginably more powerful, and while the parallels are certainly not exact, Korea in the eighteenth century was much more comparable to France in the seventeenth. Just as Louis XIV ruled a state that emerged from at least theoretical subservience to the pope in Rome and so, perhaps, he sought to demonstrate his Catholic credentials, so too did Chŏngjo, whose state had cast off theoretical subservience to the Qing Emperor in Beijing (though tribute missions continued, as they were both economically valuable and realistically impossible to end), strive to legitimize himself with an even stronger commitment to Confucianism.

A testament to the power Chŏngjo centered in himself, after his death his chosen ministers were quickly ousted from their posts and a number of his reforms were rolled back or co-opted by those who had opposed them.

Chŏngjo's son Sunjo was only ten years old when his father died, and so the country was governed by Chŏngsun 貞純王后, the still-living second queen of Yŏngjo. Since Chŏngsun's family was comprised of prominent Intransigent Patriarchs, this group struck immediately, despite Chŏngsun's own attempts to rein in its excesses. Sim Hwan-ji, finally free of his old adversary, was at the vanguard, though he would follow Chŏngjo to the grave a mere two years later. The rhetoric of Chŏngjo's plan to end hereditary slavery in Chosŏn was appropriated in Sunjo's decree to free what were by then an economic liability: government-owned slaves. Further, the resulting loss of central government revenue this emancipation would supposedly generate was made up by disbanding the Robust and Brave Regiment,[8] a major threat to aristocratic power that the Intransigents could not tolerate. The Royal Library lost importance in the political arena, the special powers given to its officials being quickly eliminated. By the 1860s, it was such a shadow of its former self that the Taewŏn'gun removed the royal writings from it and moved them to the Office of the Royal Genealogy 宗親府 (Chongch'inbu).[9] After reaching their high-water mark during Chŏngjo's final years, northern yangban likely felt stymied by the refusal of southern and capital yangban to recognize them as equals and permit them to hold important offices, a strong contributing factor to the Hong Kyŏng-nae Rebellion.

A purge of Catholics immediately followed Chŏngjo's death. Scholars have usually regarded this as resulting from their loss of Chŏngjo's protection,[10] but why was Chŏngjo's protection necessary in the first place, and why was persecution so quick to follow? Many of those persecuted as Catholics were in fact people who Chŏngjo's opponents had failed to remove by other means. The purge was led by Sim Hwan-ji, but it was in collusion with a Southerner, Mok Man-jung, then serving as head of the Censorate. Despite being a Southerner, Mok had been at odds with Ch'ae Che-gong and his supporters,[11] and the purge was his opportunity to eliminate proponents of Ch'ae and, thus, of Chŏngjo. Chŏngjo successfully protected his half-brother Prince Ŭnŏn from all punishment beyond the tamest of exiles. It was only after Chŏngjo's death that Ŭnŏn was caught up in the 1801 purge and executed because of his wife's Catholicism. Similarly, Lady Hyegyŏng's brother Hong Nag-im had been exonerated by Chŏngjo when he was accused of involvement in the plot to put Prince Ŭnjŏn on the throne in 1778. While Chŏngjo had been unable to shield Ŭnjŏn, he did vindicate Hong Nag-im. Almost immediately after Chŏngjo's death, Hong was again accused of a number of crimes, for which his punishment was slight until a probably baseless accusation of Catholicism emerged months, after the initial charges had failed to have much effect. It was only then that Hong could be given distant exile to Cheju Island, followed by execution.[12] Tasan was exiled, Yi Ka-hwan was executed, and Sŏ Yu-rin was exiled and died the following year. Yun Haeng-im, Chŏngjo's confidante in the planned elimination of hereditary slavery, was also executed by his fellow Patriarchs.

Chŏngjo is often blamed for instituting the system of in-law governance, as exemplified by Hong Kuk-yŏng and Kim Cho-sun, the latter being the system's architect.[13] It is worth remembering, though, that Chŏngjo quickly eliminated Hong, and Kim did not reach high office until after Chŏngjo's death. Nor was Kim's rise particularly meteoric, and even if it had been, Tasan's career was also impressive, though he had no family connections to either Chŏngjo or his queen. Certainly Lady Hyegyŏng's clan benefited from her marriage to Sado during Yŏngjo's reign, while the Andong Kim clan did not become especially prominent during Chŏngjo's reign.

Still, even if the in-law governance system could be traced back to Chŏngjo, how much of a black mark is this? Though in-law governance was hated by both contemporaries and later historians, its merits should not be overlooked. Rather than the generational blood-letting of the years of intense factionalism, each in-law family seemed more or less to accept defeat when it failed to secure its position by marrying a girl to the heir apparent, and no heads rolled when one family replaced another, to say nothing of digging up corpses and beheading them and executing men for crimes against other men long dead. The Chosŏn government continued to operate disaster relief measures and administer justice,[14] and the state was no more given over to banditry in the first half of the nineteenth century than at any other time.

Thus, not all of Chŏngjo's achievements were undone. Though its garrison may have gone, portions of the Illustrious Fortress stand today as a part of Chŏngjo's legacy. Two centuries of factional violence were finally brought to an end.[15] The Four Colors remained important in the political arena, but their place as the dominant force was replaced by the comparatively benign and nonviolent in-law governance. The Yi family remained on the throne—surviving the serious Hong Kyŏng-nae Rebellion—and the government continued to operate without major disruption until the modern world crashed on Korean shores in 1876. Tens of thousands of slaves were freed, and even if their economic status was not much improved and their humble origins not quickly forgotten, at least they had some respite from the lowliness of the slave label. The Royal Library remained; though quickly pushed out of real political power, it continued to function in some capacity down to the institution today that bears its name. Just as supporters of Chŏngjo lost out after the death of their patron, the Intransigents did not fare well after the deaths of Sim Hwan-ji and

Queen Dowager Chŏngsun, and in 1804 it was the Expedients who emerged triumphant. Their man Kim Cho-sun orchestrated the beginning of the in-law government that would dominate the political scene until the arrival of the Taewŏn'gun thereon.[16]

The issues surrounding Chŏngjo's reign are too numerous for any one study to address, and this book has raised a number of questions that are beyond its scope to answer. First, as revealed in Chŏngjo's letters to Sim Hwan-ji, despite the cohesiveness of late Chosŏn factions, there remained cleavages even within factions, as men vied for leadership. Studies of power struggles in Chosŏn have focused on struggles between factions, but those within factions have not been widely addressed, especially those that did not lead to splitting into new factions. Second, whether a result of conscious imitation or not, Chŏngjo's creation of the Royal Library is strikingly similar to King Sejong's 世宗 (r. 1418–1450) establishment of the Hall of Worthies, which also served as both a repository of the king's writings and an instrument of royal policy. Though the connection between the two has been noted,[17] it may be fruitful to explore in-depth the different ways the two institutions, separated by nearly four centuries, functioned, along with their "fates." The Hall of Worthies was abolished by Sejo, only to be reestablished later as the Office of Special Advisers, an obstacle to royal autonomy, while the Royal Library persisted but faded into political obscurity. Third, there is the question of what effects the construction of the Illustrious Fortress—built largely by hired rather than coerced labor—and the attending attempt to loosen restrictions on commercial activity in Suwŏn had on both the local and the national economy. Did Suwŏn become a bustling center of trade on a larger scale than was typical of late Chosŏn? Was Chŏngjo's use of hired labor a natural outgrowth of changing economic conditions, or was it instead a driving force behind such change? Fourth, did in-law governance result primarily as a result of Chŏngjo's policies? I have suggested, though by no means demonstrated, that it did not, and further investigation would be needed to build a strong case in either direction. Fifth, this book, focused as it is on the court and to a lesser extent the military, does not explore Chŏngjo's dealings with local government. Here is another area, perhaps, in which the King may have attempted to expand royal autonomy: appointment of local magistrates, collection of taxes, registration of land, registration of men for military service, and so forth. Finally, Chosŏn experienced a relatively sudden and precipitous drop-off in the percentage of its population locked in the bonds of slavery. An institution that shaped Korean society since at least the eleventh century, the eighteenth century saw a fall in the slave population from above 30 percent to much less than 10 percent.[18] Further study is needed of the influence of slavery on the political and legal history of Chosŏn Korea in a comparative perspective to both the rest of East Asia, and to slave-holding in other regions and their vastly different cultural and geopolitical contexts, such as Europe and the Islamic world. A state governing a population so heavily reliant on slave labor for so long must be profoundly affected by this state of affairs in ways that scholars have scarcely conceived, and more comparative work is sorely needed to investigate these influences.

This book also suggests larger comparative issues that might be addressed by future research. Why does there seem to be an ever-tightening monopolizing of high office in Western and Central Europe and Korea, but seemingly not in China? In addition, a comparative study of the petition systems in place in China, Korea, and Joseph's Austria would shed light on this almost totally unexplored area. Finally, taking account of recent work by Hyeok Hweon Kang and others on military technology in East Asia, the question of the relationship between expanding military power and absolutism deserves further attention. There is a strong possibility that only through sustained comparative work can we hope to answer these questions.

In the end, we are left much where we started with King Chŏngjo, a man who was in many ways a contradiction. He built a fortress that has stood for two hundred years yet was obsolete within fifty—a stronghold that never served to protect the country even when the state most needed to fight the Japanese. His new military unit was disbanded to make up for the loss of slaves that had probably been more expensive to maintain than their labor was worth. His father was fully rehabilitated one hundred years after his death, barely ten years before the family would lose its throne altogether. His son issued in his name a decree that harshly punished the Catholics that he himself had taken pains to shield from harsh punishment, and men like Tasan who had supported him were laid low as Catholics, whether they were or not. He labored under his father's long shadow while becoming in many ways the man Yŏngjo had wanted Sado to be.

If Chŏngjo had two major political goals—to maximize royal action and to maintain it beyond his own reign—we might say that he succeeded in the first but failed in the second. As long as Chŏngjo himself was alive and dedicated his considerable intellect and indefatigable energy toward playing the game of thrones—expounding on Confucian rhetoric; cajoling, manipulating, and intimidating his officials; making dozens of processions; and responding to thousands of memorials and petitions—he could create a space for himself to operate with some degree of freedom. But his efforts to build institutions that would perpetuate his own power into future generations did not succeed.

It is tempting to speculate that if he had lived another twenty years—or even ten—allowing his son to take the throne at such an age that he could rule in fact as well as in name, then Sunjo might have been able to prevent the roll-back of his father's policies and keep the new institutions in place long enough that bureaucratic inertia could make them hard to dislodge. Indeed, even if Sunjo himself were a mediocre monarch, perhaps all that was needed was an adult ruler of sound mind to hold the line until the weight of time could root those institutions in place. But Sunjo was but a boy of ten, who probably had no idea what his father's intentions had really been, any more than Chŏngjo himself, also a boy of ten when he lost his father, had understood Sado's insanity. Queen Chŏngsun faced the extraordinary constraints of serving as regent rather than as sitting ruler, the Chosŏn prejudice against her gender, and her family's strong links to opponents of Chŏngjo. It is no surprise that neither she nor Sunjo was able to stop the dismantling of Chŏngjo's system, even if they had recognized what it was and desired to save it, and there is little indication that they did either. Like Louis XV and his ministers, who could not maintain Louis's highly personalized system, Chŏngjo left behind a legacy that no one but Chŏngjo could thrive in.[19]

Thus, we are left with the final contradiction. Chŏngjo, a king who built institutions to strengthen royal power, failed to provide perhaps the most basic source of royal strength in the early modern world, when power as yet resided more in men than in institutions: an adult heir to succeed him. If Chŏngjo, like James K. Polk after him, worked so hard at governing that he condemned himself to an early grave, then his two goals were fundamentally in conflict, and he could never have accomplished them both. Perhaps that is the simplest way to describe King Chŏngjo: The light that burns twice as bright burns half as long.

NOTES

INTRODUCTION

1. *Chŏngjo sillok*, 1776.10.10.[1]

2. In the diary, Yi Kwanghyŏn claims to have been serving as recorder on the day Sado was sealed in the rice chest and provides his eyewitness account of the day's events. For a discussion of the document's authenticity and a translation of the relevant section, see JaHyun Kim Haboush, *The Confucian Kingship in Korea* (New York: Columbia University Press, 2001), 219–320 and 251–53.

3. The 2005 *New History of Korea* (*Saeroun Han'guksa*) by Yun, Pak, and Yi, despite purporting to be a "new" history, free from the domination of Japanese colonial historiography, simply gives standard nationalist responses to colonialist claims about Chosŏn, which are themselves based on colonial assumptions. With chapter titles like "Minjung Ŭisik ŭi Hwakdae (Expansion of Mass Consciousness)," the colonial model of "feudal" Chosŏn is turned on its head to show that Korea was on the verge of becoming a modern capitalist state rather than attempting to understand the dynasty on its own terms.

4. Gregory Henderson and Key P. Yang. "Outline History of Korean Confucianism, Part I: The Early Period and Yi Factionalism," *Journal of Asian Studies* 18, no. 1 (1958): 94.

5. Gregory Henderson, "Chŏng Ta-san: A Study in Korea's Intellectual History," *Journal of Asian Studies* 16, no. 3 (1957): 379. Emphasis added.

6. Ki-baik Lee, *A New History of Korea* (Cambridge: Harvard University Press, 1984), 239–40.

---

1   Although I am using solar-calendar dating in the text for clarity, primary sources are dated according to the lunar calendar, so I have chosen to use the accurate lunar dating system in citations. Due to discordance between lunar and solar dating systems, these dates may appear mismatched but are indeed accurate.

7. Lee Song-Mu, "On the Causes of Factional Strife in Late Chosŏn," in *Korean Studies: New Pacific Currents*, ed. Dae-Sook Suh (Honolulu: University of Hawaii Press, 1994).

8. Sohn, Pokee, *Social History of the Early Chosŏn Dynasty: The Functional Aspects of Governmental Structure* (Seoul: Jisik-saṅup, 2000), esp. ch. II.

9. Park Hyunmo, *Chŏngch'i ka Chŏngjo* (Seoul: P'urŭn Yŏksa, 2001), 8. Yi Tae-Jin makes a similar point in "Chosŏn wangjo yugyo jŏngch'i wa wanggwŏn," *Han'guk saron*: 23, 216.

10. Compare James Palais's realist view of Song Si-yŏl's position on the Ritual Controversies (1659/1674) in his chapter of *Political Leadership in Korea* (1976) with JaHyun Kim Haboush's realist/ideological view of the same in her chapter of *Culture and State in Late Chosŏn Korea* (1999).

11. This is a theme in each of these authors' chapters in *Culture and State in Late Chosŏn Korea* (1999).

12. Kim Paekchol, "1990 nyŏndae Han'guk sahoe ŭi 'Chŏngjo sindŭrom' taedu wa paekyŏng," *Kukhak yŏn'gu* 18 (2011): 187-230.

13. "Democratic consciousness" is discussed on page 203 in the context of the King looking out for the common people against the depredations of the aristocracy. The reference to maximizing autocracy appears on page 60.

14. Song Ki-ch'ul, *T'onghap ŭi chŏngch'i ka Yi San* (Seoul: Kukhak charyowŏn, 2012).

15. Yi Tae-Jin. "Ch'aek mŏri e," in *Chosŏn hugi t'angp'yŏng chŏngchi ŭi chaejomyŏng*, ed. Yi Tae-Jin and Kim Paekchol, 9.

16. Kim Ki-bong, "T'aeyang'wang kwa manch'ŏn myŏng'wŏl chuin'ong—Lui 14se kwa Chŏngjo," in *Chŏngjo wa 18 segi*, ed. Yŏksa hakhoe, 304.

17. Ch'ae Che-gong explained democracy to the King this way: "When I say [Westerners] have no ruler, I mean that it is the custom in their countries that they, originally having no ruler, select an outstanding person from amongst the common people and set him up as ruler. This leads to the most extreme brutality [無君云者其國俗。本無君長。 擇於凡民中純陽者。立以爲君云。尤極凶惡]." *Chŏngjo sillok*, 1791.10.25.

18. Chŏng Ch'ae-hun, "18 segi kukka unyŏng ŭi chaechŏngbi," in *Chŏngjo wa Chŏngjo sidae* (Seoul: Seoul National University Press, 2011); Park Hyunmo, *Chŏngch'i ka Chŏngjo*; Yi Tae-Jin, "Chŏngjo: Yugyojŏk kyemong chŏldae kunju," *Hanguksa simin kangjwa* 13; Yi Han-u, *Chŏngjo: Chosŏn ŭi hon i chida.* (Seoul: Haenaem, 2007); Yu Pong-hak, *Kaehyŏk kwa kaltŭng ŭi sidae: Chŏngjo wa 19-segi* (Sŏngnam: Sin'gu Munhwasa, 2009.) Park focuses on Chŏngjo's response to political changes, while Yu emphasizes social and economic change.

19. Dee, *Expansion and Crisis*, 177. Dee is commenting on Louis XIV and French society, but I contend the statement also applies to Chŏngjo and Korean society.

20. Peter H. Wilson. *Absolutism in Central Europe*, 59.

21. *Chŏngjo sillok*, 1782.5.26.

22. John B. Duncan. "Proto-nationalism in Premodern Korea," in *Perspectives on Korea*, ed. Lee, Sang-oak and Duk-Soo Park (Sydney: Wild Peony Press, 1998, 199–221); Alexander Woodside, *Lost Modernities: China, Vietnam, Korea and the Hazards of World History* (Cambridge: Harvard University Press, 2006).

23. Chŏngjo, *Chŏngjo ŏch'al'ch'ŏp*, 224, 1797.10.20. The reply he refers to can be found in the *Annals* entry for that day.

24. Doyle, *Old Regime France*, 193.

25. Page x of the preface to the paperback edition of *The Confucian Kingship in Korea*. Francis Oakley in 2006 called for more attention on European kingship as well. See Francis Oakley, *Kingship: The Politics of Enchantment* (Malden: Blackwell, 2006), 4.

26. To choose just two examples, the dynastic founder is described in a certain battle as firing a number of arrows, *all* of which were successful headshots without a single miss. The same record also has him shooting a single arrow that killed one deer, passing through its body to kill not just one but *two* more, and killing five birds with one arrow. See Baker, "Rhetoric, Ritual, and Political Legitimacy," 158–59. A second fine example was pointed out by an anonymous reviewer of this manuscript: The *Veritable Records* claim on April 13, 1453 that eight elephants were so frightened at the mere sight of the future King Sejo that they retreated before him. *Tanjong sillok*, 1453.2.26.

CHAPTER 1

1. Wilson, *Absolutism in Central Europe*, 90.

2. Victor Lieberman, "Introduction: Eurasian Variants," in *Beyond Binary Histories: Re-imagining Asia to c. 1830*, ed. Victor Liebermanan (Ann Arbor: University of Michigan Press), 14.

3. See (in roughly Lieberman's order): Seonmin Kim, "Ginseng and Border Trespassing Between Qing China and Chosŏn Korea," *Late Imperial China* 28, no. 1 (2007), 33–61; Tonio Andrade, Hyeok Hweon Kang, and Kirsten Cooper, "A Korean Military Revolution? Parallel Military Innovations in East Asia and Europe," *Journal of World History* 25, no.1 (2014), 51–84; Hyeok Hweon Kang, "Big Heads and Buddhist Demons: The Korean Musketry

Revolution and the Northern Expeditions of 1654 and 1658," *Journal of Chinese Military History* 2 (2013), 127-89; Alexander Woodside, *Lost Modernities*, Cambridge: Harvard University Press, 2006; James B. Palais, *Confucian Statecraft and Korean Institutions: Yu Hyŏngwŏn and the Late Chosŏn Dynasty* (Seattle: University of Washington Press, 1996), 980-89; Eugene Y. Park. *Between Dreams and Realty: The Military Examination in Late Chosŏn Korea* (Cambridge: Harvard University Press, 2007); Eugene Y. Park, *A Family of No Prominence: The Descendants of Pak Tŏkhwa and the Birth of Modern Korea* (Stanford University Press, 2014); Emanuel Yi Pastreich, "The Transmission and Translation of Chinese Vernacular Narrative in Chosŏn Korea: Han'gŭl Translations and Gentry Women's Literature," *Korean Studies* 39 (2015), 75-105; Duncan, "Proto-nationalism in Premodern Korea"; Anders Karlsson, "Confucian Ideology and Legal Developments in Choson Korea: A Methodological Essay," in *The Spirit of Korean Law: Korean Legal History in Context*, ed. Marie Seong-Hak Kim (Boston: Brill, 2016), 97-98; Han Sang-kwŏn, "Chosŏn sidae ŭi kyohwa wa hyŏngjŏng," *Yŏksa wa hyŏnsil* 79 (2011): 271-303.

4. Duncan, "Proto-nationalism in Premodern Korea"; Haboush. *Confucian Kingship*, 261n86; Karlsson, "Confucian Ideology and Legal Developments," 97.

5. Duncan, "Historical Memories of Koguryŏ," Haboush, *Confucian Kingship*, 25-26; Yi Song-mi, *Korean Landscape Painting: Continuity and Innovation through the Ages* (Elizabeth: Hollym, 2006), ch. 5.

6. Duncan, "Proto-nationalism in Premodern Korea"; Park, *Between Dreams and Reality*.

7. Subrahmanyam, "Connected Histories," 745.

8. Starn, "The Early Modern Muddle," 299.

9. Stanley, "Maidservants' Tales," 455, 460.

10. Stanley, "Maidservants' Tales," 447.

11. Stanley. "Maidservants' Tales," 441, 459.

12. Stanley, "Maidservants' Tales," 458.

13. Starn, "The Early Modern Muddle," 303.

14. Mary Elizabeth Berry, "Defining 'Early Modern,' " *Japan Emerging: Premodern History to 1850*, ed. Karl F. Friday (Boulder: Westview Press, 2012), 43.

15. Zmora, *Monarchy, Aristocracy, and the State*, 2.

16. Zmora, *Monarchy, Aristocracy, and the State*, 4-5, 25, 29.

17. Wilson, *Absolutism in Central Europe*, 64.

18. Sixiang Wang, "The Sounds of Our Country: Interpreters, Linguistic Knowledge, and the Politics of Language in Early Chosŏn Korea," in *Rethinking*

East Asian Languages, Vernaculars, and Literacies, 1000–1919, ed. Benjamin A. Elman (Leiden: Brill, 2014), 58–95.

19. Martina Deuchler, *The Confucian Transformation of Korea: A Study of Society and Ideology* (Cambridge: Harvard University Press, 1992); Duncan, "Proto-nationalism in Premodern Korea," esp. 210–14.

20. Zmora, *Monarchy, Aristocracy, and the State*, 65.

21. Zmora, *Monarchy, Aristocracy, and the State*, 5, 19–20, 26–28, 43–44, 80–82.

22. Haboush, *Confucian Kingship*, 141–42.

23. Scott, "Introduction: The Problem of Enlightened Absolutism," in *Enlightened Absolutism*, 1.

24. Nicholas Henshall, "Early Modern Absolutism 1550–1700: Political Reality or Propaganda?" in *Der Absolutismus—ein Mythos? Strukturwandel monarchischer Herrschaft in West- und Mitteleuropa (ca. 1550–1700)*, ed. Ronald G. Asch and Heinz Duchardt (Köhn: Böhlau, 1996), 52; Dee, *Expansion and Crisis*, 177.

25. Wilson, *Absolutism in Central Europe*, 113.

26. Rappaport, "France," in *A Companion to Eighteenth-Century Europe*, 341.

27. Dee, Expansion and Crisis, 5.

28. Cuttica and Burgess, "Introduction," in *Monarchism and Absolutism*, 1–5; James B. Collins also notes that "surprisingly few" scholars have attempted to define absolutism. See *The State in Early Modern France*, xiv.

29. Johann P. Sommerville, "Early Modern Absolutism in Practice and Theory," in *Monarchism and Absolutism*, 119–20, 129.

30. Beales, *Enlightenment and Reform in Eighteenth-Century Europe*, 263.

31. Beales, *Enlightenment and Reform in Eighteenth-Century Europe*, 264.

32. Chen Xunwu, "A Rethinking of Confucian Rationality," *Journal of Chinese Philosophy* 25, no. 4 (1998), 483–504.

33. Beales, *Enlightenment and Reform in Eighteenth-Century Europe*, 41.

34. Lossky, "The Absolutism of Louis XIV," 2.

35. Wilson, *Absolutism in Central Europe*, 122.

36. Qtd. in Lossky, "The Absolutism of Louis XIV," 13.

37. Qtd. in Collins, *The State in Early Modern France*, 88.

38. Beik, "The Absolutism of Louis XIV," 195.

39. Collins, *The State in Early Modern France*, xvii.

40. Wilson, *Absolutism in Central Europe*, 54.

41. Wilson, *Absolutism in Central Europe*, 48.

42. Ronald G. Asch, *Sacral Kingship Between Disenchantment and Re-enchantment: The French and English Monarchies, 1587–1688* (New York: Berghahn, 2014), 7.

43. Haboush, *Confucian Kingship*, 9-10, 15.

44. Asch, *Sacral Kingship between Disenchantment and Re-enchantment*, 123; Haboush, *Confucian Kingship*, 15-17.

45. Fukuyama, *The Origins of Political Order*, 426.

46. Fukuyama, *The Origins of Political Order*, 305.

47. Fukuyama, *The Origins of Political Order*, 334.

48. Palais, *Politics and Policy*, 61-67.

49. Fukuyama, *The Origins of Political Order*, 337. For a contrary view, see Wilson. *Absolutism in Central Europe*, 13. Wilson, despite having no problem applying the concept of absolutism, originating in the study of Western Europe, to Central Europe, objects to stretching it beyond its breaking point by applying it to China, where it is "misused simply as a byword for political centralization." Unfortunately, Wilson does not offer an argument or any evidence for this intriguing claim.

50. Asch, "Absolutism and Royal Government," in *A Companion to Eighteenth-Century Europe*, 454-56; Collins, *The State in Early Modern France*, 238.

51. Asch, "Absolutism and Royal Government, in *A Companion to Eighteenth-Century Europe*, 457. For a dissenting view, that Louis XIV acted most like an absolutist in the financial sector, see Dee, *Expansion and Crisis*, 177.

52. Asch, "Absolutism and Royal Government," in *A Companion to Eighteenth-Century Europe*, 451, 459.

53. Palais, *Confucian Statecraft and Korean Institutions*, 988-89.

54. Zmora, Monarchy, *Aristocracy, and the State*, 95-96.

55. Elmarsafy, *Freedom, Slavery, and Absolutism*, 19.

56. Peter H. Wilson, "Military Culture and the Reich, c.1680-1806," in *Cultures of Power in Europe*, 40; Wilson, *Absolutism in Central Europe*, 50-52. See also Henshall. *The Myth of Absolutism*, 24, where absolutism increases with the emphasis on the monarch's unique ability to choose among competing claims.

57. Elmarsaf, *Freedom, Slavery, and Absolutism*, 17.

58. Collins, *The State in Early Modern France*, 88.

59. Zmora, *Monarchy, Aristocracy, and the State*, 6.

60. Wilson, *Absolutism in Central Europe*, 3.

61. Wilson, *Absolutism in Central Europe*, 77; See also Zmora. *Monarchy, Aristocracy, and the State*, 4-5.

62. Beales, *Enlightenment and Reform in Eighteenth-Century Europe*, 170-73; Shaw. Legal Norms, 90-92, 97-99, 106-8.

63. Richardson, *Renaissance Monarchy*, 2.

64. Wilson, *Absolutism in Central Europe*, 32-33.

65. Price. "The Court Nobility and the Origins of the French Revolution," in *Cultures of Power in Europe*, 271.

66. Dee, *Expansion and Crisis*, 8.

67. Dee, *Expansion and Crisis*, 8.

68. Dee, *Expansion and Crisis*, 178.

69. Dee, *Expansion and Crisis*, 126-27.

70. Zmora, *Monarchy, Aristocracy, and the State*, 90.

71. Dee, *Expansion and Crisis*, 13. For the argument that Chŏngjo had no master plan, see Park Hyunmo, *Chŏngch'iga Chŏngjo*.

72. Zmora, *Monarchy, Aristocracy, and the State*, 5.

73. Lossky, *Louis XIV and the French Monarchy*, 37.

74. Henshall, *The Myth of Absolutism*, 4.

75. Lossky, "The Absolutism of Louis XIV," 11; see also Henshall. "The Myth of Absolutism," 11-12. On Qianlong, see Kahn. *Monarchy in the Emperor's Eyes*, 9.

76. Beik, "The Absolutism of Louis XIV," 214, 223.

77. Lossky. "The Absolutism of Louis XIV," 6.

78. Dee, *Expansion and Crisis*, 179.

79. Collins, *The State in Early Modern France*, 195-97. Chŏngjo did not even begin the building of the Illustrious Fortress until he had been on the throne for two decades.

CHAPTER 2

1. *Chŏngjo sillok*, 1776.9.22.

2. John B. Duncan, *The Origins of the Chosŏn Dynasty* (Seattle: University of Washington Press, 2000).

3. James Palais was the most prominent advocate of this "hybrid" model. See, among others, "Confucianism and the Aristocratic/Bureaucratic Balance in Korea," *Harvard Journal of Asiatic Studies* 44, no. 2 (1984): 427-68.

4. Lee Song-Mu, "Kwagŏ System and Its Characteristics: Centering on the Koryŏ and Early Chosŏn Periods," *Korea Journal* 21, no. 7 (1981): 12-13.

5. Deuchler, " 'Heaven Does Not Discriminate,' " 140-41.

6. Collins, *The State in Early Modern France*, 207.

7. Park, *A Family of No Prominence*; Palais. *Confucian Statecraft and Korean Institutions*, 208-71.

8. Park, *Between Dreams and Realty: The Military Examination in Late Chosŏn*.

9. Collins, *The State in Early Modern France*, 172.

10. Scott, "The Nobility," in *A Companion to Eighteenth-Century Europe*, 97.

11. Scott, "The Nobility," in *A Companion to Eighteenth-Century Europe*, 98.

12. This section is largely drawn from the work of James Palais. See *Politics and Policy in Traditional Korea* and *Confucian Statecraft and Korean Institutions*. The different factions' degree of openness to new ideas is discussed extensively in Mark Setton's *Chŏng Yagyong*.

13. Collins, *The State in Early Modern France*, 130–31; Palais, "Political Leadership," 15; Rappaport, "France," in *A Companion to Eighteenth-Century Europe*, 340–41.

14. Nicolas Tackett, *The Destruction of the Medieval Chinese Aristocracy* (Cambridge: Harvard University Press, 2014).

15. *Chungjong sillok*, 1539.10.7. "*Sajok*" 士族 is a Korean term for a noble family.

16. Palais, "Confucianism and the Aristocratic/Bureaucratic Balance in Korea," 448–55.

17. Collins, *The State in Early Modern France*, 207–8; Zmora, *Monarchy, Aristocracy, and the State*, 36.

18. Duncan, *Origins of the Chosŏn Dynasty* (Seattle: University of Washington Press, 2000); Park. *Between Dreams and Reality*.

19. For a recent discussion of Chosŏn factionalism, see Lee Song-Mu, *Chosŏn sidae tangjaengsa* (Seoul: Tongbang midiŏ, 2000).

20. Palais, *Politics and Policy*, 8.

21. Fukuyama, *The Origins of Political Order*, 455.

22. Zmora, *Monarchy, Aristocracy, and the State*, 43.

23. Asch, "Absolutism and Royal Government," in *A Companion to Eighteenth-Century Europe*, 454.

24. Beales, *Enlightenment and Reform in Eighteenth-Century Europe*, 9.

25. Park, *Between Dreams and Reality*, 179.

26. Fukuyama, *The Origins of Political Order*, 352.

27. Zmora, *Monarchy, Aristocracy, and the State*, 97; Collins, *The State in Early Modern France*, 194.

28. Orr, "Dynasticism and the World of the Court," in *A Companion to Eighteenth-Century Europe*, 437.

29. Andrew David Jackson, *The 1728 Musin Rebellion: Politics and Plotting in Eighteenth-Century Korea* (Honolulu: University of Hawaii Press, 2016), 119–20.

30. Some qualification is in order here. It is true that the Hongwu Emperor never granted full investiture to the King T'aejo, the founder of Chosŏn, and later Ming emperors delayed granting investiture to Sejo and Chungjong because each came to the throne after their predecessor had been overthrown.

Still, both Sejo and Chungjong were both invested, and it is likely that T'aejo would have as well if he had continued to reign after Hongwu's death, if his successor Yongle's hasty investiture of T'aejo's son is any indication. Ming emperors occasionally hesitated to recognize the Chosŏn when there appeared to be shenanigans going on, but they never actively supported one candidate over another and eventually accepted the choice of the Korean elite in every case.

31. On the lunar calendar, 1800.5.5.

32. Martina Deuchler, " 'Heaven Does Not Discriminate': A Study of Secondary Sons in Chosŏn Korea," *Journal of Korean Studies* 6 (1988–89): 121–63; Haboush, *Confucian Kingship*, 53–63, 94–95.

33. For a full discussion of the rebellion's effects on Yŏngjo, see Haboush, *Confucian Kingship*, esp. 136–42.

34. For the former view, see Sŏng Nakhun, "Han'guk tangjaengsa," in *Han'guk munhwasa taegye*, 2, 378–80; Lee Song-Mu. *Chosŏn sidae tangjaengsa*, 2, 188–93. For the latter, see Haboush, *Confucian Kingship*, ch. 5.

35. To the objection that the testimony of women was not valued in Chosŏn, it will be remembered that the sources—including the *Annals*—agree that Yŏngjo executed his own son due to the testimony of Lady Sŏnhŭi, a woman.

36. Haboush, *Confucian Kingship*, 208–9.

37. Because the adoption meant she was no longer the King's legal mother, Lady Hyegyŏng could not properly accept gifts inside the city gates.

38. *Chŏngjo sillok*, 1776.3.10.

39. *Chŏngjo sillok*, 1776.3.20.

40. *Chŏngjo sillok*, 1776.3.19.

41. Lady Hyegyŏng, *Memoirs*, 203.

42. *Chŏngjo sillok*, 1794.1.20.

43. A temporary hut for an outdoor funeral to protect against rain and sunlight.

44. *Chŏngjo*, 1789.8.12.

45. *Chŏngjo sillok*, 1789.8.20.

46. *Chŏngjo sillok*, 1794.1.1.

47. Choi Seong-hwan, "Chŏngjo ŭi ŭiri t'angp'yŏng kwa Noron pyŏkp'a ŭi taehŭng," *passim*, but esp. 339, 383.

48. Kim Sung-Yun, "T'angpyŏng and Hwasŏng," 146–48.

49. *Chŏngjo sillok*, 1776.3.30, 1777.8.23.

50. *Chŏngjo sillok*, 1776.3.30, 1776.4.2, and 1777.8.23. Hong Kye-hŭi's grandson Hong Sang-bŏm and some of his relatives were killed after they were implicated in a plot to assassinate Chŏngjo, not for the Sado affair.

51. *Chŏngjo sillok*, 1776.4.2.

52. One may wonder why Lady Hyegyŏng did not make this clear to her son, as she attempts to do for her grandson in her 1805 memoir detailing Sado's madness. One possibility is that, as JaHyun Kim Haboush carefully documents in her English translation of the *Memoirs*, Hyegyŏng was extremely reluctant to discuss Sado's illness, and indeed the first three memoirs refer to it elliptically; only the fourth and final memoir brings out the horrific details. If Hyegyŏng so struggled to share these details with Sunjo, who was born long after Sado was dead, how much more difficult would it have been to discuss them with Chŏngjo? Another possibility is that Chŏngjo did not want to understand, and Hyegyŏng either recognized this and so did not share what she knew, or did share and was ignored. As we saw, Chŏngjo had certain records regarding his father, likely symptoms of his madness, expunged. He was certainly capable of eliminating information that he did not like.

CHAPTER 3

1. *Louis XIV and the French Monarchy*, viii, 182.

2. See, among others, Chaibong Hahm and Wooyeal Paik, "Legalistic Confucianism and Economic Development in East Asia," *Journal of East Asian Studies* 3, no. 3 (2003): 461-91; David Ackerman, Jing Hu, and Liyuan Wei, "Confucius, Cars, and Big Government: Impact of Government Involvement in Business on Consumer Perceptions under Confucianism," *Journal of Business Ethics* 88, no. 3 (2009): 473-82; Ming-Yih Liang. "Confucianism and the East Asian Miracle," *American Economic Journal: Macroeconomics* 2, no. 3 (2010): 206-34. For a contrary view (that authoritarianism in Singapore is not primarily due to Confucianism), see Neil A. Englehart, "Rights and Culture in the Asian Values Argument: The Rise and Fall of Confucian Ethics in Singapore," *Human Rights Quarterly* 22, no. 2 (2000): 548-68.

3. A recent example of the latter can be found in Brooke A. Ackerly, "Is Liberalism the Only Way toward Democracy? Confucianism and Democracy," *Political Theory* 33, no. 4 (2005): 547-76.

4. Collins, *The State in Early Modern France*, 101.

5. Haboush, "Constructing the Center," in *Culture and State in Late Chosŏn Korea*, 68-70; Yamauchi Koichi, "Chōsen o motte tenka ni ō tarashimu— Gakushūin daigauzō *Kija p'alchoji* ni miru zaiya Rorōn chishiki-jin no yume," *Tōyō gakuhō* 84, no. 3 (2002): 1-31. Haboush compares the Korean devotion to Confucianism as compared with China to Liah Greenfield's assertion that

the "French were more Catholic than the Pope." She points out that the Korean nationalization of Confucianism was even more pronounced than the French nationalization of Catholicism since the French kings contested the popes' authority but not their very legitimacy, while Korean intellectuals rejected the Manchus' legitimacy as representatives of Confucianism. She quotes King Yŏngjo saying that China "exude[s] the stenches of the barbarians," and so Korea was left alone as the only remaining civilization.

6. Haboush and Deuchler, eds., *Culture and State in Late Chosŏn Korea*; Jung Ok-ja. "New Approaches to the History of Ideas," *Seoul Journal of Korean Studies* 5 (1992): 152-70; Keum Jang-tae, *Confucianism and Korean Thoughts*; Lee Kyungku, "The *Horak* Debate"; Lovins, "The King's Reason"; Setton, *Chŏng Yagyong*, 3-15.

7. The Xia (legendary), Shang (c. 1600-1046 BC), and Zhou (1046-256 BC) dynasties of ancient China, regarded as a golden age in traditional times.

8. Qin (221-206 BC) and Han (206 BC–AD 220) are the beginning of "imperial China," when the First Emperor (r. 220-210 BC) brought most of the Chinese heartland under his control and coined the term *emperor* 皇帝 (*huangdi*). The Han dynasty was traditionally well-regarded, since China was united, but still far below the glory days of the Three Dynasties.

9. Chŏngjo, *Hongjae chŏnsŏ*, 165; "Ildŭngnok," 5; "Munhak," 5. The *Ildŭngnok* 日得錄 is a record of the discussions the King held with officials of the Royal Library from 1781 to 1787. Contained in Chŏngjo's *Complete Works*, they are undated and grouped by subject, so it is difficult to pinpoint exactly when each discussion occurred. Still, their six-year representation of Chŏngjo's views agrees well with other sources.

10. *Chŏngjo sillok*, 1797.6.11.

11. *Yŏnsan'gun ilgi*, 1505.1.4; 1505.1.10; Sohn, *Social History*, 43; Edward Wagner, *The Literati Purges*, 16.

12. JaHyun Kim Haboush, "Confucian Rhetoric and Ritual," 39-62.

13. I have chosen to translate *ch'ŏnha* 天下 (lit. "All-under-Heaven") as "the realm" throughout this manuscript. I believe this better captures its ambiguous meaning of "the area over which the ruler's influence extends," rather than more modern terms such as *the world* or *the empire*.

14. Chŏngjo, *Hongjae chŏnsŏ*, "Ildŭngnok"; "Hun'ŏ," 4.

15. Jung Jae-hoon, "Eighteenth-Century *Yŏnhaeng*," 67.

16. Chŏngjo, *Hongjae chŏnsŏ*, 162; "Ildŭngnok," 3; "Munhak," 2 and 3.

17. Chŏngjo, *Hongjae chŏnsŏ*, 161; "Ildŭngnok," 1; "Munhak," 1.

18. Lovins, "Making Sense of the Imperial Pivot."

19. Kim Moon-sik, *Chŏngjo ŭi kyŏnghak kwa chujahak*, 18-20, 111, 120 (table 7); Kim Moon-sik, *Chŏngjo ŭi chewanghak*, 252-54; Paek Min-jŏng, "Chŏngjo ŭi sadaebu insik kwa chŏngch'i ch'ŏrhakchŏk ipjang yŏngu"; Park Hyunmo, *Chŏngch'i ka Chŏngjo*, 99.

20. Tasan, *Yŏyudang chŏnsŏ*, "Munjip," "Taech'aek," "Chungyongch'aek."

21. William T. Rowe, *China's Last Empire: The Great Qing* (Cambridge: Harvard University Press, 2009), 86-88.

22. The translation is JaHyun Kim Haboush's. See *Memoirs*, 205.

23. Karlsson, "Confucian Ideology and Legal Development," 98. William Shaw, in the context of Chosŏn legal history, disagrees, arguing that this reluctance is better understood as the king's failure to get officials' approval for major changes to the dynastic law code. See *Legal Norms* 37-38.

24. Richardson, *Renaissance Monarchy*, ix. For Korea, see Haboush. *Confucian Kingship*, 29-63.

25. Han Feizi made this point in his "Five Vermin" chapter through the famous story of the Song farmer.

> "In [the state of] Song there was a tiller of the field. In his field, there was a tree stump. A rabbit ran into the stump, broke its neck, and died. Following this, [the tiller] cast aside his plough and stood watch at the stump, hoping to obtain a rabbit again. A rabbit could not be obtained, and [the tiller] himself was laughed at by [everyone in] the state of Song. Now if we desire to use the [methods of] government of the Former Kings [of antiquity] to govern the common people of this age, we are standing watch at the stump." That is, if we do what the Former Kings did without taking account that things have changed, we will not succeed.

> [宋人有耕田者。田中有株。兔走觸株。折頸而死。因釋其耒而守株。冀復得兔。兔不可復得。而身為宋國笑。今欲以先王之政。治當世之民。皆守株之類也。]

26. Collins, *The State in Early Modern France*, xix.

27. *Mencius*, "Li Lou I," 17.

28. Peter H. Wilson, "Military Culture and the Reich, c.1680-1806," in *Cultures of Power in Europe*, 41; Park Sohyeon, "Crime, Law, and Confucian Justice in Korean Case Literature," *Korea Journal* 53, no. 3 (2013): 19-21.

29. *Chŏngjo sillok*, 1783.10.21. Chŏng's defense of discretion is so forceful that one is tempted to speculate that Chŏngjo himself was involved in articulating it, though there is no way to show that with the current evidence. Again, the official record obscures as much as it reveals.

30. *Chŏngjo sillok*, 1795.3.25.

31. Hong Yang-bo, *Igejip*, 17, "Ron," "Kyŏnggwŏllon."

32. I discuss an example of Chŏngjo's use of the Imperial Pivot metaphor in detail in "Making Sense of the Imperial Pivot."

33. Tasan, *Yŏyudang chŏnsŏ*, "Yŏmch'ŏl koha."

34. Tasan, *Yŏyudang chŏnsŏ*, "Sangsŏ kohu," 4.

35. *Chŏngjo sillok*, 1798.9.8.

36. This is a reference to Cheng Yi. The text can be found in *Texts of the Southern Song* 南宋文範, book 70, *waibian*, book 4, vol. 1, no. 8.

37. *Chŏngjo sillok*, 1783.7.4. Emphasis added.

38. *Chŏngjo sillok*, 1786.1.22.

39. *Chŏngjo sillok*, 1785.5.22.

40. *Chŏngjo sillok*, 1777.1.29. Emphasis added.

41. *Chŏngjo sillok*, 1788.1.23.

42. *Chŏngjo sillok*, 1799.3.24.

43. *Chŏngjo sillok*, 1793.10.11.

44. *Chŏngjo sillok*, 1798.6.21.

45. *Yŏngjo sillok*, 1776.1.1.

46. *Chŏngjo sillok*, 1776.8.8.

47. *Chŏngjo sillok*, 1779.2.22. Yao and Shun were archetypically great rulers from Chinese antiquity. Jie and Zhou were archetypically abysmal rulers from Chinese antiquity.

48. Chŏngjo, *Hongjae chŏnsŏ*. "Ildŭngnok," "Chŏngsa" 8.

49. *Chŏngjo sillok*, 1794.9.30.

50. *Chŏngjo sillok*, 1792.2.14.

51. *Chŏngjo sillok*, 1791.1.26.

52. The partial quotation "ministers cannot but be loyal" is from Dong Zhongshu's *Chun qiu fan lu*, "Tiandi zhi xing," 2; it also appears in the *Household Rituals of Confucius*. For a discussion of Chŏngjo's employment of body-based metaphors, see Lovins, "Making Sense of the Imperial Pivot."

53. Chŏngjo is incorrect here, as the *History of Song* was published in 1346, nearly fifty years before the founding of Chosŏn. It is possible that by "publish" (*ch'ullae*) Chŏngjo is referring to its circulating in Korea.

54. *Chŏngjo sillok*, 1791.4.30.

55. Zmora, *Monarchy, Aristocracy, and the State*, 51. Zmora is comparing Western and Central Europe, but this book argues the statement also applies in the eastern extremities of Eurasia.

CHAPTER 4

1. Martina Deuchler, "Despoilers of the Way—Insulters of the Sages: Controversies over the Classics in Seventeenth-Century Korea," in *Culture and State in Late Chosŏn Korea*, 91–98.

2. Lady Hyegyŏng confirms this in her *Memoirs*, noting that Yŏngjo required all lists of candidates for office to include both Patriarchs and Disciples; the Southerners are not mentioned (154).

3. Chŏngjo, *Hongjae chŏnsŏ*, "Ildŭngnok," 13; "Inmul," 3.

4. Lady Hyegyŏng, *Memoirs*, 205.

5. Chŏngjo, *Chŏngjo ŏch'alch'ŏp*, 142, 1797.6.25; 331, 1798.8.8; 641, n.d.; 534, 1799.11.2.

6. Ch'oe Hong-gyu, *Chŏngjo ŭi Hwasŏng kŏnsŏl*, 222; Park Hyunmo. *Chŏngch'iga Chŏngjo*, 320; Park Hyunmo, "18 segi Noron," in *Chŏngjo ŭi pimil ŏch'al*, 314–15; Yu Pong-hak, *Kaehyŏk kwa kaldŭng ŭi sidae*, 193.

7. Chŏngjo, *Chŏngjo ŏch'alch'ŏp* 449, 1799.4.15; 448, 1799.4.10; 252, n.d.

8. Lady Hyegyŏng, *Memoirs*, 171–74.

9. Collins, *The State in Early Modern France*, 83. Collins notes that "[t]he absence of an adult king crippled the government because of the importance of personalities between the king and the grandees in maintaining stability."

10. Shin Myung-ho, *Joseon Royal Court Culture: Ceremonial and Daily Life*, trans. Timothy V. Atkinson (Paju: Dolbegae Publishers, 2004), 98–99.

11. *Chŏngjo sillok*, 1779.5.7; 1779.6.22; 1779.6.18; 1781.9.14; Lady Hyegyŏng, *Memoirs*, 172–75. A full account of the controversy that led to Song's execution can be found in Haboush's "Constructing the Center," in *Culture and State in Late Chosŏn Korea*, 46–90. Once again, it is impossible to know how sincere Chŏngjo's professions of reluctance were, because such were politically necessary in any case considering Song Si-yŏl's reputation.

12. The first Prince of Great Abundance I could find was one Yi Sŏ (1580–1637), a royal clansman prominent in the installation of Injo on the throne in 1623. The title includes the Sinograph "p'ung" 豊 that also appears in the name of Hong's clan seat (P'ungsan 豊山), probably not coincidentally.

13. *Chŏngjo sillok*, 1780.8.15; 1779.9.26; Lady Hyegyŏng, *Memoirs*, 173.

14. Lady Hyegyŏng, *Memoirs*, 176–77. An Tae-hoe argues that Kim Chong-su's memorial was an indirect attack on Hong directed by Chŏngjo himself. See An. "Chŏngjo ŭi pimil p'yŏnji," 76.

15. Chŏng Pyŏng-sŏl, *Kwŏllyŏk kwa in'gan*, 255–58.

16. For an account of Sado's regency and all the troubles it entailed, see Haboush, *Confucian Kingship*, ch. 5.

17. *Yŏngjo sillok*, 1775.11.20; Lady Hyegyŏng, *Memoirs*, 100.

18. Palais, *Politics and Policy*, 240.

19. *Chŏngjo sillok*, 1776.7.5 and 6. Being ordered to commit suicide was the most honorable way for a Chosŏn aristocrat to be executed. See Takeshi Yagi. "Death by Royal Favor: An Analysis of Punishment in the Literati Purges and Conflicts of the Joseon Dynasty," in *Capital Punishment in East Asia*, ed. Itaru Tomiya (Kyoto: Kyoto University Press, 2012), 209–42.

20. *Chŏngjo sillok*, 1777.8.11. The reference to the Duke of Zhou can be found in the *Book of Documents*, "Zhou Shu," "Kang Gao," "Cai Zhong zhi Ming," 1. It is also recorded there that the Duke rewarded the son of the Prince of Cai despite punishing the father.

21. *Chŏngjo sillok*, 1799.3.4.

22. Park Hyunmo, *Chŏngch'i ka Chŏngjo*, 65–66; *Chŏngjo sillok*, 1777.8.11.

23. *Chŏngjo sillok*, 1794.4.10; 1794.4.11; 1794.4.13; Park Hyunmo, *Chŏngch'i ka Chŏngjo*, 67–69.

24. *Sunjo sillok*, 1801.3.16; 1801.3.18; 1801.5.29.

25. Setton, *Chŏng Yag- yong*, 27, 44; *Chŏngjo sillok*, 1791.10.25.

26. *Hongjae chŏnsŏ*, *Ildŭngnok*, "Chŏngsa," 20.

27. On September 12, 1784 (the twenty-eighth day of the seventh lunar month), a royal secretary named Yi Che-hak accused Kim of showing him a letter he had written criticizing Chŏngjo for being lacking in Virtue. For a detailed account of this incident, see Sung Soon Park. "Chŏngjodae 'Kim Ha-jae sa'gŏn' ŭi chŏnmal kwa sŏngkyŏk," *Chosŏn sidae sahakpo* 47 (2008): 121-50.

28. *Chŏngjo sillok*, 1784.12.8.

29. Haboush, *The Confucian Kingship in Korea*, 125.

30. Haboush, *The Confucian Kingship in Korea*, 135.

31. Jackson, "Causes and Aims," esp. 27-28.

32. Haboush, *Confucian Kingship*, 152-53.

33. *Chŏngjo sillok*, 1776.9.22.

34. Kim Hae-yŏng, "Chŏngjo ŭi ŭiri t'angp'yŏng kwa Noron pyŏkp'a ŭi taehŭng," 223-37.

35. Kim Sungmoon, "Too Rational to Be Modernized?," 156-57; Paek Minjŏng, "Chŏngjo ŭi sadaebu insik kwa chŏngch'i ch'ŏrhakchŏk ipjang yŏngu," Park Hyunmo, "King Chŏngjo's Political Role," 208.

36. Choi Seong-hwan, "Chŏngjo ŭi ŭiri t'angp'yŏng kwa Noron pyŏkp'a ŭi taehŭng," 338.

37. Yi Han-u, *Chŏngjo: Chosŏn ŭi hon i chida*, 236-39; *Chŏngjo sillok*, 1776.9.22.

38. Chŏngjo, *Chŏngjo ŏch'alch'ŏp* 145, 1797.7.6.

39. Chŏngjo, *Chŏngjo ŏch'alch'ŏp* 237, 1797.12.21.

40. Ibid. 143, 1797.6.27.

41. *Chŏngjo sillok*, 1786.9.7; 1788.2.11; 1788.2.15; 1788.2.12; 1788.9.7; 1788.9.9; 1788.9.10.

42. *Chŏngjo sillok*, 1789.5+.10.

43. A full translation of this quite lengthy memorial can be found in Hwisang Cho, trans. "Joint Memorials: Scholars' Channel of Communication to the Throne," in *Epistolary Korea: Letters in the Communicative Space of the Chosŏn, 1392-1910*, ed. JaHyun Kim Haboush (Columbia University Press, 2009): 59-67. I use here Cho's name for the Joint Memorial.

44. *Chŏngjo sillok*, 1790.11.14; 1792.4+.17; 1793.6.4.

45. *Chŏngjo sillok*, 1792.4+.27

46. This is but a small excerpt from his long reply to the long Memorial, in which the King talks around the issue at some length, reiterating that he has made a decision on his own but cannot openly discuss it. The reply is so long that it is difficult to believe Chŏngjo articulated it as recorded on the spot. Considering the evidence from Chŏngjo's letters that he saw at least some memorials before they were officially presented to him, it seems likely that he had seen this one, or at least some version of it, in order to have such a lengthy response prepared.

47. Yi Han-u, *Chŏngjo: Chosŏn ŭi hon i chida*, 361-64, 399-406.

48. Kwŏn Tu-hwan, "Chŏngjo ŏch'alch'ŏp ŭi sŏldŭngnyŏk kwa nolli," in *Chŏngjo ŭi pimil ŏch'al*, 162.

49. Beales, *Enlightenment and Reform in Eighteenth-Century Europe*, 166.

50. Collins, *The State in Early Modern France*, 143.

51. An recounts the discovery and subsequent study of the letters in his book, *Chŏngjo ŭi pimil p'yŏnji*, 18-21.

52. An Tae-hoe, *Chŏngjo ŭi pimil p'yŏnji*, 13, 16, 18.

53. An Tae-hoe, *Chŏngjo ŭi pimil p'yŏnji*, 18; Pak Ch'ŏl-sang, "Saero palgul-han Chŏngjo ŏch'alch'ŏp ŭi charyojŏk kach'i," in *Chŏngjo ŭi pimil ŏch'al*, 30-33, "Manch'ŏn" ("Ten Thousand Streams") is an abbreviation of Chŏngjo's long and illustrious second pen name.

54. Chŏngjo, *Chŏngjo ŏch'alch'ŏp* 120, 1797.2.20; 522, 1799.9.28.

55. *Chŏngjo ŏch'alch'ŏp*, letters 342 and 344.

56. Letters 319, 320, 340, 342, 344, 418, 435, and 606.

57. Letters 342, 344, 347, 348, 402, 503, 504, 535, and 634.

58. Letters 405 and 406.

59. Letters 117 and 435.

60. Letter 432.

61. Letters 118 and 308.

62. Letter 225.

63. Letters 423 and 536.

64. Chŏngjo *Chŏngjo ŏch'alch'ŏp* 302, 1798.4.6. Emphasis added.

65. Chŏngjo, *Chŏngjo ŏch'alch'ŏp* 404, 1798.10.14.

66. *Sŭngjŏngwŏn ilgi*, 1798.11.1.

67. Chŏngjo, *Chŏngjo ŏch'alch'ŏp* 643, n.d.

68. 1797.12.4, as recorded in the *Records of the Royal Secretariat*.

69. This is the Intransigent-authored account of the purge that accompanied Chŏngjo's accession.

70. *Chŏngjo sillok*, 1799.3.7.

71. Chŏngjo, *Chŏngjo ŏch'alch'ŏp* 442, 1799.3.6. Emphasis added.

72. Chŏngjo, *Chŏngjo ŏch'alch'ŏp* letters 120, 209, 431, and 503.

73. Chŏngjo, *Chŏngjo ŏch'alch'ŏp* 138, 1797.6.5.

74. Ibid., 432, 1799.1.28.

75. Louis XIV, *Memoirs*, 176.

CHAPTER 5

1. Han Sang-gwŏn, "Chŏngjo ŭi kunjugwan," 166. Secret inspectors were officials sent to investigate a locality without announcing or revealing their presence as investigators. They sent the king confidential reports on what they observed. Despite the significant power they wielded while holding the office, inspectors were often reluctant to openly expose corruption, since the implicated officials or their allies could and did exact retribution on them once they had moved on to other posts.

2. Park, *Chŏngch'i ka Chŏngjo*.

3. Ki-baik Lee, *A New History of Korea*, 208.

4. Lee Song-Mu, "Factional Strife in Late Chosŏn," 3; Park Hyunmo, "18 segi Noron ŭi chŏngch'igwan kwa chŏngguk unyŏng kisul," 330–31; Song Chan-sik, "The Power Structure of Sarim Politics," in *The Institutional Basis of Civil Governance in the Chosŏn Dynasty*.

5. Yi Han-u, Chŏngjo: Chosŏn ŭi hon i chida, 280–81; Park Hyunmo, Chŏngch'i ka Chŏngjo, 154; Kim Sung-Yun, "T'angpyŏng and Hwasŏng," 150.

6. *Chŏngjo sillok*, 1789.12.8. It was rather convenient for Chŏngjo that, now that he was ready to do this, a number of officials were calling for him to do so.

7. Chŏngjo, *Hongjae chŏnsŏ* 174, "Ildŭngnok 14," "Hun'ŏ."

8. Yi Tae-Jin, "King Chŏngjo," 181.

9. Kim, "T'angpyŏng and Hwasŏng," 153–54.

10. *Chŏngjo sillok*, 1792.2.11.

11. Sŏl Sŏk-gyu, "Kyujanggak yŏngu (sang)," 22.

12. Yi Tae-Jin, "King Chŏngjo," 169–76.

13. *Chŏngjo sillok*, 1792.2.11.

14. Park Hyunmo, "Sejong kwa Chŏngjo ŭi ridŏsip sŭt'ail pigyo," 143.

15. Ki-baik Lee, *A New History of Korea*, 173.

16. Sŏl Sŏk-gyu, "Kyujanggak yŏngu (sang)," 13–14; Hucker, *Dictionary of Official Titles*, 290, #3382.

17. *Chŏngjo sillok*, 1776.9.25.

18. Haboush, "Confucian Rhetoric," 45–48.

19. Palais, *Confucian Statecraft*, 616; Yi Tae-Jin. "King Chŏngjo," 177.

20. Ibid., 176.

21. Kim Sung-Yun, "T'angpyŏng and Hwasŏng," 149; Park Hyunmo, *Chŏngch'i ka Chŏngjo*, 154.

22. Kim Sung-Yun, "T'angpyŏng and Hwasŏng," 149–50.

23. Han Sang-gwŏn, *Chŏngjo ŭi kunjugwan*, 153.

24. Lossky, *Louis XIV and the French Monarchy*, 17.

25. Yi Tae-Jin, "King Chŏngjo," 177–78.

26. Jung Ok-ja, *Chŏngjo sidae ŭi sasang kwa munhwa*, 26; Pak Kwang-yong. *Yŏngjo wa Chŏngjo ŭi nara*, 229.

27. Chŏngjo's affinity for the *Documents* was discussed earlier. The *Rites of Zhou* was presumably included for its focus on government offices, organization, administration, and the relationships between them.

28. Han Sang-gwŏn, *Chŏngjo ŭi kunjugwan*, 150.

29. Jung Ok-ja, *Chosŏn hugi munhwa undongsa* (Seoul T'ŭkpyŏlsi: Ilchogak, 1988), 114; Kim Moon-sik, *Chŏngjo ŭi chewanghak*, 251–55; Park Hyunmo, *Chŏngch'i ka Chŏngjo*, 157. For a detailed description of the contents and structure of the lessons, see *Chosŏn hugi munhwa undongsa*, 125–49. Kim says the four graduates' names were omitted from the official record.

30. Kim Moon-sik, *Chŏngjo ŭi chewanghak*, 254–56.

31. Michael Nylan, "The 'Chin Wen/Ku Wen' Controversy in Han Times," *T'oung Pao* 80, no. 1 (1994): 83–145. Ironically, according to Nylan, the controversy over the Old Texts and New Texts was minor during the Han Dynasty. It is not until the Qing that it becomes a major cleavage.

32. Chŏngjo, *Hongjae chŏnsŏ* 50, "Ch'aengmun 3," "Sangsŏ."

33. Kim Moon-sik, *Chŏngjo ŭi chewanghak*, 255.

34. Kim Moon-sik, *Chŏngjo ŭi chewanghak*, 253. Kim gives the publication year for the *Responses* as 1795, but the catalog entry at the Kyujanggak Institute at Seoul National University lists 1792.

35. Chŏngjo, *Hongjae chŏnsŏ* 50, "Ch'aengmun 3," "Non'ŏ."

36. Kim Sung-Yun, "T'angpyŏng and Hwasŏng, 151-52.

37. *Hongjae chŏnsŏ, Ildüngnok*, "Chŏngsa," 17.

38. Zhuge Liang lived from 181–234. He was a renowned general and statesman of the state of Shu during the Chinese Three Kingdoms Period.

39. *Chŏngjo sillok*, 1776.9.22. This is the same conversation about factionalism discussed in chapter 3.

40. Hongjae chŏnsŏ, Ildüngnok, "Chŏngsa," 19.

41. Hongjae chŏnsŏ, Ildüngnok, "Chŏngsa," 16.

42. Chŏngjo, Chŏngjo ŏch'alch'ŏp.449, 1799.4.15.

43. Haboush, "Ritual Controversy," in *Culture and State in Late Chosŏn Korea*, 82-83.

44. Chŏngjo, Hongjae chŏnsŏ, "Ildŭngnok" 8, "Chŏngsa" 3.

45. Deuchler, " 'Heaven Does Not Discriminate,' " passim; Moon, "From Dirt to Heaven," 154-65.

46. Scott, "The Nobility," in *A Companion to Eighteenth-Century Europe*, 100.

47. It is worth mentioning again that the name of "Southerner" faction did not refer to a regional basis. Resistance to Ch'oe Che-gong's position was not based on his regional origins.

48. Park, *Between Dreams and Reality*, 115.

49. *Chŏngjo sillok*, 1781.6.22.

50. Park, *Between Dreams and Reality*, 114-15.

51. Sun Joo Kim, *Marginality and Subversion in Korea*, passim.

52. *Yŏngjo sillok*, 1772.12.28.

53. *Chŏngjo sillok*, 1791.4.16.

54. The sinographs look very similar: 魚 and 魯.

55. *Chŏngjo sillok*, 1777.7.22.

56. *Chŏngjo sillok*, 1777.5.6.

57. *Chŏngjo sillok*, 1778.8.1.

58. *Chŏngjo sillok*, 1785.2.17.

59. Park. *Between Dreams and Reality*, 198n4.

60. Jaeyoon Song, "Debates on Just Taxation in Ma Duanlin's *Comprehensive Survey*," in *State Power in China, 900-1325*, ed. Patricia Buckley Ebrey and Paul Jakov Smith (Seattle: University of Washington Press, 2016), 244-45.

61. Palais, *Confucian Statecraft*, 8.

62. *Chŏngjo sillok*, 1788.5.5.

63. Collins, *The State in Early Modern France*, xix.

64. Yi Tae-Jin, "King Chŏngjo"; Han Sang-gwŏn, *Chosŏn hugi sahoe wa sowŏn chedo*.

65. Ko Donghwan, "Development of Commerce and Commercial Policy," 215-16.

66. Cole, *The Portable Queen*, 1.

67. Yi Tae-Jin, "King Chŏngjo," 171-72; Park Hyunmo. *Chŏngjo sahu 63 nyŏn*, 74. His first trip to the tomb was actually in 1764, when he was still a child. The visit in 1776, when he was on the verge of ascending the throne, had far more symbolic importance.

68. Kim Ji-young, "Chosŏn hugi kugwang haengch'a wa kŏdunggil," 36; Park Hyunmo, *Chŏngjo sahu 63 nyŏn*, 80.

69. Chang, *A Court on Horseback*; Cole, *The Portable Queen*, 22-24. Elizabeth undertook twenty-three processions outside of London in her forty-four-year reign, a rate of 1.9 percent.

70. Haboush, "Gender and the Politics of Language in Chosŏn Korea," in *Rethinking Confucianism*, 249.

71. Cole, *The Portable Queen*, 163-64.

72. Han Sang-gwŏn, "Active Use of Petitions," 233-34; *Chŏngjo sillok*, 1777.2.20; 1777.6.10.

73. *Chŏngjo sillok*, 1777.2.20.

74. *Chŏngjo sillok*, 1777.6.10.

75. *Chŏngjo sillok*, 1781.7.16.

76. Han Sang-gwŏn, "Active Use of Petitions," 235.

77. *Chŏngjo sillok*, 1783.7.12.

78. Beales, "Joseph II, Petitions and the Public Sphere," in *Cultures of Power in Europe*, 256.

79. Beales, "Joseph II, Petitions and the Public Sphere," in *Cultures of Power in Europe*, 253, 261. Jisoo Kim has done groundbreaking work on petitions from the other side, that is, of the petitioner. Historians of government and monarchy, on the other hand, have yet to take advantage of these resources for understanding the function of political systems that made use of them. See Jisoo Kim, *The Emotions of Justice: Gender, Status, and Legal Performance in Chosŏn Korea* (University of Washington Press, 2016).

80. Beales, "Joseph II, Petitions and the Public Sphere," in *Cultures of Power in Europe*, 249.

81. Han Sang-gwŏn, "Chŏngjo ŭi kunjugwan," 165; Kim Hae-yŏng, *Ch'ŏlhakcha, Chŏngjo ŭi hyoch'i rŭl punsŏkhada*, 207.

82. Kim, "Women's Legal Voices." JaHyun Kim Haboush. *The Great East Asian War and the Birth of the Korean Nation*, New York: Columbia University Press, 2016.

83. Beales, "Joseph II, Petitions and the Public Sphere," in *Cultures of Power in Europe*, 256–57.

84. Beales, "Joseph II, Petitions and the Public Sphere," in *Cultures of Power in Europe*, 257–58, 260.

85. Qtd. in Beales, "Joseph II, Petitions and the Public Sphere," in *Cultures of Power in Europe*, 257, 259.

86. Hong *Sŭng-gi, Koryŏ kwijok sahoe wa nobi*; Salem, *Slavery in Medieval Korea*.

87. *Book of Former Han*, "Treatise on the Lay of the Land [地理志]."

88. Palais, *Confucian Statecraft*, 212.

89. Ibid., 228, 258.

90. Ibid., 249–52.

91. Beales, *Enlightenment and Reform in Eighteenth-Century Europe*, 9.

92. Shaw, *Legal Norms in a Confucian State*, 123, 133–34, 143, 171–72.

93. Shaw, *Legal Norms in a Confucian State*, 112–13.

94. *Chŏngjo sillok*, 1791.3.27.

95. Palais notes in *Confucian Statecraft* (266) that "this discussion presaged a significant liberalization of the rules for escaping the burdens of slavery."

96. Hiraki Minoru, *Chosŏn hugi nobije yŏn'gu*, 195.

97. Palais, *Confucian Statecraft*, 266.

98. Yi Tae-Jin, "King Chŏngjo," 195.

99. *Sunjo sillok*, 1801.1.28, quoted in Palais, *Confucian Statecraft*, 267. The translation is Palais's.

100. Chŏngjo, *Hongjae chŏnsŏ*, "Sŏin 5," "Ikjŏng kongju kojae puryusŏ."

101. For a discussion of Yu Su-wŏn's critique of slavery, see Palais. *Confucian Statecraft*, 253–57. Chŏngjo likely did not intend to abolish *all* slavery, since he continued to the practice of enslaving criminals and their immediate relatives, people who "deserved" the mistreatment given to slaves. What he objected to was the perpetuation of that treatment (and, more practically, tax exemption) through generations.

CHAPTER 6

1. Palais, *Confucian Statecraft*, 1108.

2. Hur Nam-lin, "National Defense in Shambles: Wartime Military Buildup in Chosŏn Korea, 1592–98," *Seoul Journal of Korean Studies* 22, no. 2 (2009): 113–35. Hur argues the strategic weakness of Chosŏn's army resulted from structural problems endemic to its military organization that prevented it from

fielding a force large enough to repel a major invasion. On the other hand, Andrade, Kang, and Cooper present a strong case that the Chosŏn army's musketeers were well-drilled and could be devastatingly effective in small-scale engagements, particularly when their manpower was supplemented by an ally. See their article "A Korean Military Revolution?"

3. Chong Da-ham, "Making Chosŏn's Own Tributaries: Dynamics between the Ming-Centered World Order and a Chosŏn-Centered Regional Order in the East Asian Periphery," *International Journal of Korean History* 15, no. 1 (2010): 29–63; Kenneth R. Robinson. "Centering the King of Chosŏn: Aspects of Korean Maritime Diplomacy, 1392–1592," *Journal of Asian Studies* 59, no. 1 (2000), 109–25.

4. Zmora, *Monarchy, Aristocracy, and the State*, 106.

5. Park Hyunmo, *Chŏngch'i ka Chŏngjo*, 307.

6. Roh Young-koo, "Hwasŏng Fortress," 194; *Chŏngjo sillok*, 1793.12.8.

7. Roh Young-koo, "Hwasŏng Fortress," 169, 186.

8. Kim Sung-Yun, "T'angpyŏng and Hwasŏng," 159.

9. Ibid.; Roh, "Hwasŏng Fortress," 195.

10. *Chŏngjo sillok*, 1790.2.19.

11. *Chŏngjo sillok*, 1790.6.10.

12. *Chŏngjo sillok*, 1790.1.22.

13. Palais, *Confucian Statecraft and Korean Institutions*, 980–88. Palais portrays the Commercial Equalization Law as Ch'ae Che-gong's own idea, only approved by Chŏngjo. This opens the question, familiar to scholars of Henry VIII and Thomas Cromwell, among others, over the respective contributions of the king and a favored minister to policies. While the question is likely impossible to answer definitively, the *Veritable Records*' portrayal of the king as not initiating policy sorely needs correcting, so I lean toward Chŏngjo being the more active party here.

14. Kim Sung-Yun, "T'angpyŏng and Hwasŏng," 156.

15. Roh Young-koo, "Hwasŏng Fortress," 187; Ch'oe Hong-gyu. *Chŏngjo ŭi Hwasŏng kŏnsŏl*, 11.

16. *Chŏngjo sillok*, 1793.1.12.

17. For comparison, the annual land tax revenue from Kyŏngsang Province, one of the richest in the country, was 628,770 *yang*. See James B. Lewis. *Frontier Contact between Chosŏn Korea and Tokugawa Japan* (New York: Routledge, 2003), ch. 4.

18. Roh Young-koo, "Hwasŏng Fortress," 200. As an example, a cartwright working the Fortress was paid a daily wage comparable to that paid to royal

sculptors and painters, "an impressive remuneration." See Park, *A Family of No Prominence*, 62.

19. *Chŏngjo sillok*, 1794.7.11.
20. *Chŏngjo sillok*, 1794.10.19.
21. *Kojong sillok*, 1899.8.3.
22. Tasan, *Tasan simunjip* 10, "Sŏl," "Sŏngsŏl."
23. Park Hyunmo, *Chŏngch'i ka Chŏngjo*, 318.
24. Kim Sung-Yun, "T'angp'yŏng and Hwasŏng," 160.
25. Kim Sung-Yun, "T'angp'yŏng and Hwasŏng," 159-60.
26. Haboush, *Confucian Kingship*, 138.
27. Ch'oe Hong-gyu, *Hwasŏng kŏnsŏl*, 23, 238-39, 270-72; *Chŏngjo sillok* 1797.8.7. Yi said,

> Now among those who serve at Your Majesty's court, could it be that no one is shocked and fearful? If there is truly no other reason for this [use of the army], and the only desire is to display the army's capabilities, then I your servant, though I worry it is a crime worthy of death, suggest that Your Majesty's behaviour is excessive.
>
> [則今日北面於殿下之廷者。其不有瞠然而驚。慄然而駴乎。設使眞無他事。而只欲觀保障軍容。臣愚死罪。以爲殿下過擧]。

28. Wilson, *Absolutism in Central Europe*, 76.
29. Lady Hyegyŏng, *Memoirs*, 164, 205.
30. Haboush, *Confucian Kingship*, 185-87, 233.
31. Roh Young-koo, "Hwasŏng Fortress," 195.
32. Kim Sung-Yun, "T'angpyŏng and Hwasŏng," 159-60.
33. Ibid., 161.
34. *Chŏngjo sillok*, 1795.2.28; Kim Sung-Yun, "T'angpyŏng and Hwasŏng," 161.
35. Letter 121, Kim Sung-Yun, "T'angpyŏng and Hwasŏng," 161.
36. Jackson, "Histories in Stone," 12.
37. Park Hyunmo, *Chŏngch'i ka Chŏngjo*, 307, 328.
38. *Chŏngjo sillok*, 1788.1.23.
39. *Chŏngjo sillok*, 1793.1.12.
40. *Chŏngjo sillok*, 1793.1.12.
41. Park Hyunmo, "18 segi Noron ŭi chŏngch'igwan kwa chŏngguk unyŏng kisul," 314-15.
42. *Chŏngjo sillok*, 1796.7.2; 1797.8.7; 1794.9.15.
43. Chŏngjo, *Chŏngjo ŏch'alch'ŏp* 121, 1797.2.25. Yi's memorial can be found in the *Annals* entry for the same date.

44. Chŏngjo, *Chŏngjo ŏch'alch'ŏp* 123, 1797.3.5.

45. The coiled dragon and crouching tiger were auspicious geomantic formations.

46. Feng and Pei are proper names for places that served as the core for their respective dynasties.

47. *Chŏngjo sillok*, 1793.1.12.

48. *Chŏngjo sillok*, 1795.8.18; 1795.8.19.

49. Park, *Between Dreams and Reality*, 137-38.

50. Hur, "National Defense in Shambles," 117-18.

51. Frank Tallett, *War and Society in Early Modern Europe, 1495-1715*, New York: Routledge. 2003, chapter 3. The quotation is of Lord Herbert of Cherbury writing in 1600, on page 84.

52. For some comparison, the largest force fielded by Chosŏn according to the official records was 25,000 troops in 1598, during the second phase of the Imjin War against Japan. See Hur, "National Defense in Shambles," 115-18.

53. Dee, *Expansion and Crisis*, 177; Wilson, *Absolutism in Central Europe*, 99.

CHAPTER 7

1. Daniel Lord Smail, *On Deep History and the Brain*, (Berkeley: University of California Press, 2008), 168.

2. Jisoo Kim, "Women's Legal Voice: Language, Power, and Gender Performativity in Late Chosŏn Korea," *Journal of Asian Studies* 74, no. 3: 661.

3. Fukuyama, *The Origins of Political Order*, 422.

4. Population figures for China come from Andre Gunder Frank, *ReOrient: Global Economy in the Asian Age* (Berkeley: University of California Press, 1998), 109. Figures for Korea come from Palais, *Confucian Statecraft*, 366-68

5. Park Hyunmo, "Sejong kwa Chŏngjo ŭi ridŏsip sŭt'ail pikyo," 147.

6. In this period, the eventual third king of Chosŏn struggled with his brothers over the throne. The dynastic founder abdicated in disgust while private armies fought in the streets of the capital.

7. Park Hyunmo, "King Sejong's Deliberative Politics: With Reference to the Process of Tax Reform," *Review of the Korean Studies* 8, no. 3 (2005): 62; "Sejong kwa Chŏngjo ŭi ridŏsip sŭt'ail pikyo," 151.

8. Mi-rim Yoo, "King Sejong's Leadership and the Politics of Inventing the Korean Alphabet," *Review of Korean Studies* 9, no. 3 (2006): 24-25.

9. *Sejong sillok*, 1444.2.20.

10. Milan Hejtmanek, "Chiphyŏnjŏn," in *King Sejong the Great*, 21; Park Hyunmo, "Sejong kwa Chŏngjo ŭi ridŏsip sŭt'ail pikyo," 143.

11. Park Hyunmo, "King Sejong's Deliberative Politics," 59-61.

12. Park Young-do, "King Sejong's Confucian Rule by Law," 124.

13. Park Hyunmo. "King Sejong's Deliberative Politics," 63-72, 82-86. Absolutism, as I have argued, is also a kind of "cogovernment." But the devil is in the details. Absolutism puts the king out front, not mixed in with the other nobles. Though in practice it was cogovernment, it was never *framed* as such. Absolutism is at least as much about the image of power and authority as about its actual use.

14. Park Byoung-ho, "King Sejong's Contributions to the Development of Legal Institutions," in *King Sejong the Great*, trans. Mark Peterson, 113-16.

15. Karlsson, "Confucian Ideology and Legal Development," 97; Kim Paekchol, "*Taejŏn t'ongjŏn pyŏngjŏn* p'yŏn ŭi sŏngkyŏk," 89-119; Kwak Nak-hyŏn, "Taejŏn t'ongp'yŏn pyŏngjŏn rŭl shichwi t'onghae pon muye," 43-51.

16. Karlsson, "Confucian Ideology and Legal Developments," 98; Kim and Kim, *Wrongful Deaths*, 6-8, 19. There are at least three extensive legal histories covering Chŏngjo's reign, and each translates *Simnirok* quite differently. Jisoo Kim renders it "Record of Stating and Hearings," in *Emotions of Justice*. Sun Joo Kim and Jungwon Kim opt for "Records of Royal Reviews" in *Wrongful Deaths*. William Shaw translates it as the "Record of Difficult Cases" in *Legal Norms in a Confucian State*. In her article "Thinking with Chinese Cases," Sohyeon Park offers "Record of Judicial Review." I adopt Kim and Kim's rendering to emphasize the king's involvement in the judicial process in these "difficult" or protracted cases. For a legal history of a broader time scale, see Kim, *Law and Custom in Korea* and Kim, *The Spirit of Korean Law*.

17. Yi Tae-Jin, "Ch'aengmori e," 7.

18. Elmarsafy, *Freedom, Slavery, and Absolutism*, 12-13.

19. Haboush, *The Confucian Kingship in Korea*, 33-35.

20. Haboush, *The Confucian Kingship in Korea*, 59, 62-63.

21. Haboush, *The Confucian Kingship in Korea*, 95.

22. Haboush, *The Confucian Kingship in Korea*, 68, 189-90.

23. Haboush, *The Confucian Kingship in Korea*, 146.

24. Haboush, *The Confucian Kingship in Korea*, 60; Han Sang-gwŏn. "Chŏngjo ŭi kunjugwan," 163.

25. Kim Hae-yŏng, *Ch'ŏlhakcha, Chŏngjo ŭi hyoch'i rŭl punsŏkhada*, 222.

26. Haboush, *The Confucian Kingship in Korea*, 61.

27. Haboush, *The Confucian Kingship in Korea*, 155.

28. Crossley, *A Translucent Mirror*, 42-43.

29. Adler, "The Qianlong Emperor," in *New Qing Imperial History*, 114, 117; Crossley, *A Translucent Mirror*, 18; Kahn, *Monarchy in the Emperor's Eyes*, 9, 73;

Rawski. "The Qing Empire during the Qianlong Reign," in *New Qing Imperial History*, 19.

30. Tsai, *Perpetual Happiness*, 210.

31. Tsai, *Perpetual Happiness*, 78-79, 88.

32. Tsai, *Perpetual Happiness*, 88, 91.

33. Tsai, *Perpetual Happiness*, 140.

34. Tsai, *Perpetual Happiness*, 142, 147.

35. Tsai, *Perpetual Happiness*, 78, 95, 96.

36. Tsai, *Perpetual Happiness*, 111.

37. Adler, "The Qianlong Emperor," in *New Qing Imperial History*, 114; Crossley, *A Translucent Mirror*, 231.

38. Benjamin A. Elman, *Classicism Politics, and Kinship: The Ch'ang-chou School of New Text Confucianism in Late Imperial China* (Berkeley: University of California Press, 1990), ch. 4.

39. Chang, *A Court on Horseback*, 295; Crossley, *A Translucent Mirror*, 267; Elliott, *Emperor Qianlong*, 77, 123-24.

40. Qtd. in Kahn, *Monarchy in the Emperor's Eyes*, 70n22. See also Elliott, *Emperor Qianlong*, 23-25.

41. On the succession struggle that brought Yongzheng to the throne, see Huang, *Autocracy at Work*, ch. 3. On the treason case that led to Yongzheng dealing with the rumors, see Spence, *Treason by the Book*.

42. JaHyun Kim Haboush, "The Education of the Yi Crown Prince: A Study in Confucian Pedagogy," in *The Rise of Neo-Confucianism in Korea*, ed. Wm. Theodore de Bary and JaHyun Kim Haboush (New York: Columbia University Press, 1985), 161-222. I follow Ross King and others in using the term *Literary Sinitic* rather than the more common *classical Chinese* or *literary Chinese* for the common written language of premodern East Asia. This language is known as *hanmun* 漢文 ("Chinese writing") in modern Korea and *wenyan* 文言 ("literary language") in modern China. See Sheldon Pollack, *The Language of the Gods in the World of Men: Sanskrit, Culture, and Power in Premodern India* (Berkeley: University of California Press, 2006); Ross King, "Ditching 'Diglossia': Describing Ecologies of the Spoken and Inscribed in Pre-modern Korea," *Sungkyun Journal of East Asian Studies* 15, no. 1: 1-19.

43. Elliott, *Emperor Qianlong*, 16-17.

44. Elliott, *Emperor Qianlong*, 31-32.

45. *Communication and Imperial Control in China*, 4, 7-8; see also Han Sŭng-hyŏng, "Chungguk ŭi 18-segi," in *Chŏngjo wa 18-segi*, 207.

46. Chang, *A Court on Horseback*, 7.

47. *Yŏngjo sillok*, 1753.1.11

48. Chang, *A Court on Horseback*, 88; Symons, "Qianlong on the Road," in *New Qing Imperial History*, 56-57.

49. Chang, *A Court on Horseback*, 147.

50. Chang, *A Court on Horseback*, 90-91, 170, 178, 189-95. Elizabeth I also frequently staged military displays on procession, though in her case the primary purpose was to demonstrate to both to her own subjects and to visiting foreign envoys that, despite her gender, England was militarily powerful. Chŏngjo did not have any foreign envoys on his processions to impress; for him it was purely about intimidating his own ministers and reminding them who really controlled the military. In both cases, though, it was more a symbolic act than a genuine concern with military effectiveness that "worked as diplomacy but crumbled on the battlefield," exemplified by Elizabeth's not going on procession whenever actual military threats from abroad loomed. See Cole, *The Portable Queen*, 155-56.

51. Cole, *The Portable Queen*, 36-37.

52. Chang, *A Court on Horseback*, 431.

53. Chang, *A Court on Horseback*, 263.

54. JaHyun Kim Haboush discusses Jung Ok-ja's use of the "progressive/conservative" dichotomy in her chapter of *Culture and State in Late Chosŏn Korea*, 48-49. Yi Han-u criticizes Chŏngjo for being "oriented toward the past" because he fails to divest himself of Sado. The implication is that Chŏngjo failed to "modernize" Chosŏn, *Chŏngjo: Chosŏn ŭi hon i chida* (Seoul: Haenaem, 2007), 125. For a scathing critique of the Korean nationalist response to the Japanese imperialist paradigm in the context of early Korean history, see Hyung II Pai. *Constructing Korean Origins: A Critical Review of Archaeology, Historiography, and Racial Myth in Korean State-Formation Theories* (Cambridge: Harvard University Press, 2000).

55. Collins, *The State in Early Modern France*, xiii, 83; Zmora, *Monarchy, Aristocracy, and the State*, 90.

56. Henshall, *The Myth of Absolutism*, 47.

57. Doyle, "Conclusion," 251, in *Old Regime France*.

58. Swann, "The State and Political Culture," 155-57, in *Old Regime France*, ed. William Doyle.

59. Doyle, "Conclusion," 251, in *Old Regime France*, ed. William Doyle.

60. Henshall, *The Myth of Absolutism*, 4.

61. Sturdy, *Louis XIV*, 162.

62. Lossky, "The Absolutism of Louis XIV," 12.

63. Swann, "The State and Political Culture," 140, in *Old Regime France*, ed. William Doyle.

64. Lossky, "The Absolutism of Louis XIV," 5.

65. Lossky, *Louis XIV and the French Monarchy*, 8. See also Schalk, "Under the Law," passim; Kim Ki-bong, "T'aeyang wang kwa manch'ŏn myŏngwŏl chuin'ong," 271, in *Chŏngjo wa 18 segi*.

66. Doyle, "Introduction," 4. In *Old Regime France*.

67. Lossky, *Louis XIV and the French Monarchy*, 7; Swann. "The State and Political Culture," 144. In *Old Regime France*; Henshall, *Myth of Absolutism*, 39–40; Swann. "The State and Political Culture," 144. In *Old Regime France*.

68. Jones, *The Great Nation*, 83.

69. Henshall, *Myth of Absolutism*, 140. Henshall is writing of France, but the statement is equally applicable to late Chosŏn Korea.

70. Henshall, *Myth of Absolutism*, 39.

71. Parker, "Absolutism, Feudalism, and Property Rights," 62.

72. Lossky, *Louis XIV and the French Monarchy*, 16.

73. Henshall, *Myth of Absolutism*, 39.

74. Henshall, *Myth of Absolutism*, 38; Hurt. *Louis XIV and the Parlements*, 3.

75. Parker, "Absolutism, Feudalism, and Property Rights," 63.

76. Doyle, "Introduction," 4, in *Old Regime France*; Sturdy, *Louis XIV*, 41.

77. Henshall, *Myth of Absolutism*, 50.

78. Louis XIV, *Memoirs*, 54.

79. Sturdy, *Louis XIV*, 164.

80. Zmora, *Monarchy, Aristocracy, and the State*, 90.

81. Fukuyama, *The Origins of Political Order*, 354; Lossky, *Louis XIV and the French Monarchy*, 9; Scott, "The Nobility," in *A Companion to Eighteenth-Century Europe*, 96; Rappaport, "France," in *A Companion to Eighteenth-Century Europe*, 347–48; Sturdy. *Louis XIV*, 164.

82. Lossky, *Louis XIV and the French Monarchy*, 26. See also Henshall, *Myth of Absolutism*, 51 and Doyle, "Politics: Louis XIV," in *Old Regime France*, 172.

83. Lossky, *Louis XIV and the French Monarchy*, 8; Swann. "The State and Political Culture," in *Old Regime France*, 146. This did not apply to an official convicted of serious offenses such as treason.

84. Sturdy, *Louis XIV*, 39–40.

85. Zmora, *Monarchy, Aristocracy, and the State*, 7. Zmora points out that the states of Western Europe tended to lose authority to private actors as a result of the vast scale of European warfare. See also Wilson, *Absolutism in Central Europe*, 97. Wilson criticizes the pervasive belief that foreign aggression is part and parcel of absolutism.

86. Wilson, *Absolutism in Central Europe*, 89.

87. The latter title is part of the new pen name Chŏngjo adopted for himself the

year before his death, "the Lord of the Shining Moon and the Myriad Streams" 滿川明月主人翁 (*manch'ŏn myŏng'wŏl chuin'ong*). The name was not accepted by scholars after he died, as evidenced by the title of his posthumously collected works, which used his original pen name "Expansive Study" 弘齋 (Hongjae).

88. Qtd. in Schalk, "Under the Law," 287.

89. *Manch'ŏn myŏngwŏl chuinong chasŏ.*

90. Sturdy, *Louis XIV*, 2.

91. Qtd. in Lossky, *Louis XIV and the French Monarchy*, 69.

92. Ronald G. Asch, *Sacral Kingship between Disenchantment and Re-enchantment: The French and English Monarchies, 1587–1688* (New York: Berghahn, 2014), 170n31.

93. Qtd. in Jones, *The Great Nation*, 5. See also Sturdy, *Louis XIV*, 15.

94. Richardson, *Renaissance Monarchs*, 23.

95. Collins, *The State in Early Modern France*, 165–66.

96. Lossky, *Louis XIV and the French Monarchy*, 7.

97. Lossky, *Louis XIV and the French Monarchy*, 85; Louis IV. *Memoirs*, 176.

98. Doyle, "Politics: Louis XIV," 170–71, in *Old Regime France.*

99. Lossky, *Louis XIV and the French Monarchy*, 70.

100. *Memoirs*, 50, 53; Sturdy, *Louis XIV*, 10, 12.

101. Sturdy, *Louis XIV*, 164; *Chŏngjo sillok*, 1797.5.25.

102. Henshall, *Myth of Absolutism*, 35.

103. Sturdy, *Louis XIV*, 163–64.

104. Henshall, *Myth of Absolutism*, 71–72.

105. Lossky, *Louis XIV and the French Monarchy*, 295.

106. Swann, "The State and Political Culture," 158, in *Old Regime France*, ed. William Doyle.

107. Rose, "Kingship and Counsel in Early Modern England," 58, 52–53. Emphasis in original. Nicholas Henshall in *The Myth of Absolutism* also argues that the English king was stronger than his French counterpart, turning the Whiggish argument that Parliament restrained royal absolutism on its head.

108. Rose, "Kingship and Counsel in Early Modern England," passim, but esp. 49–50, 62, and 67.

109. "The Absolutism of Louis XIV," 3.

CONCLUSION

1. *Chŏngjo sillok*, 1787.1.25.

2. This phrase is part of an exchange between Duke Ding and Confucius: "Duke Ding asked, 'A single saying that can cause a state to perish—is there

such a thing as this?' Confucius replied, 'There is no saying that can have *that* sort of effect. There is, however, something close. People have a saying, "I take no joy in being a ruler, except that no one dares to oppose what I say." If what the ruler says is good, and no one opposes him, is this not good? On the other hand, if what he says is not good, and no one opposes him, does this not come close to being a single saying that can cause a state to perish?' " This exchange neatly illustrates the inherent tension in classical Confucian political philosophy. It permits opposition to the ruler, but only if what he says is "not good." The passage also implies that if what the ruler says *is* good, then opposing him is wrong.

3. Zmora, *Monarch, Aristocracy, and the State*, 90.

4. Henshall, *Myth of Absolutism*, 173.

5. Asch, "Absolutism and Royal Government," in *A Companion to Eighteenth-Century Europe*, 455.

6. Palais, *Politics and Policy*, passim, but esp. 247-51. Palais remarks on page 250 that Kojong "lacked a proper understanding of the political process and the extent of monarchical power in his own country."

7. King, "Ditching 'Diglossia,' " 6. King argues for adopting the term "Sinographic cosmopolis" to describe premodern East Asia because "the unifying feature was not so much Chinese *characters* themselves, as it was the common training in Literary Sinitic and the culture it embodied." Avoiding the term "Chinese" emphasizes its supraregional dimension, and the term "cosmopolis" as defined by Sheldon Pollack emphasizes the shared political culture. Emphasis in original.

8. *Sunjo sillok*, 1801.1.28; 1802.1.20.

9. Yi Tae-Jin, *Kyujanggak sosa*, (Seoul National University Library, 1990), 28-29.

10. Palais, *Politics and Policy*, 304n16 carries this implication.

11. Lee Song-Mu, *Chosŏn hugi tangjaensa*, 260.

12. Lady Hyegyŏng, *Memoirs*, 194n16.

13. Pak Hyunmo, *Chŏngch'iga Chŏngjo*, 397-98 is one example, Choi Seong-hwan, "Chŏngjo ŭi ŭiri t'angp'yŏng kwa Noron pyŏkp'a ŭi taehŭng," 384 is another.

14. Karlsson, "Royal Compassion and Disaster Relief in Chosŏn Korea."

15. Choi Seong-hwan, "Chŏngjo ŭi ŭiri t'angp'yŏng kwa Noron pyŏkp'a ŭi taehŭng," 383.

16. Lee Song-Mu, *Chosŏn hugi tangjaensa*, 268-69.

17. An example is Ch'oe Tu-jin's "Chŏngjo sidae Kyujanggak ŭi kyoyuk ŭiŭi."

18. Hiraki, *Chosŏn hugi nobije yŏn'gu*, James Palais disputes the extent of the drop in slaves Hiraki finds but concedes that it was a dramatic drop. See *Confucian Statecraft* 249–51.

19. Dee, *Expansion and Crisis*, 128.

BIBLIOGRAPHY

PRIMARY SOURCES

Ban, Gu. *Hanshu* [*Book of Han*]. Zhonghua shuju: Beijing, China, 1962. https://ctext.org/han-shu.

Ch'ae, Che-gong. *Pŏn'amjip* [*The Collected Works of Ch'ae Che-gong*]. Seoul, South Korea: Han'guk kojŏn pŏnyŏgwŏn, 2017. http://db.itkc.or.kr/itkcdb/mainIndexIframe.jsp.

Chŏng, Yag-yong. *Tasan simunjip* [*The Collected Poetry and Prose of Tasan*]. http://db.itkc.or.kr/itkcdb/mainIndexIframe.jsp.

——. *Yŏyudang chŏnsŏ* [*The Collected Works of Tasan*]. Seoul, South Korea: Tasan haksul munhwa chaedan, 2001. http://db.itkc.or.kr/itkcdb/mainIndexIframe.jsp.

Chŏngjo. *Hongjae chŏnsŏ* [*The Collected Works of Chŏngjo*]. Seoul, South Korea: Minjok munhwa ch'ujinhoe, 2001. http://db.itkc.or.kr/itkcdb/mainIndexIframe.jsp.

——. *Chŏngjo ŏch'alch'ŏp* [*The Royal Letters of Chŏngjo*]. Translated by Paek Sŭng-ho and Chang Yu-sŭng. Seoul, South Korea: Sungkyunkwan University Press, 2009.

Chŏngjo sillok [*The Veritable Records of King Chŏngjo's Reign*]. Seoul, South Korea: Kuksa pyŏnch'an wiwŏnhoe, 1958. http://sillok.history.go.kr/main/main.jsp.

Chungjong sillok [*The Veritable Records of King Chungjong's Reign*]. Seoul, South Korea: Kuksa pyŏnch'an wiwŏnhoe, 1956. http://sillok.history.go.kr/main/main.jsp.

Hong, Yang-bo. *Igyejip* [*The Collected Works of Hong Yang-bo*]. Seoul, South Korea: Chaep'an parhaeng kyŏngin munhwasa, 2001. http://db.itkc.or.kr/itkcdb/mainIndexIframe.jsp.

Kojong Sunjong sillok [*The Veritable Records of King Kojong's and King Sunjong's Reign*]. Seoul: South Korea: T'amgudang, 1986. http://sillok.history.go.kr/main/main.jsp.

Lady Hyegyŏng. *The Memoirs of Lady Hyegyŏng: The Autobiographical Writings of a Crown Princess of Eighteenth-Century Korea*. Translated by JaHyun Kim Haboush. Berkeley: University of California Press, 1996.

Louis XIV. *A King's Lessons in Statecraft*. Translated by Herbert Wilson. London: T. Fisher Unwin, 1924.

Sejong sillok. [*The Veritable Records of King Sejong's Reign*]. Seoul, South Korea: Kuksa pyŏnch'an wiwŏnhoe, 1956. http://sillok.history.go.kr/main/main. jsp.

Sunjo sillok. [*The Veritable Records of King Sunjo's Reign*]. Seoul, South Korea: Kuksa pyŏnch'an wiwŏnhoe, 1958. http://sillok.history.go.kr/main/main. jsp.

Sŭngjŏngwŏn ilgi [*Records of the Royal Secretariat*]. Seoul, South Korea: Kuksa pyŏnch'an wiwŏnhoe, 1961-1970. http://sjw.history.go.kr/.

Tanjong sillok. [*The Veritable Records of King Tanjong's Reign*]. Seoul, South Korea: Kuksa pyŏnch'an wiwŏnhoe, 1956. http://sillok.history.go.kr/main/ main.jsp.

Yŏngjo sillok. [*The Veritable Records of King Yŏngjo's Reign*]. Seoul, South Korea: Kuksa pyŏnch'an wiwŏnhoe, 1957. http://sillok.history.go.kr/main/main. jsp.

Yŏnsan'gun ilgi [*The Daily Records of Prince Yŏnsan's Reign*]. Seoul, South Korea: Kuksa pyŏnch'an wiwŏnhoe, 1956. http://sillok.history.go.kr/main/main. jsp.

Zhang, Zhongfang. *Nan Song wenfan* [*Texts of the Southern Song*]. Jiangsu shuju: China, 1888.

SECONDARY SOURCES

Works in Korean and Japanese

An, Tae-hoe. *Chŏngjo ŭi pimil p'yŏnji: Kuk'wang ŭi konoe wa t'ongch'i ŭi kisul* [*Chŏngjo's Secret Letters: The King's Troubles and His Ruling Technique*]. P'aju, South Korea: Munhak tongnae, 2010.

Cho, Sŏngŭl. "Chŏng Yagyong ŭi Chung'ang kwanje kaehyŏknon [*Tasan's Central Government Reforms*]." *Tongbang hakchi* 89/90 (1995), 299-331.

Chŏng, Pyŏng-sŏl. *Kwŏllyŏk kwa in'gan: Sado seja ŭi chugŭm kwa Chosŏn wang-sil* [*Power and Person: Crown Prince Sado's death and the Chosŏn Dynasty*]. P'aju, South Korea: Munhak tongnae, 2012.

Chŏng, Sŏkchong. *Chosŏn hugi ŭi chŏngch'i wa sasang* [*Late Chosŏn Politics and Thought*]. Seoul, South Korea: Han'gilsa, 1994.

Ch'oe, Hong-gyu. *Chŏngjo ŭi Hwasŏng kŏnsŏl* [*The Construction of Chŏngjo's Illustrious Fortress*]. Seoul, South Korea: Ilchisa, 2001.

———. *Chŏngjo ŭi Hwasŏng kyŏngyŏng yŏn'gu* [*A Study of the Administration of Chŏngjo's Illustrious Fortress*]. Seoul, South Korea: Ilchisa, 2005.

Ch'oe, Tu-jin. "Chŏngjo sidae Kyujanggak ŭi kyoyuk ŭiŭi [The Educational Significance of the Royal Library in Chŏngjo's Time]." *Susan haeyang kyoyuk yŏn'gu* 25, no. 1 (2013): 273–86.

Han, Sang-gwŏn. *Chosŏn hugi sahoe wa sowŏn chedo: Sang'ŏn, kyŏkchaeng yŏngu* [*Late Chosŏn Society and the Petition System: A Study of Sang'ŏn and Kyŏkchaeng*]. Seoul, South Korea: Ilchogak, 1996.

———. "Chŏngjo ŭi kunjugwan [Chŏngjo's Views on Monarchy]." *Chosŏn sidae sahakpo* 41 (2007), 141–77.

———. "Chosŏn sidae ŭi kyohwa wa hyŏngjŏng [Edification and Punishment in the Chosŏn Period]." *Yŏksa wa hyŏnsil* 79 (2011): 271–303.

Han, Seunghyun [Han Sŭng-hyŏn]. "Chungguk ŭi 18-segi- Sŏ Yurŏp kwa Chosŏn kwa ŭi pigyo rŭl chungsimŭro [China's 18th Century, Focusing on Comparison with Chosŏn and Western Europe]." *Yŏksa hakbo* 213 (2012): 127–53.

Hiraki, Minoru. *Chosŏn hugi nobije yŏn'gu* [*A Study of the Slavery System of Late Chosŏn*]. Seoul, South Korea: Chisik Sanŏpsa, 1982.

Hong, Sŭng-gi. *Koryŏ kwijok sahoe wa nobi* [*Koryŏ Slavery and Aristocratic Society*]. Seoul: Ilchogak, 1983.

Jung, Ok-ja [Chŏng Ok-cha]. "Chŏngjo ŭi hakye sasang: Hongjae chŏnsŏ Ilsŏngnok munhakcho rŭl chungsimuro [Chŏngjo's Literary and Artistic Thought: Focusing on Literary Passages in his *Diaries*]." *Hanguk hakbo* 4, no. 2 (1978): 2–37.

———. *Chosŏn hugi munhwa undongsa* [*History of Late Chosŏn Cultural Movements*]. Seoul T'ŭkpyŏlsi, South Korea: Ilchogak, 1988.

———. "Chŏngjo ŭi sahoe t'onghap sasang [Chŏngjo's Thought on Social Integration]." *Hanguk hakbo* 24 (1998): 148–76.

———. *Chŏngjo sidae ŭi sasang kwa munhwa* [*Thought and Culture during the Reign of Chŏngjo*]. Tolbegae, 1999.

———. *Chŏngjo ŭi munye sasang kwa Kyujanggak* [*Chŏngjo's Literary Thought and the Royal Library*]. Seoul T'ŭkpyŏlsi: Hyohyŏng Ch'ulp'an, 2001.

Kang, Man'gil, and Chŏng Chang-yŏl. *Tasan ŭi chŏngch'i kyŏngje sasang* [*Tasan's Political and Economic Thought*]. Ch'angjak Kwabi P'yŏngsa, 1990.

Kim, Chun-hyŏk. *Yi San Chŏngjo, kkum ŭi tosi Hwasŏng ŭl seuda* [*Chŏngjo: Setting up the Illustrious Fortress, City of Dreams*]. Seoul, South Korea: Yŏyudang, 2008.

Kim, Hae-yŏng. *Ch'ŏlhakcha, Chŏngjo ŭi hyoch'i rŭl punsŏkhada* [*A Philosophical Analysis of Chŏngjo's Filial Piety*]. Seoul, South Korea: Antiquus, 2012.

Kim, Hyŏn-mok. "Chŏngjo ŭi ch'aekmun e nat'anan aemin sasang yŏngu [A Study of 'Loving the People' Thought as Revealed in Chŏngjo's Policy Question]." *Hanmun kojŏn yŏngu* 17 (2008): 127–54.

Kim, In-gŏl, et al. *Chŏngjo wa Chŏngjo sidae* [*King Chŏngjo and His Times*]. Seoul, South Korea: Seoul National University Press, 2011.

Kim, Ji-young [Kim Chi-yŏng]. "Chosŏn hugi kugwang haengch'a wa kŏdunggil [Late Chosŏn Royal Processions and Their Routes]." *Seoulhak Yŏn'gu* 30 (2008): 33–69.

Kim, Kyŏng-hŏn, ed. *Chŏngjo wa 18-segi: yŏksa rosŏ 18-segi, Sŏgu wa Tong Asia ŭi pigyosajŏk sŏngch'al* [*Chŏngjo's 18th Century: Reflections on a Historial Comparison of East Asia and the Western Hemisphere*]. Seoul, South Korea: P'urŭn Yŏksa, 2013.

Kim, Man-il. *Chosŏn 17-18 segi Sangsŏ haesŏk ŭi saeroun kyŏnghyang* [*New Influences on the Understanding of the* Book of Documents *in 17th-and 18th-Century Chosŏn*]. Seoul, South Korea: Kyŏngin Munhwasa, 2007.

Kim, Moon-sik [Kim Mun-sik]. *Chŏngjo ŭi kyŏnghak kwa chujahak* [*Chŏngjo's Study of the Classics and Zhu Xi Neo-Confucianism*]. Seoul, South Korea: Munhŏn kwa Haesŏk, 2000.

———. *Chŏngjo ŭi chewanghak* [*Chŏngjo's Royal Learning*]. Kyŏnggi-do P'aju: T'aehaksa, 2007.

Kim, Paekchol [Kim Paek-ch'ŏl]. "Chosŏn hugi Chŏngjo dae *Taejŏn t'ongjŏn pyŏngjŏn* p'yŏn ŭi sŏngkyŏk [The Publication Nature of the 'Military Tactics' Chapter of the *Complete Compilation of the Great Code* in Chŏngjo's Reign]." *Kunsaji* 76 (2010): 89–119.

———. *Chosŏn hugi Yŏngjo ŭi t'angp'yŏng chŏngch'i* [*Yŏngjo's Policy of Impartiality Politics in Late Chosŏn*]. P'aju, South Korea: T'aehaksa, 2010.

———. "1990 nyŏndae Han'guk sahoe ŭi 'Chŏngjo sindŭrom' taedu wa paekyŏng: Nayakhan imgum esŏ chŏldae kyemong kunjuro ŭi chaet'ansaeng [The Background and Rise of 'Chŏngjo Syndrome' in Korean Society in the 1990s: The Rebirth of a Weak King as an Enlightened Despot]." *Kukhak yŏn'gu* 18 (2011): 187–230.

Kim, Sung-Yun [Kim Sŏng-yun]. "Chŏngjo ch'ŏlhak sasang ŭi chŏngch'ijŏk chomyŏng [Illuminating Chŏngjo's Political Philosophy]." *Pusan sahak* 25/26 (1994): 47-79.

Kim T'ae-yŏng. "Tasan kyŏngseron-esŏ wanggwŏnnon [Tasan's Theory of Royal Power from His Theory of Governance]." *Tasanhak* 1 (2000): 162-262.

Kwak, Nak-hyŏn. "*Taejŏn t'ongp'yŏn* pyŏngjŏn rŭl shichwi t'onghae pon muye [Determining Military Skill through Examination in the *Complete Compilation of the Great Code*]." *Mudo yŏn'gu soji* 22, no. 2 (2011): 43-51.

Lee, Song-Mu [Yi Sŏng-mu]. *Chosŏn sidae tangjaengsa* [*A History of Factional Struggle in the Chosŏn Period*]. Seoul, South Korea: Tongbang midiŏ, 2000.

Paek, Minjŏng. "Tasan ŭi *Chungyong kang'ŭi(bo)* chodae naeyong punsŏk: Chŏngjo ŭi *Kyŏngsa kang'ŭi, Chungyong* ŏje cho'gan mit kit'a chodae waŭi pigyo rŭl chungsimŭro [A Philosophical Analysis of Chŏng Yak-yŏng's Replies to Chŏngjo's Questions in his *Lectures on the* Doctrine of the Mean: In Comparison to the *Doctrine of the Mean* Portion of his *Lectures on the Classics and Histories*]." *Tongbang hakchi* 147 (2009), 399-448.

———. "Chŏngjo ŭi sadaebu insik kwa chŏngch'i ch'ŏrhakchŏk ipjang yŏngu [A Study of Political Philosophy and Scholar-Official Understanding under Chŏngjo]." *Hanguk sirhak yŏngu* 20 (2010): 399-474.

Paek Sŭngjong, ed. *Chŏngjo ŭi pimil ŏch'al: Chŏngjo ka kŭ ŭi sidae rŭl malhada* [*Chŏngjo's Secret Letters: Chŏngjo Talks of His Times*]. Seoul, South Korea: P'urŭn yŏksa, 2011.

———. *Chŏngjo wa pullyang sŏnbi Kang Yi-ch'ŏn: 18-segi Chosŏn ŭi munhwa t'ujaeng* [*Chŏngjo and the Bad Scholar Kang Yi-ch'ŏn: Cultural Conflict in 18tg Century Chosŏn*]. Seoul, South Korea: P'urŭn yŏksa, 2011.

Park, Hyunmo [Pak Hyŏn-mo]. "Chŏngjo ŭi chŏngch'i hyŏnsil insik kwa kwŏndoron [Chŏngjo's Politically Realistic Consciousness and Theory of Discretion]." *Hanguk hakbo* 25, no. 4 (1999): 85-127.

———. "Chŏngjo ŭi kunsaron pip'an: Ch'ogye munsin wa munch'e panjŏng ŭl chungsimŭro [A Critique of Chŏngjo's Scholar-king Discourse, Focusing on the *ch'ogye munsin* and the Style Controversy]." *Hanguk silhak yŏngu* 2 (2000): 143-72.

———. "Chŏngjo ŭi t'angp'yŏng chŏngch'i yŏngu: Sŏngwangron ŭi i'nyŏm kwa hangye [A Study of Chŏngjo's T'angp'yŏng Politics: The Ideology and Limits of Sage-King Discourse]." *Hanguk chŏngch'i hakhuibo* 34, no. 1 (2000): 45-62.

———. "Chŏngch'i ka Chŏngjo ŭi yŏksajŏk p'yŏngga: Yŏksa sok ŭi Chŏngjo wa Chŏngjo an ŭi yŏksa [A Historical Evaluation of Chŏngjo the Politician:

Chŏngjo in History and History in Chŏngjo]." *Hanguk hakbo* 27, no. 2 (2001): 131-54.

———. *Chŏngch'i ka Chŏngjo* [*Chŏngjo the Politician*]. Seoul, South Korea: P'urŭn Yŏksa, 2001.

———. "Chŏngjo ŭi chŏngch'i wa Suwŏnsŏng: Hwasŏng kŏnsŏl ŭi chŏngch'ijŏk ŭimi [Chŏngjo's Politics and Suwŏn: The Political Meaning of the Illustrious Fortress's Construction]." *Hanguk kwa kukje chŏngch'i* 17, no. 1 (2001): 65-100.

———. "Chŏng Yagyong ŭi kunjunon: Chŏngjo wa ŭi kwankye rŭl chungsim ŭro [Tasan's Theory of Kingship: Focusing on His Relationship with Chŏngjo]." *Chŏngchi sasang yŏn'gu* 8 (2003): 7-30.

———. "Sejong kwa Chŏngjo ŭi ridŏsip sŭt'ail [Sejong's and Chŏngjo's Leadership Styles]." *O'nŭl tong'yang sasang* 17 (2007): 133-52.

———. *Chŏngjo sahu 63 nyŏn: Sedo chŏngch'igi (1800-1863) ŭi kungnaeoe chŏngch'i yŏngu* [*63 Years after Chŏngjo's Death: A Study of the Internal and External Politics of the Period of In-Law Rule*]. P'aju, South Korea: Ch'angbi, 2011.

Pak, Kwang-yong. *Yŏngjo wa Chŏngjo ŭi nara* [*The Country of Yŏngjo and Chŏngjo*]. P'urŭn Yŏsa, 1998.

Park, Sung Soon [Pak, Sŏng-sun]. "Chŏngjodae 'Kim Ha-jae sa'gŏn' ŭi chŏnmal kwa sŏngkyŏk [An Account of the 'Kim Ha-jae Incident' in Chŏngjo's Reign]." *Chosŏn sidae sahakpo* 47 (2008), 121-50.

Sin, Tong-jun. *Chosŏn ŭi wang kwa sinha, puguk kangbyŏng ŭl nonhada* [*Chosŏn Royal Discussions of Strengthening the Country*]. P'aju, South Korea: Sallim Ch'ulp'ansa, 2007.

———. *Chosŏn kugwang vs. Chungguk hwangje: sidae rŭl ttwiŏnŏmnŭn kwŏllyŏk ŭi pŏpch'ik* [*Korean King vs. Chinese Emperor: Principles of Power to Overcome the Times*]. P'aju, South Korea: Yŏksa ŭi Ach'im, 2010.

Sŏl, Sŏk-gyu. "Kyujanggak yŏn'gu (sang): Chŏngjo tae ŭi chŏngguk kwa kwallyŏnhayŏ [A Study of the Royal Library and Its Connection to the Political Conditions in the Chŏngjo Period, Part I]." *Taegu sahak* 29 (1986): 117-43.

———. "Kyujanggak yŏn'gu (ha): Chŏngjo tae ŭi chŏngguk kwa kwallyŏnhayŏ [A Study of the Royal Library and Its Connection to the Political Conditions in the Chŏngjo Period, Part II]." *Taegu sahak* 31 (1986): 73-107.

Song Ki-ch'ul. *T'onghap ŭi chŏngch'i ka Yi San* [*Chŏngjo, the Complete Politician*]. Seoul, South Korea: Kukhak charyowŏn, 2012.

Sŏng, Nakhun, et al. *Han'guk munhwasa taegye 2* [*Outline of Korean History, volume 2*]. Seoul, South Korea: Korea University Korean Culture Institute, 2011.

Yamauchi, Koichi. "Chōsen o motte tenka ni ō tarashimu—Gakushūin daigauzō *Kija p'alchoji* ni miru zaiya Rorōn chishiki-jin no yume [Chosŏn as the Legitimate Ruler of the Realm—A Dream of an Out-of-Power Patriarch Intellectual as Seen in the *Purpose of the Lord of Ji's Eight Laws* in the Gakushūin University Collection]." *Tōyō gakuhō* 84, no. 3 (2002): 1–31.

Yi, Han-u. *Chŏngjo: Chosŏn ŭi hon i chida [Chŏngjo: The Soul of Chosŏn Fades]*. Seoul, South Korea: Haenaem, 2007.

Yi, Kŭnsun. *Chosŏn hugi tangjaengsa yŏn'gu [Studies in the History of Late Chosŏn Factional Struggle]*. Seoul, South Korea: Iljogak, 1988.

Yi, Tae-Jin [Yi T'ae-jin]. *Chosŏn yugyo sahoesaron [A Social History of Chosŏn Confucianism]*. Chisik sanŏpsa, 1989.

———. "Chosŏn wangjo ŭi yugyo chŏngch'i wa wanggwŏn [Confucian Politics and Royal Power in Chosŏn]" *Han'guk saron* 23 (1990): 215–32.

———. *Kyujanggak sosa [A Brief History of the Royal Library]*. Seoul National University Library, 1990.

———. "Chŏngjo ŭi taehak t'amgu wa saeroun kunjunon [Chŏngjo's New Theory of Kingship and His Study of the *Greater Learning*]." *Taedong munhwa yŏn'gu ch'ongsŏ* XI (1992), 219–69.

———. "Chŏngjo: Yugyojŏk kyemong chŏldae kunju [Chŏngjo: Enlightened Confucian Absolute Monarch]." *Hanguksa simin kangjwa* 13 (1993): 61–85.

———. *Chosŏn sidae chŏngch'isa ŭi chae chomyŏng [Illuminating Chosŏn Political History]*. Seoul, South Korea: T'aehaksa, 2003.

Yi Tae-Jin, and Kim Paekchol, eds. *Chosŏn hugi t'angp'yŏng chŏngch'i ŭi chejo-myŏng (ha) [Reexamining Late Chosŏn Policy of Impartiality Politics, vol. 2]*. P'aju, South Korea: T'aehaksa, 2011.

Yi, Yi-hwa. "Kyujanggak sogo [A Brief Examination of the Royal Library]." *Kyujanggak* 3 (1979): 149–65.

Yŏksa hakhoe. *Chŏngjo wa 18 segi: Yŏksa rosŏ 18 segi, Sŏgu wa Tong Asia ŭi pigyosajŏk sŏngch'al [Chŏngjo and the 18th Century: Comparative Reflections on the 18th Century, the West and East Asia as History]*. Seoul, South Korea, Purŭn yŏksa, 2013.

Yu, Mi-rim. *Chosŏn hugi ŭi chŏngch'i sasang [Late Chosŏn Political Thought]*. Seoul, South Korea: Chisik san'ŏpsa, 2002.

Yu, Pong-hak. *Kkum ŭi munhwa yusan, Hwasŏng: Chŏngjo tae yŏksa, munhwa chae chomyŏng [The Illustrious Fortress, Cultural Legacy of Dreams: Another Look at Culture and History under Chŏngjo]*. Seoul, South Korea: Sin'gu Munhwasa, 1996.

———. *Chŏngjo Taewang ŭi kkum: Kaehyŏk kwa kaltŭng ŭi sidae* [*The Dream of Chŏngjo the Great: A Period of Reform and Discord*]. Seoul, South Korea: Sin'gu Munhwasa, 2001.

———. *Kaehyŏk kwa kaltŭng ŭi sidae: Chŏngjo wa 19-segi* [*A Period of Reform and Discord: Chŏngjo and the 19th Century*]. Sŏngnam: Sin'gu Munhwasa, 2009.

Yun, Nae-hyŏn, Pak Sŏng-su, and Yi Hyŏn-hŭi. *Saeroun Han'guksa* [*New History of Korea*]. Paju, South Korea: Chipmundang, 2005.

Works in English

Andrade, Tonio, Hyeok Hweon Kang, and Kirsten Cooper. "A Korean Military Revolution? Parallel Military Innovations in East Asia and Europe." *Journal of World History* 25, no. (2014): 51-84.

Asch, Ronald G. *Sacral Kingship between Disenchantment and Re-enchantment: The French and English Monarchies, 1587-1688*. New York: Berghahn, 2014.

Asch, Ronald G., and Heinz Duchardt, eds. *Der Absolutismus—ein Mythos? Strukturwandel monarchischer Herrschaft in West- und Mitteleuropa (ca. 1550-1700)*. Köhn: Böhlau. 1996.

Baker, Donald L. "Factionalism in Perspective: Causes and Consequences of Political Struggles during the Chosŏn Dynasty." *Korean Studies in Canada* 2 (1994): 2-10.

———. "Rhetoric, Ritual, and Political Legitimacy: Justifying Yi Sŏng-gye's Ascension to the Throne." *Korea Journal* 53, no. 4 (2013): 141-67.

Bartlett, Beatrice. *Monarchs and Ministers: The Grand Council in Mid-Qing China, 1723-1820*. Berkeley: University of California Press, 1991.

Beales, Derek. *Enlightenment and Reform in Eighteenth-Century Europe*. New York: I. B. Tauris, 2005.

Beik, William. "The Absolutism of Louis XIV as Social Collaboration." *Past & Present* 188 (2005): 195-224.

Bjornstad, Hall. "The Marginalization of the Mémoires of Louis XIV." *European Legacy* 17, no. 6 (2012): 779-89.

Ebrey, Patricia Buckley, and Paul Jakov Smith, eds. *State Power in China, 900-1325*. Seattle: University of Washington Press, 2016.

Chang, Michael G. "Fathoming Qianlong: Imperial Activism, the Southern Tours, and the Politics of Water Control, 1736-1765." *Late Imperial China* 24, no. 2 (2003): 51-108.

———. *A Court on Horseback: Imperial Touring and the Construction of Qing Rule, 1680-1785*. Cambridge: University of Harvard Press, 2007.

Ch'oe, Yŏng-ho. "The Private Academies (Sŏwŏn) and Neo-Confucianism in Late Chosŏn Korea." *Seoul Journal of Korea Studies* 21, no. 2 (2008): 139-91.

Chong, Da-ham [Chŏng Ta-ham]. "Making Chosŏn's Own Tributaries: Dynamics between the Ming-Centered World Order and a Chosŏn-Centered Regional Order in the East Asian Periphery." *International Journal of Korean History* 15, no. 1 (2010): 29-63.

Cole, Mary Hill. *The Portable Queen: Elizabeth I and the Politics of Ceremony.* Amherst: University of Massachusetts Press, 1999.

Collins, James B. *The State in Early Modern France.* 2nd ed. Cambridge: Cambridge University Press, 2009.

Crossley, Pamela Kyle. *A Translucent Mirror: History and Identity in Qing Imperial Ideology.* Berkeley: University of California Press, 1999.

Cuttica, Cesare, and Glenn Burgess, eds. *Monarchism and Absolutism in Early Modern Europe.* Brookfield: Pickering & Chatto, 2012.

De Bary, Wm. Theodore, and JaHyun Kim Haboush, eds. *The Rise of Neo-Confucianism in Korea.* New York: Columbia University Press, 1985.

Dee, Darryl. *Expansion and Crisis in Louis XIV's France: Franche-Comté and Absolute Monarchy, 1674-1715.* Rochester: University of Rochester Press, 2009.

Deuchler, Martina. " 'Heaven Does Not Discriminate': A Study of Secondary Sons in Chosŏn Korea." *Journal of Korean Studies* 6 (1988-89): 121-63.

——. *The Confucian Transformation of Korea: A Study of Society and Ideology.* Cambridge. MA: Harvard University Press, 1992.

Doyle, William, ed. *Old Regime France.* New York: Oxford University Press, 2001.

Duncan, John B. "Proto-nationalism in Premodern Korea." *Perspectives on Korea.* Sydney, AU: Wild Peony, 1998.

——. *The Origins of the Chosŏn Dynasty.* Seattle: University of Washington Press, 2000.

——. "Historical Memories of Koguryŏ in Koryŏ and Chosŏn Korea." *Journal of Inner and East Asian Studies* 1 (2004): 118-36.

Duncan, John B., et al., eds. *The Institutional Basis of Civil Governance in the Chosŏn Dynasty.* Seoul, South Korea: Seoul Selection, 2009.

Elliott, Mark C. *Emperor Qianlong: Son of Heaven, Man of the World.* New York: Longman, 2009.

Elman, Benjamin A. *Classicism Politics, and Kinship: The Ch'ang-chou School of New Text Confucianism in Late Imperial China.* Berkeley: University of California Press, 1990.

Elman, Benjamin A., ed. *Rethinking East Asian Languages, Vernaculars, and Literacies, 1000–1919.* Leiden, the Netherlands: Brill, 2014.

Elman, Benjamin A., Herman Ooms, and John B. Duncan, eds. *Rethinking Confucianism: Past and Present in China, Japan, Korea, and Vietnam.* Los Angeles: University of California Press, 2002.

Elmarsafy, Ziad. *Freedom, Slavery, and Absolutism: Corneille, Pascal, Racine.* Lewisburg: Bucknell University Press, 2003.

Fox, Paul W. "Louis XIV and the Theories of Absolutism and Divine Right." *Canadian Journal of Economics and Political Science/Revue canadienned'Economique et de Science politique* 26, no. 1 (1960): 128–42.

Frank, Andre Gunder. *ReOrient: Global Economy in the Asian Age.* Berkeley: University of California Press, 1998.

Friday, Karl F., ed. *Japan Emerging: Premodern History to 1850.* Boulder, CO: Westview Press, 2012.

Fukuyama, Francis. *The Origins of Political Order: From Prehuman Times to the French Revolution.* New York: Farrar, Straus and Giroux, 2011.

Haboush, JaHyun Kim. "Confucian Rhetoric and Ritual as Techniques of Political Dominance: Yŏngjo's Use of the Royal Lecture." *Journal of Korean Studies* 5 (1984): 39–62.

———. *The Confucian Kingship in Korea.* New York: Columbia University Press, 2001.

———. *The Great East Asian War and the Birth of the Korean Nation.* New York: Columbia University Press, 2016.

Haboush, JaHyun Kim, ed. *Epistolary Korea: Letters in the Communicative Space of the Chosŏn, 1392–1910.* Columbia University Press: 2009, 59–67.

Haboush, JaHyun Kim, and Martina Deuchler, eds. *Culture and State in Late Chosŏn Korea.* Cambridge: Harvard University Press, 1999.

Han, Sang-gwŏn. "Social Problems and the Active Use of Petitions during the Reign of King Chŏngjo." *Korea Journal* 40, no. 4 (2000): 227–46.

Henderson, Gregory. "Chŏng Ta-san: A Study in Korea's Intellectual History." *Journal of Asian Studies* 16, no. 3 (1957): 377–86.

Henderson, Gregory, and Key P. Yang. "An Outline History of Korean Confucianism, Part I: The Early Period and Yi Factionalism." *Journal of Asian Studies* 18, no. 1 (1958): 81–101.

Henshall, Nicholas. *The Myth of Absolutism: Change and Continuity in Early Modern European Monarchy.* London: Longman, 1992.

Hucker, Charles O. *A Dictionary of Official Titles in Imperial China.* Stanford, CA: Stanford University Press, 1985.

Huang, Pei. *Autocracy at Work: A Study of the Yung-cheng Period, 1723-1735.* Bloomington: Indiana University Press, 1974.

Hur, Nam-lin. "National Defense in Shambles: Wartime Military Buildup in Chosŏn Korea, 1592-98." *Seoul Journal of Korean Studies* 22, no. 2 (2009): 113-35.

Hurt, John J. *Louis XIV and the Parlements.* New York: Manchester University Press, 2002.

Hwang, Kyung Moon [Hwang Kyŏng-mun]. "From the Dirt to Heaven: Northern Koreans in the Chosŏn and Early Modern Eras." *Harvard Journal of Asiatic Studies* 62, no. 1 (2002): 135-78.

Jackson, Andrew. "The Causes and Aims of Yŏngjo's Chŏngmihwan'guk." *Papers for the British Association of Korean Studies* 13 (2011): 17-34.

———. "Histories in Stone: Stelae Commemorating the Suppression of the Musin Rebellion and Contested Factional Histories." *International Journal of Asian Studies* 11, no. 1 (2014): 53-75.

———. *The 1728 Musin Rebellion: Politics and Plotting in Eighteenth-Century Korea.* Honolulu: University of Hawaii Press, 2016.

Jones, Colin. *The Great Nation: France from Louis XV to Napoleon.* New York: Columbia University Press, 2002.

Jung Jae-Hoon [Chŏng Chae-hun]. "Meeting the World through Eighteenth-Century *Yŏnhaeng.*" *Seoul Journal of Korean Studies* 23, no. 1 (2010): 51-69.

Jung, Ok-ja [Chŏng Ok-cha]. "New Approaches to the History of Ideas in the Late Joseon Period." *Seoul Journal of Korean Studies* 5 (1992): 152-70.

Kahn, Harold L. *Monarchy in the Emperor's Eyes: Image and Reality in the Ch'ien-lung Reign.* Cambridge, MA: University of Harvard Press, 1971.

Kang, Hyeok Hweon. "Big Heads and Buddhist Demons: The Korean Musketry Revolution and the Northern Expeditions of 1654 and 1658." *Journal of Chinese Military History* 2 (2013): 127-89.

Karlsson, Anders. "Royal Compassion and Disaster Relief in Chosŏn Korea." *Seoul Journal of Korean Studies* 20, no. 1 (2007): 71-98.

Kim, Jisoo. "Women's Legal Voice: Language, Power, and Gender Performativity in Late Chosŏn Korea." *Journal of Asian Studies* 74, no. 3 (2015): 667-86.

———. *The Emotions of Justice: Gender, Status, and Legal Performance in Chosŏn Korea.* Seattle: University of Washington Press, 2016.

Kim, Marie Seong-Hak, ed. *The Spirit of Korean Law: Korean Legal History in Context.* Boston: Brill, 2016.

Kim, Moon-sik [Kim Mun-sik]. "Royal Visits and Protocols in the Chosŏn Dynasty: Focusing on Wŏnhaeng Ŭlmyo Chŏngni Ŭigwe Compiled during King Chŏngjo's Reign." *Korea Journal* 48, no. 2 (2008): 44-72.

Kim, Paekchol [Kim Paek-ch'ŏl]. "King Yŏngjo's T'angp'yŏng Policy and Its Orientation." *International Journal of Korean History* 16, no. 1 (2011): 51-80.

Kim, Seonmin [Kim Sŏn-min]. "Ginseng and Border Trespassing Between Qing China and Chosŏn Korea." *Late Imperial China* 28, no. 1 (2007): 33-61.

Kim, Sun Joo. *Marginality and Subversion in Korea: The Hong Kyongnae Rebellion of 1812.* Seattle: University of Washington Press, 2009.

Kim, Sun Joo, and Jungwon Kim, trans. *Wrongful Deaths: Selected Inquest Records from Nineteenth-Century Korea.* Seattle: University of Washington Press, 2004.

Kim, Sungmoon [Kim Sŏng-mun]. "Too Rational to Be Modernized? Confucian Rationality and Political Modernity in Traditional Korea." *Review of Korean Studies* 9, no. 4 (2006): 135-68.

Kim, Sung-Yun [Kim Sŏng-yun]. "T'angpyŏng and Hwasŏng: The Theory and Practice of Chŏngjo's Politics and Hwasŏng." *Korea Journal* 41, no. 1 (2001): 137-65.

Kim-Renaud, Young-Key, ed. *King Sejong the Great: The Light of 15th Century Korea.* The International Circle of Korean Linguistics, 1992.

King, Ross. "Ditching 'Diglossia': Describing Ecologies of the Spoken and Inscribed in Pre-modern Korea." *Sungkyun Journal of East Asian Studies* 15, no. 1, 1-19.

Ko, Donghwan [Ko Tong-hwan]. "Development of Commerce and Commercial Policy during the Reign of King Chŏngjo." *Korea Journal* 40, no. 4 (2000): 202-26.

Lee, Ki-baik [Yi Ki-baek]. *A New History of Korea.* Cambridge, MA: Harvard University Press, 1984.

Lee, Kyungku [Yi Kyŏng-ku]. "The *Horak* Debate from the Reign of King Sukjong to King Sunjo." *Korea Journal* 51, no. 1 (2011): 14-41.

Lee, Sang-oak, and Duk-Soo Park, eds., *Perspectives on Korea.* Sydney, AU: Wild Peony Press, 1998.

Lewis, James B. *Frontier Contact Between Chosŏn Korea and Tokugawa Japan.* New York: Routledge, 2003.

Lieberman, Victor. *Beyond Binary Histories: Re-imagining Eurasia to c. 1830.* Ann Arbor: University of Michigan, 1999.

Lee Song-Mu [Yi Sŏng-mu]. "Kwagŏ System and Its Characteristics: Centering on the Koryŏ and Early Chosŏn Periods." *Korea Journal* 21, no. 7 (1981), 12-13.

Lossky, Andrew. "The Absolutism of Louis XIV: Reality or Myth?" *Canadian Journal of History* 19 (1984): 1-15.

——. *Louis XIV and the French Monarchy*. New Brunswick, NJ: Rutgers University Press, 1994.

Lovins, Christopher. "The King's Reason: Yi Sŏng-gye and the Centralization of Power in Early Chosŏn." *Korea Review of International Studies* 9, no. 1 (2006): 51–60.

——. "Making Sense of the Imperial Pivot: Metaphor Theory and the Writings of King Jeongjo." *Korea Journal* 52, no. 3 (2012): 177–200.

Millward, James A., et al., eds. *New Qing Imperial History: The Making of Inner Asian Empire at Qing Chengde*. New York: RoutledgeCurzon, 2004.

Nylan, Michael. "The 'Chin Wen/Ku Wen' Controversy in Han Times." *T'oung Pao* 80, no. 1 (1994): 83–145.

Oakley, Francis. *Kingship: The Politics of Enchantment*. Malden, MA: Blackwell, 2006.

Pai, Hyung Il. *Constructing Korean Origins: A Critical Review of Archaeology, Historiography, and Racial Myth in Korean State-Formation Theories*. Cambridge, MA: Harvard University Press, 2000.

Palais, James B. "Confucianism and the Aristocratic/Bureaucratic Balance in Korea." *Harvard Journal of Asiatic Studies* 44, no. 2 (1984): 427–68.

——. *Politics and Policy in Traditional Korea*. Cambridge, MA: Harvard University Press, 1991 [1975].

——. "Political Leadership and the *Yangban* in the Chosŏn Dynasty." *Etudes Thematiques: La Societe Civile face a l'Etat dans Les Traditions Chinoise, Japonaise, Coreenne et Vietnaiennnes* 3 (1994): 391–408.

——. *Confucian Statecraft and Korean Institutions: Yu Hyŏngwŏn and the Late Chosŏn Dynasty*. Seattle: University of Washington Press, 1996.

Park, Eugene Y. *Between Dreams and Realty: The Military Examination in Late Chosŏn Korea*. Cambridge, MA: Harvard University Press, 2007.

——. "Imagined Connections in Early Modern Korea, 1500–1894: Representations of Northern Elite Miryang Pak Lineages in Genealogies." *Seoul Journal of Korean Studies* 21, no. 1 (2008): 1–28.

——. *A Family of No Prominence: The Descendants of Pak Tŏkhwa and the Birth of Modern Korea*. Stanford, CA: Stanford University Press, 2014.

Park, Hyunmo [Pak Hyŏn-mo]. "King Chŏngjo's Political Role in the Conflicts between Confucianism and Catholicism in Eighteenth-Century Korea." *Review of Korean Studies* 7, no. 4 (2004): 205–28.

——. "King Sejong's Deliberative Politics: With Reference to the Process of Tax Reform." *Review of the Korean Studies* 8, no. 3 (2005): 57–89.

Park, Jae-Woo [Pak Chae-wu]. "Consultative Politics and Royal Authority in the Goryeo Period." *Seoul Journal of Korea Studies* 24, no. 2 (2011): 203–218.

Park, Sohyeon [Pak So-hyŏn]. "Thinking with Chinese Cases: Crime, Law, and Confucian Justice in Korean Case Literature." *Korea Journal* 53, no. 3 (2013), 5-28.

Park, Young-do [Pak Yŏng-do]. "King Sejong's Confucian Rule by Law: Focusing on the Relationship between Law and Rule by Benevolence." *Review of the Korean Studies* 9, no. 3 (2006): 103-31.

Parker, David. "Sovereignty, Absolutism and the Function of the Law in Seventeenth-Century France." *Past & Present* 122 (1989): 36-74.

——. "Absolutism, Feudalism and Property Rights in the France of Louis XIV." *Past & Present* 179 (2003): 60-96.

Pastreich, Emanuel Yi. "The Transmission and Translation of Chinese Vernacular Narrative in Chosŏn Korea: Han'gŭl Translations and Gentry Women's Literature." *Korean Studies* 39 (2015): 75-105.

Pollack, Sheldon. *The Language of the Gods in the World of Men: Sanskrit, Culture, and Power in Premodern India.* Berkeley: University of California Press, 2006.

Richardson, Glenn. *Renaissance Monarchy: The Reigns of Henry VIII, Francis I and Charles V.* Oxford University Press, 2002.

Robinson, Kenneth R. "Centering the King of Chosŏn: Aspects of Korean Maritime Diplomacy, 1392-1592." *Journal of Asian Studies* 59, no. 1 (2000): 109-25.

Roh, Young-koo [No Yŏng-gu]. "The Construction and Characteristics of Hwaseong Fortress in the Era of King Jeongjo." *Korea Journal* 41, no. 1 (2001): 166-212.

Rose, Jacqueline. "Kingship and Counsel in Early Modern England." *Historical Journal* 54, no. 1 (2011): 47-71.

Rowe, William T. *China's Last Empire: The Great Qing.* Cambridge, MA: Harvard University Press, 2009.

Salem, Ellen. "Slavery in Medieval Korea." PhD diss. Columbia University, 1978.

Schalk, Ellery. "Under the Law or Laws unto Themselves: Noble Attitudes and Absolutism in Sixteenth and Seventeenth-Century France." *Historical Reflections/Réflexions Historiques* 15, no. 1 (1988): 279-92.

Scott, Hamish, ed. *Enlightened Absolutism.* London: Macmillan, 1990.

Scott, Hamish, and Brendan Sims, eds. *Cultures of Power in Europe during the Long Eighteenth Century.* Cambridge, UK: Cambridge University Press, 2007.

Setton, Mark. "Factional Politics and Philosophical Development in the Late Chosŏn." *Journal of Korean Studies* 8 (1992): 37-80.

——. *Chŏng Yagyong: Korea's Challenge to Orthodox Neo-Confucianism.* Albany: State University of New York Press, 1997.

Shaw, William. *Legal Norms in a Confucian State*. Berkeley: Institute of East Asian Studies, 1981.

Shin, Myung-ho [Sin Myŏng-ho]. *Joseon Royal Court Culture: Ceremonial and Daily Life*. Translated by Timothy V. Atkinson. Paju, South Korea: Dolbegae Publishers, 2004.

Smail, Daniel Lord. *On Deep History and the Brain*. Berkeley: University of California Press, 2008.

Sohn, Pokee [Son Po-ki]. *Social History of the Early Chosŏn Dynasty: The Functional Aspects of Governmental Structure*. Seoul, South Korea: Jisiksanup, 2000.

Spence, Jonathan. *Treason by the Book*. New York: Viking, 2001.

Stanley, Amy. "Maidservants' Tales: Narrating Domestic and Global History in Eurasia, 1600–1900." *American Historical Review* 121, no. 2 (2016): 437–60.

Starn, Randolph. "The Early Modern Muddle." *Journal of Early Modern History* 6, no. 3 (2002): 296–307.

Struve, Lynn, ed. *The Qing Formation in World-Historical Time*. Cambridge, MA: Harvard University Press, 2004.

Sturdy, David J. *Louis XIV*. New York: St. Martin's Press, 1998.

Subrahmanyam, Sanjay. "Connected Histories: Notes towards a Reconfiguration of Early Modern Eurasia." *Modern Asian Studies* 31, no. 3 (1997): 735–62.

Suh, Dae-sook [Sŏ Tae-suk], ed. *Korean Studies: New Pacific Currents*. Honolulu: Center for Korean Studies, University of Hawaii, 1994.

Suh, Dae-sook Suh, and Chae-jin Lee [Yi Chae-jin], eds. *Political Leadership in Korea*. Seattle: University of Washington Press, 1976.

Tallett, Frank. *War and Society in Early Modern Europe, 1495–1715*, New York: Routledge, 2003 [1992].

Tackett, Nicolas. *The Destruction of the Medieval Chinese Aristocracy*. Cambridge, MA: Harvard University Press, 2014.

Tomiya, Itaru, ed. *Capital Punishment in East Asia*. Kyoto, Japan: Kyoto University Press, 2012.

Tsai, Shih-Shan Henry. *Perpetual Happiness: The Ming Emperor Yongle*. Seattle: University of Washington Press, 2001.

Wagner, Edward. *The Literati Purges: Political Conflict in Early Yi Korea*. Cambridge, MA: Harvard University Press, 1974.

Wilson, Peter H. *Absolutism in Central Europe*. New York: Routledge, 2000.

Wilson, Peter H., ed. *A Companion to Eighteenth-Century Europe*. Malden, MA: Blackwell, 2008.

Woodside, Alexander. *Lost Modernities: China, Vietnam, Korea and the Hazards of World History*. Cambridge, MA: Harvard University Press, 2006.

Yi, Song-mi [Yi Sŏng-mi]. *Korean Landscape Painting: Continuity and Innovation through the Ages.* Elizabeth: Hollym, 2006.

Yi, Tae-Jin [Yi T'ae-jin]. "King Chŏngjo: Confucianism, Enlightenment, and Absolute Rule." *Korea Journal* 40, no. 4 (2000): 168–201.

Yoo, Mi-rim [Yu Mi-rim]. "King Sejong's Leadership and the Politics of Inventing the Korean Alphabet." *Review of Korean Studies* 9, no. 3 (2006): 7–38.

Zmora, Hillay. *Monarchy, Aristocracy, and the State in Europe, 1300–1800.* New York: Routledge, 2001.

INDEX

absolutism:
  and aristocratic-bureaucratic
    balance, 9, 15–21, 128, 153–154
  "conservative innovation" concept
    of William Beik, xvii, 157
  and early modern states, 1
  effect of war on, 143
  and the English monarchy,
    147–148, 189n107
  European monarchs compared
    with Chinese emperors, xx, 8,
    166n49
  as a kind of "cogovernment,"
    185n13
  "strong" and "weak" absolutism of
    Francis Fukuyama, 7–8, 126
  See also discretion; royal power
—of Chŏngjo:
  and his direct interaction with the
    people, 2, 95–100
  and the Imperial Pivot
    (*hwanggŭk*) metaphor, 35, 38,
    39, 145, 173n32
  and ruler-based interpretations of
    Zhu Xi, 34
  and the ruler's discretion (*kwŏn*),
    38–47, 85–86
  summary of, xii, xvi–xvii
  Yŏngjo's rule contrasted with,
    128–131
An, Tae-hoe, 64, 65, 174n14, 176n51
Analects (*Lunyu*), 33–34, 85
  Chongjo's paraphrasing of, 149

Andrade, Tonio, Hyeok Hweon
  Kang, and Kirsten Cooper,
  181–82n2
aristocratic-bureaucratic balance:
  and absolutism, 9, 15–21, 128
  the Chinese bureaucracy
    compared with Korea's, 132–33
  and the "hybrid" model, 167n3
  and Joseph II of Austria, 20, 101
Asch, Ronald G., 8, 144

Baker, Donald L., xiv
Beales, Derek:
  enlightened despotism defined by,
    5–6
  on Holy Roman Emperor Joseph
    II, 64, 99–100
Beik, William, xvii, 10–11, 147
Berry, Mary Elizabeth, 3
Book of Changes (*Yijing*), 33, 84
Book of Documents (*Shujing*):
  Duke of Zhou, 57, 175n20
  "Great Plan" (*Hongfan*) of, 33, 35
  as one of the Five Classics, 33
  and the study of history and
    statecraft, 31
Book of Former Han, slavery of the
  Lord of Ji's law recorded in, 100

Catholicism:
  and early modern France, 130
  Louis XIV's defense of, 144–145
Catholic Purge of 1801, 58, 147, 155